THE MODERNIST NOVEL AND THE DECLINE OF EMPIRE

In the early twentieth century, subjects of the British Empire ceased to rely on a model of centre and periphery in imagining their world and came instead to view it as an interconnected network of cosmopolitan people and places. English language and literature were promoted as essential components of a commercial, cultural, and linguistic network that spanned the globe. John Marx argues that the early twentieth century was a key moment in the emergence of modern globalization, rather than simply a period of British imperial decline. Modernist fiction was actively engaged in this transformation of society on an international scale. The very stylistic abstraction that seemed to remove modernism from social reality in fact internationalized the English language. Rather than mapping the decline of Empire, modernist novelists such as Conrad and Woolf celebrated the shared culture of the English language as more important than the waning imperial structures of Britain.

JOHN MARX is Assistant Professor of English at the University of Richmond. He has published in *Modernism/Modernity*, *Novel*, *Diaspora*, *Victorian Studies*, *Victorian Institutes Journal*, *Research in African Literatures*, and the *Cambridge Companion to Postcolonial Literary Studies*.

THE MODERNIST NOVEL AND THE DECLINE OF EMPIRE

JOHN MARX

CAMBRIDGE
UNIVERSITY PRESS

CAMBRIDGE UNIVERSITY PRESS
Cambridge, New York, Melbourne, Madrid, Cape Town, Singapore, São Paulo

Cambridge University Press
The Edinburgh Building, Cambridge CB2 2RU, UK

Published in the United States of America by Cambridge University Press, New York

www.cambridge.org
Information on this title: www.cambridge.org/9780521856171

© John Marx 2005

First published 2005

Printed in the United Kingdom at the University Press, Cambridge

A catalogue record for this book is available from the British Library

ISBN-13 978-0-521-85617-1 hardback
ISBN-10 0-521-85617-5 hardback

Contents

v

Acknowledgements

I have incurred debts of all sorts during the writing of this book. I could not have written it without the financial assistance of the University of Richmond Faculty Research Committee and the Office of the Dean of Arts and Sciences. Nor would I have completed it without the support of my students and colleagues in the Department of English.

I have benefited from the professional, intellectual, and personal help of friends, colleagues, and teachers. Ellen Rooney taught me to attend to the details of argument through the details of writing. Although I claim no mastery of this principle, I can say that it guided me through every stage of the book's composition. I have consistently thought of this project as an inquiry into a long twentieth century. My sense of that century's culture owes much to Neil Lazarus, who has been the most valued of interlocutors for more than a decade as well as the most gracious of hosts. Nancy Armstrong's confidence in the book's larger claims allowed me to finish what I started, and I am grateful for her detailed attention to the manuscript. The argument of this book took shape amidst ongoing discussions with Brown University comrades Lois Cucullu, Nicholas Daly, Steve Evans, Tamar Katz, Mark McMorris, Jennifer Moxley, Caroline Reitz, Jennifer Ting, and Annette Van. It received an early shot in the arm from Ronald R. Thomas, then of Trinity College, Hartford. For pointed and timely criticism of various chapters, I thank Christy Burns, Tammy Clewell, Barry Faulk, Benita Parry, and Leonard Tennenhouse. I am grateful to Ray Ryan and the anonymous readers from Cambridge University Press, whose guidance enabled me to bring the book into its present form. Mark Cooper read every damn word of this book, most more than twice, and gave me the gift of litotes. My sense of obligation to him is in no way insignificant. Beth Anderson, meanwhile, put up with all of it. We first met in the card catalogue while I was doing initial research on this project and I have been entirely dependent on her ever since.

Earlier and shorter versions of the first and third chapters appeared in *Modernism/Modernity* 6.1 (1999) and *Novel: A Forum on Fiction*, Vol. 32, No. 1, Fall 1998. Copyright *Novel* Corp. © 1998. I am grateful to the editors of these journals for permission to reprint.

Introduction: The decline of Britain and the rise of English

> In the nation that is not
> Nothing stands that stood before
>
> A. E. Housman

This book contends that British modernism imagined the world as an array of discrete yet interconnected localities. It argues that modernist writing abjured the Victorian fantasy of a planet divided into core and periphery, home and colony in favour of the new dream of a decentred network of places and peoples described, analyzed, and managed by a cosmopolitan cast of English-speaking experts. Far from representing the last gasp of a nation on the wane, a 'structure of compensation' for a culture tortured by a sense of its 'belatedness', modernism joined hands with an interdisciplinary archive of scholarship and commentary to imagine a world of which England was no longer the centre but in which English language and literature were essential components of an abstract or virtual differential system that spanned the globe.[1] To substantiate this claim, I concentrate on the infamous narratives of decline that characterize early twentieth-century fiction. I read these tales not only for the myriad ways they argued that England no longer occupied the core of an ever-expanding empire, but also for how they revised the very distinctions between British nation and English culture on which empire-building depended. I observe that such stories elevated English while devaluing Great Britain. In the process, they helped authorize immigrants and colonial subjects to write fiction in English that privileged marginality for a cosmopolitan readership.

In the hands of Virginia Woolf, James Joyce, and Joseph Conrad, English became exotic. Their writings accustomed readers to finding the

---

[1] For an account of modernism as the literary participant in an English culture convinced of its twilight status, see Meisel (5). This perception of modernism is, of course, widespread. For elaborations of the thesis that modernist narratives of decline reflected economic and social malaise, see also Bongie and Simpson.

very essence of high art in nonstandard, idiosyncratic prose. At the same time, they acquainted readers with a host of alien locales, many of which lay within England itself. In such places readers discovered English mongrelized into a various yet global, particular yet universal, popular yet elite medium.[2] This transformation did not repudiate linguistic tradition per se, so much as transgress the rules that governed English culture in the Victorian era. *Mrs Dalloway, Ulysses,* and *Lord Jim* portrayed languages that were neither fully English nor fully foreign. From the islands of the South Pacific to the London suburbs, these novels discovered vernaculars that could be described only through a rhetoric of neither/nor. This is the rhetoric of litotes, or the double negative, which Michel Foucault characterizes as an attempt to move beyond arguments 'for' or 'against', and instead emphasize 'what is not or is no longer indispensable' ('What is Enlightenment?' 43). What was no longer indispensable for modernism, as it turned out, was English's status as a standardized imperial language. The English vernaculars that appear in the pages of early twentieth-century fiction can best be understood as not *not* English, languages shaped by British imperialism that nevertheless represent clear attempts to reject the inside/outside alternatives that organized the peoples, cultures, and idioms of the British Empire in previous centuries.

This rhetorical innovation should be read as a key part of a broad and multifaceted social and cultural transformation habitually invoked by historians, economists, and other scholars of the early twentieth century. Although there is no end of discussion about exactly when modernity occurs or exactly what it entails, critics generally agree that one of its pivotal features is the emergence of systems and networks that reconfigured modes of communication and the lived experience of time and space. This contention is evident in writing that credits technologies with the dual effect of violating boundaries and establishing new types of interconnection.[3] Barriers break down 'horizontally across the face of the land and vertically across social strata', according to Stephen Kern, as transportation improvements speed movement across continents and communication devices rapidly transmit privileged information to the

---

2 '[G]lobalization [enacts] the uncoupling of the "natural" link between languages and nations, languages and national memories, languages and national literatures', writes Mignolo (42). Although he takes this to be a largely late-twentieth-century phenomenon, I argue that it is a process that properly began in the nineteenth century, and developed aggressively during the modernist era.

3 Kern's list of significant technologies entering general use around the turn of the century includes the 'telephone, wireless telegraph, x-ray, cinema, bicycle, automobile, and airplane' (1).

ears of the hoi polloi (316). Friedrich Kittler identifies psychophysical alteration that new technology engenders when he describes how human thoughts, bodies, and actions begin to appear as supplements to machinic activity. 'Our writing tools are also working on our thoughts', Kittler quotes from Nietzsche, 'the first mechanized philosopher' (*Gramophone* 200). He observes that to think of the human body as a kind of machine is to understand it in a comprehensively different manner. 'Instead of the classical question of what people would be capable of if they were adequately and affectionately "cultivated"', Kittler notes, 'one asks what people have always been capable of when autonomic functions are singly and thoroughly tested' (*Discourse* 214). One also asks what other kinds of machines people can be plugged into. And, further, one notes that to raise the problem of being embedded in a potentially expansive mechanical system also raises the problem of describing such a network.

Connectivity has a rather different valence in Rudolf Hilferding's classic account *Finance Capital: A Study of the Latest Phase of Capitalist Development.* Technological innovation was spurred on by and enabled economic transformation, according to Hilferding. Railroads spearhead nothing less than a 'revolution in transport' that allowed producers to improve their turnover time and retailers to respond more rapidly to demand, especially in foreign markets (323). The export of capital was a signal event for producers and consumers, but it meant the most to specialists engaged in the activities of banking and speculation Hilferding associates with 'finance capital', an emergent economic segment dominated by Britain at the twentieth century's dawn (315). 'The export of capital was . . . an English monopoly', he contends, 'and it secured for England the domination of the world market' (323). Although Britain soon lost its commanding position to Germany and especially the United States, according to Hilferding and Giovanni Arrighi it established the shape of what was to come: a model of international finance organized not only to ensure the rapid mobility of capital but also to focus economic activity on speculation in and accumulation of financial instruments.[4]

Envisioning the globe as an abstract system criss-crossed by economic and technological pulses of information and exchange had the paradoxical

---

4 On this transition from British to American hegemony, see Hilferding 323 and Arrighi, *Long Twentieth Century* 219. The literature on this transformation of the economy is voluminous. Accounts that articulate it to changes in literature, the arts, and culture include Harvey's description of the 'casino economy' in *The Condition of Postmodernity* and Jameson's Arrighi-inspired 'Culture and Finance Capital'.

effect of increasing interest in location. 'The free flow of capital across the globe', David Harvey explains, combined with 'the shrinkage of space that brings diverse communities across the globe into competition with each other implies localized competitive strategies and a heightened sense of awareness of what makes a place special' (271). Kern makes a similar point, observing that technological spread affirmed the 'plurality of time and spaces' rather than social, cultural, and geographic homogeneity (8). Even as capital went global, it directed attention to small differences and local variations.

Niklas Luhmann argues that this process of differentiation went so far as to beg the 'question of whether the self-description of the world society is possible' (430). Since 'there is no longer a "good society"', the broad terms of culture as civilization proffered by the Victorians must necessarily give way to more 'regional delimitations' and more or less connected communication subsystems (430, xii). These feature vernaculars specific to institutions and disciplines as well as idioms localized geographically. Fredric Jameson takes the Luhmannian process of differentiation as a defining feature of modernity – 'the gradual separation of areas of social life from each other, their disentanglement from some seemingly global and mythic . . . overall dynamic, and their reconstitution as distinct fields with distinct laws and dynamics' (*Singular* 90). But Jameson also sees this process as modernism's condition of possibility, since this same differentiation encourages an unprecedented sense of aesthetic autonomy and literary specialization (*Singular* 146).

By imagining the proliferation of local Englishes on a planet-wide scale, modernism laid the ground for the most utopian accounts of globalization as free intellectual and commercial exchange.[5] It also anticipated globalization's neocolonial aspects by identifying an English that was a cut above the rest.[6] Novelists established a highly specialized literary language that, in retrospect, seems clearly related to the rising authority of the professions. Edward Said observes that 'the intellectual hegemony of Eliot, Leavis, Richards, and the New Critics coincides not only with the work of masters like Joyce, Eliot himself, Stevens, and Lawrence, but also with the serious and autonomous development of literary studies in the university' (*The World, the Text and the Critic* 164). Louis Menand

---

5 On globalization as a freeing of exchange, see the *Foreign Policy* special study 'Measuring Globalization'. The widespread conclusion that globalization and less regulated trade go together appears in Giddens as well and in Bhagwati's essays in *Stream*.
6 On globalization as neocolonialism, see Lazarus and Paul Smith.

identifies further grounds for embedding modernism amidst a range of developing professions, arguing that the 'manner in which the modern artist tried to keep his ideological distance from the businessman, to guard the autonomy of his work, was also one of the ways in which the artist and the businessman were both, in spite of their self-conceptions, bound together' (101).[7]

As Harold Perkin explains in *The Rise of Professional Society: England Since 1880*, the modernist period saw the consolidation of a professional-managerial class fed by the growing institutions of the welfare state, a modern university system, and the financial service sector that made London the hub of global commerce. 'The professionals are not just another ruling class', Perkin claims, for their hierarchical rearrangement of labour around such notions as qualification and specialization 'reach[es] much further down the social pyramid than ever landlordship or even business capital did' (3). With the benefits of professional designation widespread, including the capacity to restrict the market for specific types of labour from plumbing to preaching, it is perhaps not surprising that professionalism spawned an ideology appealing even to those who did not benefit from it at work. Perkin argues:

[S]ince the professional's status and income depend less on the market than on his power to persuade society to set an agreed value on his service, the ideal implied the principle of a just reward not only for the particular profession but for every occupation necessary to society's well-being. Since, too, the ideal is justified by social efficiency and the avoidance of waste, particularly the waste of human talent, it implied a principle of social justice which extended to the whole population. (8–9)

As Perkin goes on to note, professionalism could never fully live up to its social ideal. Not every form of social activity could lead to the sorts of benefits associated with established professions and even those were unevenly empowered and rewarded. Professionalism did away with the inequality of class society by shedding the 'binary model [of] a small ruling class exploiting a large underclass', but it replaced this with new 'inequalities and rivalries of hierarchy' (9).

The contradiction between professionals as a class and professionalism as an ideal resulted in tension that was both productive and broadly

---

7 Based on such arguments, Robbins sums up the critical situation in his *Secular Vocations*. He observes that it is 'no longer shocking' to associate developments in English literature with professionalism (64).

transformative. The notion that all varieties of human talent were potentially valuable offered the possibility of redefining activities of all sorts.
This was so because the primary bar to professionalization was not
academic accreditation, Perkin argues, but rather successful persuasion:
'The professions in general . . . live by persuasion and propaganda, by
claiming that their particular service is indispensable' (6). Accreditation
and publicly verifiable qualifications were means for persuading people to
treat a particular activity as specialized and even professional labor, but
they were far from the only means.

Novelists of difficult fiction, for instance, could not earn diplomas or
pass exams to gain recognition for their work. Their tactics were different,
as I show in my first chapter chronicling the efforts of Joseph Conrad to
persuade his friends, agents, and publishers to judge him by rules other
than those applied to some run-of-the-mill author. His campaign to get
himself designated as an elevated sort of writer, an expert who transformed adventure fictions into art, should be treated as an effort to
professionalize his endeavour, despite the fact that it lacks the familiar
institutional signs of accreditation. Conrad's attempt appeared, we must
remember, at a time when many of the professions we now recognize as
such were only just beginning to form. In Chapter 2 I demonstrate that an
ethnographer like Malinowski needed to do as much persuading as any
modernist novelist, and that in this effort he borrowed liberally from the
very fictional genres writers such as Conrad also sought to revise. I attend
to another aspect of expertise in my third chapter when I focus on gender
and imperial representation. I consider, for instance, how the pictorial
representation of landscape, which in the nineteenth century might
have been executed by any ordinary middle-class woman, came to seem
a more demanding task featuring the sort of careful attention to cultural
difference one finds in the likes of E.M. Forster's *A Passage to India*.

The success of Conrad and similarly inclined writers may well explain
why literature provides Perkin with '[p]erhaps the best example' of a field
that successfully professionalized work on 'subject matter [previously]
accessible to the laity' (*Rise* 395–6). Inside and outside the academy,
literature sought to 'become *the* humane discipline, the modern substitute
for philosophy and theology' (396). Not surprisingly, Perkin has in mind
F.R. Leavis's famed insistence that 'liberal education should be centred in
the study of creative literature [and] that for English-speaking people it
must be centred in the literature of the English language' (*Critic* 166).
Leavis's nativism notwithstanding, his definition of English as a linguistic
rather than national category is apparent from the literary selections that

receive his attention. Francis Mulhern reminds us that in *The Great Tradition*, only one of Leavis's chosen novelists – George Eliot – is English ('English Reading' 254). As Gauri Viswanathan's foundational *Masks of Conquest: Literary Study and British Rule in India* demonstrates furthermore, the notion of English literature as the foundation of liberal education was not an entirely homegrown idea but one nurtured by colonial administrators in nineteenth-century India.

Literary study of the sort recommended by Leavis reveals an imperial aspect to professionalism largely missing from Perkin's study. To be fair, *The Rise of Professional Society* does make pointed reference to the world outside England. It notes the importance of reforms to the Indian Civil Service that mandated qualifying examination in the wake of the so called Indian Mutiny (371). The Boer War looms large over a discussion of turn-of-the-century debate about national efficiency (158–89). And decolonization, when it comes, makes an appearance as well. By and large, though, Perkin describes the rise of professionalism as an internal development. Thankfully, substantial scholarship allows us to see professionalism and imperialism operating in tandem. These works include disciplinary specific studies (such as Stocking, *After Tylor*; Mitchell, *Rule*; and Errington) as well as broader social accounts (such as Kuklick, *Savage*; Desai; and Cain and Hopkins). Equally important research considers modernism and imperialism side by side.[8] I believe these accounts logically require us to take the next step and triangulate modernism, professionalism, and imperialism, which in turn allows us to redescribe them as components of a new whole.

The writing and study of literature shared strategy as well as tactics with other professions. Collaborating more or less inadvertently, experts learned to distinguish their discipline-specific idioms from one another and to categorize them as valid permutations of a fast disappearing imperial mother tongue. At the same time, literary specialists joined experts in fields ranging from anthropology to economics in focusing on regionalized social activity both inside and outside England. The local vernaculars they discovered differed from specialized professional idioms, but were similar insofar as they were idiomatic. The boundaries between them were not entirely stable, as professional writers compulsively

---

8 Criticism such as Felski; Gikandi; North, *Dialect*; and Torgovnick informs my analysis of primitivism in Chapter 4. My fifth chapter on imperialism and local culture depends on Baucom; Esty, *Shrinking Island*; and Manganaro. My sense of modernism's relationship to imperialism owes notable debts as well to scholarship that includes Said, *Culture and Imperialism*; Suleri; Duffy; and Bivona.

appropriated syntax and terminology from most every locality. Instead, specialized languages differed from regional varieties in their tendency to enforce a distinction between high and low cultural production in general. No more or less than anthropology, psychology, and economics, modernist fiction made linguistic facility necessary for understanding, administering, and mediating an infinitely divisible, multilingual, yet English-speaking globe.[9] We owe the persisting distinction between global expert languages and regionally specific creoles to such innovation.[10]

To understand modernist literature as part of a turn-of-the-century boom in increasingly authoritative specialized languages is to question a long-standing critical premise that rarefied language cannot have widespread effects. Such an assumption allows Michael Levenson, for instance, to define an aesthetic movement whose flight from tradition does little more than express a dying worldview. Here, modernism marks a historical ending, as Levenson argues that early twentieth-century novelists understood 'a declining [British] liberalism . . . [as] a distinct literary opportunity . . . and a release from extra-artistic responsibilities' (*Genealogy* 53–4).[11] By taking the novel to the level of high art, modernism appears to have abdicated any capacity to shape the social world that so clearly shaped it. An enduring formula dictates: the more complex the language, the narrower its social impact. Similarly, scholars concerned with the late twentieth century typically take modernism as an avant-garde beginning and thus restrict it to either anticipating the postmodern or going popular and losing its edge. Jameson reproduces this logic when he describes

9 On linguistic schemes for analyzing different varieties of English, see Pakir and Mufwene. See Willinsky and Pennycook on the persistence of British imperialism in the continued spread and use of English.

10 Bourdieu provides a sociological vocabulary for intellectual 'uses' of the people ('Uses'). See also the World Bank publication 'Local Dynamics in an Era of Globalization', Ching and also Hay on the 'coercive convergence' that causes regional variation to emerge as a result of transnational management, and Sunder Rajan for a formulation of the persistent question within postcolonial studies about how scholarly methods shape the circulation of local cultures (Yusuf, et al.; Hay 525; Sunder Rajan 613). Twenty-first-century US hegemony still relies on this relationship between global and local knowledge, though that debt is occluded by America's wish to inherit the mantle of British civilization while disavowing its imperial legacy. See Beard and Beard, W. Williams, and the recent writings of Ferguson. Tennenhouse observes that English fiction 'allowed Americans to think of themselves as English, despite their political separation from England' (178). See Kaplan and Pease on the notion of imperialism in American literary and cultural studies.

11 Classic iterations of this formula include Auerbach's reading of Mrs Ramsay's brown stocking as a symbol for futile attempts to order a shattered world, and Lukács's description of formalism as solipsistic elitism (*Realism* 39). More contemporary versions include Berman's treatment of modernism's 'spectacular triumphs in art and thought' as the culmination of 500 years of modernization undercut by a public 'shatter[ed] into a multitude of fragments, speaking incommensurable private languages' (17).

the 'postmodern revolt' as a commodified reiteration of early twentieth-century experimentation (*Postmodernism* 4). In either case, we are invited to understand modernist writings as cultural epiphenomena that may have reflected a wider structure of feeling but whose effects were more or less limited to a hermetically sealed realm of aesthetics. We have taken modernist autonomy at its word, in short, and granted modernist literature the authority to define the narrow confines of its influence to the scholarly and esoteric realm of the arts.[12]

I propose instead to consider modernist fiction as an influential and productive component in a pivotal discourse of administration. I believe modernism rightly belongs within a history that does not stop and start somewhere around the turn of the twentieth century, but mutates and migrates from the mid-1800s to the present day. Modernist fiction was an active participant in what Perkin refers to as the twentieth-century 'triumph' of professionalism both as an ideal and as a mechanism for remaking institutions large and small throughout England and the British Empire. Allow me to show how I see the three 'isms' of modernism, imperialism, and professionalism working together by turning to the question of how to historicize modernism's specialized aesthetics.

THE RISE OF LITOTES

To be precise in our assessment of the world as modernism depicted it, we need to be clear about the social universe twentieth-century writers sought to displace. When Linda Colley charts the consolidation of Great Britain in the 1700s, she explains that Britons 'came to define themselves as a single people not because of any political or cultural consensus at home, but rather in reaction to the Other beyond their shores' (6). Nineteenth-century writers found it equally important to preserve a British identity opposed to the foreign cultures of Europe and the larger world, but considered this endeavour increasingly difficult to sustain. With the incorporation of new and far-flung territories, a significant portion of the globe that had been considered outside the nation came to occupy a place within it.[13] At the same time, the new and strange cultures discovered in

---

12 On this point, see Jameson's chapter 'Modernism as Ideology' in *Singular Modernity*.

13 Gikandi and Baucom recount British responses to pressure to preserve some kind of British essence. Even as artists and politicians alike agreed that the 'modern British nation [could not] be imagined outside the realm of the empire', Parliament rehabilitated a feudal 'law of the soil' as the ultimate test of citizenship (Gikandi 31; Baucom 8–9).

Africa and Asia seemed to contrast neatly with a British style of life. Britain absorbed entire continents that paradoxically served as the foreign substance against which a British essence could be defined. The very territories that helped designate the political entity of the British state were perceived as its cultural opposites. Africa and Asia were assimilated into Britain and simultaneously excluded from it. As V.Y. Mudimbe explains this chiasmatic logic, colonial peoples and places appeared in Victorian writing as 'not only the Other who is everyone except me, but [also] the key which, in its abnormal differences, specifies the identity of the Same' (*Invention of Africa* 12).

Such logic was interrupted by the early twentieth-century shift towards technological, financial, and professional interconnection. In the context of such epochal change, the place of Britain in the larger world necessarily changed as well. Three particular features were especially significant to the new conjuncture. First, anti-imperial writers from the colonies ever more aggressively appropriated the putatively English terms of nationalism and human rights.[14] Second, a steady diet of imported goods and a growing immigrant population made clear that the exotic was as much an integral component of day-to-day life in the British Isles as English language and literature were part and parcel of colonial existence.[15] Third, Britain found itself suddenly vulnerable to competition with the manufacturing powerhouses belonging to a next generation of empire builders in Germany and the United States.[16]

Commentators responded both to these conjunctural changes and to the broader epochal shift by seeking to preserve some sense of English authenticity. Social critics portrayed the Empire as a threat to England's security that required the adoption of extreme protective measures. General William Booth's *In Darkest England* and William Reeves's *In Darkest London* were among the tracts indicating that the infiltration of foreign elements was well advanced. They documented an influx of migrants rapidly transforming London into an 'urban jungle' and argued that only the sternest blockade could halt the invasion (McLaughlin 4–5).[17] Popular fictions described international commerce as inherently dangerous. In the

---

14 For a good historical overview of Indian nationalism in this period, see Sarkar, *Modern India*, and on the various forms of African nationalism, see Davidson, *Let Freedom Come*.
15 On the importation of colonial objects and ideas, see Baucom, Daly, Gikandi, and Kuklick, *Savage*. For statistics on immigration, see Fryer.
16 Important histories on this geo-political contest include Robinson et al., Arrighi, and Hobsbawm.
17 Novels such as H.F. Lester's *Taking of Dover* and Rider Haggard's *She* also stoked fears of reverse colonization (Brantlinger 235).

detective stories of Arthur Conan Doyle, for instance, foreign bodies and foreign things came to represent a dissolute influence every bit as pernicious as the opium addiction slowly killing Holmes.[18] Inadvertently or not, by locating the foreign in every pore of the English body, such writing tended to undermine the very opposition of core and periphery it hoped to sustain. Newspaper commentators and politicians allied themselves with authors of potboilers in desperate attempts at reinforcement that only exacerbated the problem. The more hyperbolic their writing, the more difficult it became for them to maintain such a distinction.

In Chapter 4 of this book, I observe how novelists from Sarah Grand to D.H. Lawrence proved that such a distinction could not be maintained when they developed a literary language of primitivism that competed with, even as it borrowed from anthropological and evolutionary writing. Like-minded authors portrayed 'the underside of liberalism . . . a nightmare vision of unruly subjects . . . unamenable to. . .formal democratic calculus', '[a] popular mind', as the economist J.A. Hobson put it, 'reverted . . . into a type of primitive savagery' (quoted in Glover 41–2). To describe this popular 'type', novelists drew on the writings of Sigmund Freud, Max Nordau, Herbert Spenser, and the psychiatrist Henry Maudsley in representing the English as 'savages of a decomposing civilization' (see Arata 26). The idea of a population becoming progressively less civilized fed on newspaper reports of recruits failing Army physicals during the Boer War and was further propelled by suggestively allegorical histories of collapse such as Oswald Spengler's *Decline of the West*.[19] World War I provided more grist for the mill, as writers in every genre wallowed in a decadent England of maimed foreigners and shell-shocked soldiers (Arata 140–1; Dean 61). Lawrence summed up the discourse in a 1915 letter: 'I think there is no future for England, only a decline and fall' (*Letters* 2: 441).[20]

---

18 See Keep and Randall. Brantlinger identifies Wodehouse's *The Swoop . . . A Tale of the Great Invasion* as a sweeping imitation of this sort of narrative, while Gissing's Henry Ryecroft ridicules the chronic concern over foreign products when he stops dead in the street at the sight of imported butter: 'This is the kind of thing that makes one gloom over the prospects of England. The deterioration of English butter is one of the worst signs of the moral state of our people' (Brantlinger 235; Gissing 152; and see Trotter, 154).

19 As Trotter recounts, Boer War recruiting 'campaigns revealed that 60 per cent of Englishmen were unfit for military service' (112–13). Statistics about poor English fitness were circulated so widely in the press and were so clearly ready-made for popular exploitation that the government organized an Inter-Departmental Committee on Physical Degeneration to manage the discourse. On Spengler and modernism, especially Lawrence, see Shaffer.

20 'There is in all these works a certain atmosphere of universal doom', Auerbach noted with characteristic understatement in *Mimesis*, echoing Lawrence as he assessed Woolf's *To the Lighthouse* and postwar writing in general (551).

Lawrence's very negation paradoxically affirmed the future of English language, literature, and culture, even though he concluded that the invasion of England by foreign elements meant the end of its centrality within a larger Britain. Though a genealogy of writers leading straight to Enoch Powell persisted in attempting to reinscribe 'an old insular culture from within the bloated, multicultural empire', Lawrence and others fell in love with the discordant alien stuff they discovered from London to Glasgow, Cardiff to Kent (Esty, 'National Objects' 9; see also Baucom 10–14). They expressed their affection for foreign matter by mixing domestic romance and the romance of adventure, thus muddying literary distinctions between home and abroad. They borrowed an assortment of strange and wonderful commodities from international commerce and proceeded to redecorate the English home. They deposited lust for foreign travel in the heads of the sort of fictional heroines who for more than a century had dreamed of marriage and motherhood.

Underpinning persistent tropes of decline was a sense that a little degeneration might be a good thing. It bespoke an intoxicating exoticism and offered new means to reinvent English in all of its incipient diversity. As I argue in Chapter 5, what emerged was an English culture radically different from that associated with the 'country', the model most resonant to eighteenth- and nineteenth-century readers. Raymond Williams explains that in previous centuries England's countryside represented the ideal against which modernity was measured, a 'rural democracy' that predated the enclosure, industrialization, and privatization of land and wealth (*Country and City* 102). Paired with the city, the country generated a series of oppositions between urban opacity and rural transparency, the impersonal and the personal, learning and instinct, the modern and the premodern, the artificial and the authentic (156). Modernist country could not have been more different. It was 'a queer jumble of the old England and the new', a pastoral setting flooded with primitive sludge (Williams, 264).[21] Novelists invested the countryside with the properties of a British colony. Marlow opens Conrad's 'Heart of Darkness' by acknowledging that England 'also . . . has been one of the dark places of the earth' (48). Clarissa Dalloway declares that walking the streets of Westminster makes one feel 'out, far out to sea and alone' (*Mrs Dalloway* 11). And there was a general predilection for heroines recalling 'the type of

---

21 In Lawrence's fiction, Williams writes, 'it is rather a primitivism [that makes] accessible . . . direct living in contact with natural processes – animals and birds and flowers and trees but also the human body, the naked exploration and relationship' (*Country and City* 266).

old Egypt' (Grand 32).[22] So common was this strategy that, far from horrifying them, the transformation of English people and places must have thrilled writers and readers alike with an invigorating *frisson*.

Modernist fiction shared an understanding of what makes places feel local with diverse disciplines, most notably anthropology. Although modernist anthropology is generally thought of as the inventor of the ethnic island – the isolated culture stuck in primitive time – Arjun Appadurai shows how early twentieth-century fascination with closed cultural systems produced documents of imperial contact and historic change. 'Much that has been considered local knowledge is actually knowledge of how to produce and reproduce locality under conditions of anxiety and entropy, social wear and flux, ecological uncertainty and cosmic volatility, and the always present quirkiness of kinsmen, enemies, spirits, and quarks of all sorts' (*Modernity* 181). Modernism and anthropology did not discover these mitigating historical and political terms but invested them with new importance by making them the concern of specialists.

I explain in Chapter 5 that while anthropology and literature shared an investment in local culture, they approached it in distinct ways. Literary descriptions of various and sundry English places relied on a specialized aesthetic that allowed writers and artists to gather detailed bits and pieces from around the world and compose them into cosmopolitan local scenes. In a series of books and articles historicizing early twentieth-century art and literature, Jameson observes that modernism set out to master what it perceived as the fragmentation of social existence by transforming the fragment itself into an aesthetic object. Novelists wrote fictions whose style replicated 'the specialization and divisions of capitalist life, at the same time [seeking] . . . in precisely such fragmentation a desperate Utopian compensation for them' (*Postmodernism* 7).[23] This resistance collapsed, Jameson explains, because capitalism incorporated 'artistic production . . . into commodity production generally' (*Postmodernism* 4).

---

22 Among the host of additional examples, especially of the way primitivism became associated with the very domesticity that had once been so inviolate, one might also look at the scandalously popular short stories of George Egerton. Not even Kurtz's fiancée, the 'pale visage[d]' Intended, escaped the touch of primitivism. Though she is unaware of the mark upon her, Marlow sees it. As he gazes at her in the closing pages of 'Heart of Darkness', she appears haunted by her African double, that 'wild and gorgeous apparition of a woman' who shared Kurtz's hut and whose outstretched arms, 'bedecked with powerless charms', echo the Intended's final gesture (135, 160).

23 Modernism, Jameson writes, 'faithfully . . . reproduced and represented the increasing abstraction and deterritorialization of . . . [the] "imperialist stage"' while at the same time behaving as if through its artwork 'a stricken world . . . [might] by some Nietzschean fiat and act of the will be transformed into the stridency of Utopian color' ('Culture' 252; *Postmodernism* 9).

What Jameson considers a failure might equally be considered a successful effort to extend and intensify social fragmentation. Perhaps modernist texts deal in fragments because the modernists had to prove beyond a doubt that the world had gone to pieces before they could offer to reassemble it. To see just such a salvage operation in action, one might revisit what are surely the most generative fragments identified by Jameson, the 'sharp metallic clangs bursting out suddenly from the depths of the ship' in *Lord Jim* (*The Political Unconscious* 213). Jameson describes these clangs as remainders of an 'older repressed content' that Conrad has 'derealized' by rewriting 'in the terms of the aesthetic' (214). The older content in question is none other than the 'former real world' of working-class labour, a 'ground bass of material production [that] continues underneath the new formal structures of the modernist text' ('Culture' 265; *Political Unconscious* 215).[24]

Jameson reads *Lord Jim* as repressing the clanging fragment along with its historical origin, but the art historian Rosalind Krauss shows we could as easily understand the novel as redefining what that clang is. As she explains, modernist fragments demonstrate the linguistic thesis that signs have 'no natural relation to a referent' (28).[25] When Conrad writes of 'the harsh scrape of a shovel, the violent slam of a furnace-door [exploding] brutally, as if the men handling the mysterious things below had their breast full of fierce anger', readers who remember the Victorian industrial novel must understand his use of redolent synecdoche, familiar as they are with such gritty portraits of working-class life as those penned by Friedrich Engels and Henry Mayhew (*Lord Jim* 13).[26] Conrad's 'clangs' refer to all those works of social realism and incorporate fragments of that discourse into an even more specialized kind of writing.

---

24 Later in Jameson's narrative, postmodern art unabashedly campaigns to make a world that needs 'neither production (as capital does) nor consumption (as money does), which supremely, like cyberspace, can live on . . . [its] own internal metabolisms and circulate without any reference to an older type of content' ('Culture' 265). If repression describes the modernist text, postmodern art exhibits denial: it mirrors 'the total flow of the circuits of financial speculation . . . [as it] steers unwittingly towards a crash' ('Culture' 265).

25 The fragment, Krauss writes, is 'in itself indeterminable, for it might be almost anything – bubbles of soda, stripes of shadow, rays of sun – . . . [that] hardens and solidifies, its lines of writing now posturing as the graining of wood. Thus the piece becomes the support, or signifier, for a . . . signified' (27). One may find ample evidence for this way of interpreting the fragment in modernist fiction. Woolf, for instance, trains readers to deduce a context from often minute details. In *Orlando*, she dictates the 'reader's part in making up from bare hints dropped here and there the whole boundary and circumference of a living person' (*Orlando* 73).

26 See Gallagher, *Industrial Reformation* and Lesjak on Victorian industrial writing.

The auditory transformation of industrial description accompanies all the fragments in this section of *Lord Jim*, which melds the heavy labour of the boiler room with the professional task of piloting the ship *Patna*. While stoking the boiler produces a clang, steering the ship makes 'the links of wheel-chains [grind] heavily in the grooves of the barrel' (13). Even Jim's relatively genteel occupation yields a similar effect: 'Jim would glance at the compass . . . would stretch himself till his joints cracked with a leisurely twist of the body' (13). Though elevated through the 'leisurely' quality of its 'twist', Jim's cracking body still echoes the scraping shovels of labour.

By emphasizing this relationship, *Lord Jim* does not displace the world of material production so much as revitalize the tired description of the industrial novel. The metonymic slide from the clangs below deck to the grinding and cracking above allows Conrad to defamiliarize industrial realism. His auditory signs, meanwhile, return us to the referent and promise to present, once and for all, the unvarnished truth of toil as a multifarious activity involving not only heavy lifting but also expert navigation. Though the elevated position of the pilot's perch above the boiler room preserves a sense of hierarchy, Conrad transforms class difference between manager and worker into a precise counterpoint of clangs and cracks, manifesting the rhythmic underpinning to a veritable symphony of synergistic work. Thus *Lord Jim* gives literary substance to the administrative fantasies of early twentieth-century professionals who aspired to integrate their expertise into all sorts of economic activities. It treats the physical toil associated with labour and the intellectual knowledge of specialized services as integral parts of a larger whole. Once Conrad has disassembled the descriptive language of industrial fiction into so many auditory fragments, he reassembles them in a way that reveals a revised sense of the labour on his ship.

Tellingly, Conrad locates this retooled representation of professional work overseas rather than, say, in a mill town or urban slum. Pilots crack and stokers clang as the 'local steamer' *Patna* plies its way up the Somali coast, loaded with apparently Muslim pilgrims headed to the Holy Land. Just as Conrad reduces industrial realism to fragments in order to rewrite and recompose it, he similarly takes apart the world imagined by imperial adventure fiction to put it back together again. The *Patna*'s milieu is composed of synecdoches – the ocean rendered as 'deep folds of water', for instance (11) – while the ship is loaded down by passengers jumbled together into a tableau of fragmented body parts, 'a chin upturned, two closed eyelids, a dark hand with silver rings, a meagre limb draped in a torn covering, a head bent back, a naked foot, a throat bared and stretched as if offering itself to the knife' all 'trembling slightly to the unceasing vibration of the ship' (12).

While the constant trembling compounds earlier references to the domestic industrial novel, these shredded bodies reiterate the stereotypes of imperial romance – not to mention its undisguised violence. The pilgrims hail from the stock settings of adventure fiction: 'solitary huts in the wilderness . . . populous campongs . . . villages by the sea' (9–10). The crew, meanwhile, is a more mongrel version of the wild bunch popularized by Rider Haggard. '[O]wned by a Chinaman', the *Patna* is 'chartered by an Arab . . . commanded by a sort of renegade New South Wales German', engineered by a man of indiscriminate origin who had been 'stranded out East somewhere' and assisted by a 'weak-headed child of Wapping' (9, 13, 16–17).

There is little in this assortment of stock characters and ethnic specimens that is not the product of adventure fiction. As Said shows, Conrad makes the 'aesthetics, politics, and even epistemology' of imperial writing seem 'inevitable and unavoidable' (*Culture and Imperialism* 24). He also 'records its illusions and tremendous violence and waste', however, and 'dates' the ideology of Empire (*Culture and Imperialism* 26). In so doing, *Lord Jim* does not topple imperialism but does revise its textual raw material. Conrad assembles his stereotypes into a seaborne collective that is distinctly different from the jingoistic crew of explorers and natives that was a staple in imperial romance. Although *Lord Jim*'s allusions allow us to attach its characters to English literary tradition, the community that emerges in this novel is not British. As Marlow repeatedly intones that Jim is 'one of us', 'us' clearly does not mean Britons but rather the loose affiliation of vagabond experts, speakers of English, and specialists in cross-cultural relations that Empire engendered and Conrad captures in prose. Their chief representatives are not purebreds but oddballs like Marlow, Jim, and the Bavarian East Asian trader and amateur entomologist named Stein.

In sum, modernist fiction swept aside the chiasmatic relation of inside and out that had enabled the Victorian distinction between English and British. It did so by combining and intensively aestheticizing popular genres habitually associated with the domestic – such as the industrial novel – and the imperial – such as the adventure story. Specialization was not only the technical means to an end, for novels like *Lord Jim* took the spread of professionalism as the content of their narratives as well. They described a network of mongrel managers who shared a language if not a nation, and who laboured to administer a dazzling array of local places populated in large measure by speakers of dialects that were not entirely not English. Conrad was far from alone in separating the notion of what counts as English from the quality of being British. I make the case in Chapter 2 that Conrad's global labour relations were in tune with the state-of-the-art administrative techniques in imperial governance. In the 1890s, for instance, Britain had already started to move away from colonization on the model of Victorian India and towards more mediated rule by proxy that thrived on a cosmopolitan mix of service and industry not so different from that imagined by *Lord Jim.*[27]

THE MODERNIST PROFESSIONAL CLASS

Even pre-modernist imperialism cultivated foreigners who were well versed in English language and culture. Administrators sought to manage colonial territories and peoples, but found they could not do so without teaching their subjects. As early as 1823, officers in India complained, 'the greatest difficulty . . . springs from . . . ignorance of the spirit, principles and system of the British Government' (Pennycook 72). Part of the solution to this problem emerged as 'the content of English literary education [was adapted] to the administrative and political imperatives of British rule' (Viswanathan 3). Though English study in the colonies was intended as a tool for disciplining elites, as Salman Rushdie observes, 'those people who were . . . colonized by the language . . . [were also] rapidly remaking it, domesticating it' (64). Gauri Viswanathan describes, for instance, a father withdrawing his son from school before he was 'intellectually advanced [enough] to understand lectures on Christianity' (13). Or, consider the early Gold Coast agitator Attoh Ahuma, who sought to craft a 'thinking nation' and preserve in English a distinctive knowledge of statecraft possessed by '[o]ur forbears, . . . [who] with all their limitations and disadvantages, had occasion to originate ideas' (Ahuma 6; see Davidson, *Black Man's Burden* 39–40). Through these

---

27 In sub-Saharan Africa, for example, Native Administrations were appointed to manage the day-to-day exploitation of natural resources, while District Commissioners advised them. India saw intensified negotiations to hand off power to indigenous leaders, even as English economists set the priorities for a new Indian Central Bank. For its part, Egypt was the site of efforts to retard industrialization in favour of increased agricultural development managed, yet again, by a local class advised by English experts. For an introduction to African Native Administration, see Afigbo, as well as Crowder and Ikime. On the formation of an Indian Central Bank, see Chandavarkar, *Keynes*. Zeleza's economic history of Africa includes detailed analysis of the de-industrializing of Egypt.

small acts English language, literature, and culture were effectively In-
dianized and Africanized, in a process that simultaneously established the
particularity of the 'English-language . . . of England' as well (Rushdie
64–5).

By spreading literary study throughout the colonies, British administrators, quite unlike their seventeenth- and eighteenth-century counterparts in the Americas, facilitated the proliferation of local English dialects.
They also invited the idea that literary expertise might represent a truly
valuable form of capital, one capable of legitimating the construction of a
whole new class to organize the not entirely un-English cultures being
generated worldwide. '[S]uch a framework . . . focused attention on the
high literati', the historian Sumit Sarkar observes, making them the centre
of modernist colonial historiography as well as early twentieth-century
anticolonial politics (*Writing Social History* 189). Imperialism authorized
such readers and writers to speak for Indians and Africans in general even
as it distinguished them from 'the people' (Guha 94).[28] Such distinction
primed the colonial elite to compete with their European counterparts. It
set the stage, moreover, for what the anthropologist Aihwa Ong calls
flexible citizenship, the constant flux of economic and national loyalties
that describes the governing condition for the many twenty-first-century
experts bearing multiple passports who represent the cutting edge of
global culture (7–21). Neither fully English nor fully foreign, their specialized habits of reading and writing allow them to appropriate the
powers and privileges of English modernism as well as the English
language. Though their labour dislodges European definitions of specialized discourse, the successes and failures of European professionalism are
eminently available to them.[29] As the Singaporean scholar Wang Gungwu
tells the *New York Times*, 'Today, fewer and fewer people think of English
in terms of either England or America . . . in a funny way, it is part of the
identity of a new [global] middle class' (Mydans 6).

If it seems unclear how these polymorphous professionals with their
various revisions of English could ever be considered a class, modernist

---

28 'The only way the indigenous bourgeoisie could hope . . . to compete for hegemony', the
    historian Guha shows, 'was to mobilize the people in a political space of its own making' (101). As
    Kapur suggests, Gandhi's writing 'constructs *and* deconstructs the 'national' via (among other
    symbols) the oppressed figure of the untouchable' (194).
29 This is how Spivak describes the relationship between *The Satanic Verses* and the modernist avant-
    garde. As she writes, 'In postcoloniality, ever metropolitan definition is dislodged. The general
    mode for the postcolonial is citation, reinscription, rerouting the historical. *The Satanic Verses*
    cannot be placed within the European avent-garde, but the successes and failures of the European
    avant-garde are available to it' (*Outside* 217).

fiction provides a theory. James Joyce's *Ulysses* suggests how the plurality of English vernaculars generated by imperialism was assembled into the discursive foundation for a transnational class of English-speaking experts. Joyce imagines vernaculars to exist in parallel relationship with one another as historical and geographic differences abide, producing new combinations through juxtaposition. His 'Oxen of the Sun' chapter disassembles English into heterogeneous components before reassembling it into a fair approximation of a global tongue. The chapter begins by mimicking a Latin dialect, moves on to a bawdy Anglo-Saxon style, then Middle English, and so on and so forth until its last pages, where Joyce 'talks' what he himself described as 'a frightful jumble of pidgin English, nigger English, Cockney, Irish, Bowery slang and broken doggerel' (*Letters* 138–39). As he mimics them, Joyce turns what might otherwise resemble a narrative of historical progression into one of polyglot competition. Set side by side, these forms of English – vernacular and official, ancient and modern, written and spoken, standard and slang – become a gallimaufry of international styles. The Anglo-Saxon phrase 'Truest bed-thanes they twain are', offered early on in the chapter is no more and no less exotic than the contemporary bit of street speech, 'Hoots, mon, a wee drap to pree', that comes at the close. Neither is exactly foreign – they both resemble English – though neither is remotely standard. By the time he is done, Joyce has dragged his readers through what amounts to a densely polyvocal assemblage of almost, but not quite English sentences. In so doing, he may bring us to understand that English language and culture have been so tainted by a long history of lexical cross-pollination that they can no longer be considered national categories.[30]

Because these fragments of linguistic history make sense only when understood within the autonomous relational system that is *Ulysses*, moreover, the novel becomes the very place where English falls apart in order to receive a new formal coherence. Joyce offers the specialized milieu of modernist fiction as the venue for defining the polyglot English that imperial history has wrought and that globalization will demand.[31]

---

30 Pollack shows how vernacular languages themselves are best understood not as autochthonous but as the product of cosmopolitan contact. On global English, see Fishman, Conrad, and Rubal-Lopez.

31 Instead of presenting English as a standard language, Joyce shows English as 'a variety of broken forms of English: English as it has been invaded, and as it has hegemonized a variety of other languages without being able to exclude them' (S. Hall 179). Doyle observes that in the midst of this linguistic exchange, Joyce presents his characters mulling over eugenics and national and racial fitness, thus implying that all kinds of authenticity were being reconsidered in the light of globalization (115).

'Oxen of the Sun' refuses the core–periphery geography governing so many accounts of global English, moreover.[32] It calls into question any formula that groups English into original and derivative categories, while suggesting that the conversion of the language into a transnational accumulation of local variations neither began nor ended with modernism. Rather, Joyce helps us to imagine a loosely tied network of ongoing and reciprocal interaction between various English speakers.

The spread of this network influenced and was influenced by new economic and geopolitical realities. As Hilferding and other economic historians have shown, these centred on the City's booming financial sector. By the early decades of the twentieth century, a service sector dominated by finance had outpaced manufacturing as the prime engine of the economy.[33] With market share came increased clout, and 'management of the economy . . . [left] the hands of party politicians and transferred . . . to the Treasury and the Bank of England', which in turn took advice from the City and the economists of Oxbridge (Cain and Hopkins 1: 148–9).[34] City professionals developed a thoroughly cosmopolitan commercial model engineered and administered by international monetary experts well versed in the specialized vernacular of speculation. These specialists behaved as if the only way to save England from the decaying British Empire was to forge new and deeper ties with foreign powers. To this end, they welcomed European and American investors to park money in London's banks, encouraged town and village bankers to invest accounts abroad, urged politicians to negotiate treaties allowing them to fund development in overseas territories not controlled by Britain, and in sum created a 'marriage of English capital with foreign demand' (Goschen 23; Cain and Hopkins 1: 182, 1: 384–5; Davis and

---

32 Crystal observes that linguists generally render 'the spread of English around the world as three concentric circles', Britain and the United States typically occupy an inner circle. India and Singapore, et al. find themselves in a middle loop. While China, Russia, and the rest of the world make up an expanding zone of 'nations which recognize the importance of English' (53–4).

33 London finance acquired a position of dominance over British manufacturing by disinvesting in the nation, steering capital to foreign markets, and pocketing the fees it charged for advising and managing such transfers. Bankers 'largely ignored the problems of domestic industry', thereby stunting automobile, aircraft, and other cutting edge enterprises, and facilitating a precipitous drop in manufacturing throughout the British Isles (P. Anderson 44). By 1901, the service sector as a whole provided nearly one third of all the jobs in Britain, and by 1921 over 40 per cent of Britons were thus employed, many of them in service professions which did not exist a century before (Rubinstein 33).

34 On Keynes and the treasury, see Skidelsky Vol. 3 and 2: 190–3. By the middle of the twentieth century, the British State found itself relegated to making global policy 'from behind' the public face of the most prominent English firms (Arrighi and Silver 281–2).

Huttenback 212).[35] 'In this way, the City and sterling acquired a world role, and London became the center of a system of global payments that continued to expand right down to the outbreak of war in 1914' (Cain and Hopkins 1: 468).

These alterations coincide precisely with the shifting relationship between English culture and British Empire that I have been describing. They also coincide with the United States' efforts to finally make good on long-standing threats to displace Britain as the superpower of the English-speaking world. World War I, its aftermath, the Depression, and finally World War II confirmed America's place on the imperial stage and drove another nail into Great Britain's coffin. Nonetheless, the transnational elite that emerged from this period remained in many ways distinctly un-American.

In 1944, John Maynard Keynes reported to the House of Lords that the United States had taken control of the global clearing union that he had spent the last several years working to establish. He told them to expect the dollar to be the new global currency when the dust settled after World War II, and to understand that the new agencies of international economy, the IMF and the World Bank, would be located in Washington (*Collected Writings* 26: 211). Curiously, Keynes characterized this as good news, if not for Britain as a whole, then at least for the experts of the City. 'We are in no position . . . to set up as international bankers', he informed the Chancellor of the Exchequer, 'unless we can secure a general settlement on the basis of temporary American assistance followed by an international scheme' (25: 412). Becoming 'Vice-Chairman, so to speak, to their [American] chairmanship' was the only way for English services to hold onto their position as the facilitators of global investment (26: 234). To the House of Lords Keynes opined, 'So far from an international plan endangering the long tradition, by which most Empire countries, and many other countries, too, have centred their financial systems in London, the plan is, in my judgment, an indispensable means of maintaining this tradition' (26: 12). In response to worried editorials in *The Times*, Keynes emphatically confirmed, 'No country has more to gain from it [the plan] than ourselves' (26: 8).

35 The City housed joint stock banks from around the world. It sponsored debt in the United States and Europe, in European colonies, and in unallied regions of Central and South America, and English finance attempted to corner the market in providing the services of international 'intermediation which enabled . . . [investment in production anywhere in the world] to take place' (Ingham 48).

Perhaps Keynes merely made a virtue of necessity. Nonetheless, the manner in which he did so begs the question of who exactly constitutes 'ourselves'? It is hard to miss how the people of Britain recede behind English professionals in Keynes's speech to the Lords. British decline seems less pressing to him than preserving the influence of those specialists on global commerce. 'I dare to speak for the much abused so-called experts', Keynes informed Parliament. 'I even venture sometimes to prefer them, without intending any disrespect, to politicians. The common love of truth, bred of a scientific habit of mind, is the closest of bonds between the representatives of divers nations' (*Collected Writings* 26: 20–1).

The very ties of education and expert knowledge that helped generate a national professional-managerial class also laid the foundation for a global class of specialists linked more securely to their overseas colleagues than to their home countries. Keynes worked hard to keep the new institutions of global exchange free from patriotic interference, and in so doing helped make it possible for transnational organizations to offer a cosmopolitan alternative to national class allegiances (26: 234–8). The Bretton Woods negotiations had the not entirely intentional effect of building an institutional home away from home for London bankers. Keynes's spin on the outcome of those talks, moreover, provided English experts with their overseas vocation. 'I fancy', he mused in 1946, 'that the Americans themselves are only half self-conscious about the sea-change which has occurred' (26: 233). While the Americans may not have been capable of understanding what they had wrought, Keynes clearly believed a burgeoning population of Anglophone experts could do so.[36]

Instead of treating the dollar as the unambiguous agent of US domination, Keynes considered it a mongrel currency, the offspring of English expertise and American capital. The dollar was a 'dog of mixed origin . . . a sturdier and more serviceable animal . . . not less loyal and faithful to the purposes for which it has been bred' (26: 10). Those purposes, of course, remained the City's own of smoothing the way for international trade and creating a financial infrastructure for the fluid exchange of money, people, and things.

---

36 When reading Keynes's 'fancy', we might recall *Nostromo* where Conrad, the not not English author, gives voice to the American financier Holroyd, who predicts a brilliant future for himself and the British mine owner. 'We shall be giving the word for everything,' he announces. 'We shall run the world's business whether the world likes it or not' (77). As Subramani observes in his commentary on this passage, 'Conrad's narrative forcefully predicted the route that global finance will take' (153). In short, modernist fiction, like Keynesian economics, gave itself the job of charting the future of other peoples', and often Americans', money.

In the early twenty-first century, residues of this way of thinking about English still inform the vocabulary of globalization: as economists attempt to analyze that chimerical concept, they speak of a spreading 'Anglo-US image' of capitalism and they ask, 'Will Global Capitalism be Anglo-Saxon Capitalism?' (Hay 530, Dore). For his part, Perkin addresses the dissemination of professionalism into Europe, Asia, and the Americas through a frame of 'Anglo-Saxon attitudes' and 'Anglo-American individualism.'[37] Such semantic traces reinforce a tendency to conceive of American hegemony as a revision of British Empire. For instance, the Oxford-educated American historian and member of Nixon's 'kitchen cabinet' William Y. Elliott chaired a mid-1950s study group that described US dominance of the world market as an extension and variation of Victorian imperialism (see Arrighi 280). Questions of American stability in the late 1980s and early 90s, meanwhile, reiterated decline narratives offered by Britain a century before. As the economist Jagdish Bhagwati observes, 'As was Great Britain at that time, America ha[d] been struck by a "diminished giant syndrome"' ('Diminished Giant Syndrome' 95). The politics of leaders as different as Margaret Thatcher, whose monetarist policies preceded and might be seen as a test case for America's own, and Tony Blair, eager to serve as mediator between America, the new Europe, and the former British Empire, underscore the extent to which English experts still aspire to exert their influence from the margins. From the beginning of the century they have attempted to market themselves as valued repositories of 'local "know how"' (Cain and Hopkins 2: 295). It is not too much to say they hoped their professed mastery would only grow more valuable when the task of 'managing "localization"', as the World Bank calls it, became a central challenge for transnational corporations and as American overseas politics began to mandate thorough-going consideration of its imperial aspirations (Yusuf et al. 2). Niall Ferguson is among those who have advised the United States to learn from Britain's example. He has made his reputation arguing that 'For better, for worse – fair and foul – the world we know today is in large measure the product of Britain's age of Empire' and that 'the reality is that the Americans have taken our old role without yet facing the fact that an empire comes with it' (xxix, 370). In the midst of Britain's decline, in short, English specialists did their best to become indispensable – and did so precisely by claiming to understand that decline better than anyone else.

37 See the chapter entitled 'Towards a Global Perspective' in *Third Revolution*.

Conrad, Woolf, Joyce, and company pioneered this way of thinking. Though the network of English experts imagined by Keynes, like the English vernaculars recounted by Joyce, remains overwhelmingly European, the tactic of treating English as a medium for international exchange between specialized readers and writers has proved eminently appropriable by non-Europeans. 'English' no longer names a series of monolithic ethno-linguistic entities, each of which reproduces the nation-form of the others, but rather identifies a way to unify a number of competing English vernaculars through a logic of parallelism. A trans-national field of competing English specialists may seem like a pipe dream in the context of the European and American hypernationalism of the first half of the twentieth century, one as patently fantastic as Stephen Dedalus's desire to 'fly by those nets' of church, nation, and family (Joyce, *Portrait* 203). It remains the case, however, that modernists of various nationalities, from T.S. Eliot and Ford Madox Ford to Richard Wright, Gertrude Stein, and Jean Rhys, reproduced something very much like Stephen's dream. Understanding the imagined community of modernism, therefore, demands an explanation of the relationship between this desire and its imperial forebears, as well as the relationship of each to the political economy of professional specialization. To this end, the following chapters revisit the prose that first informed us the Empire was dead, assured us something new was on the horizon, and confirmed that new thing would be, if not traditionally English, at least English speaking. Having established the general contours of this rhetoric, I proceed to what many consider the beginning of modernist fiction, to Joseph Conrad and his efforts to elevate novel-writing into an art.

CHAPTER I

Conrad's gout

They are the same words that the Bourgeois reads every morning –
the very same! But then . . . if he finds them again in one of my
poems he no longer understands them! That's because they have
been rewritten by a poet.

Attributed to Stéphane Mallarmé

What has driven [me] into the bush . . . is the usual thing . . . I have
moved outside . . . Outside I am freer.

Wyndham Lewis

Modernists write from the margins. No less an authority than T. S. Eliot
decreed that every writer 'should, to some extent, be able to look upon,
and mix with, all classes as an outsider' ('Place' 244). Eliot offered this
prescription in the 1940s, and it has since become so habitual in criticism
that one may scarcely discover any modernist occupying other than what
Michael Levenson calls an 'ambiguous position' vis-à-vis English culture,
literature, and history (*Modernism* 79).[1] The most English of novelists
appear to be like an 'exile from his own culture', while the period as a
whole is incontrovertibly 'dominated . . . by foreigners and expatriates', as
Terry Eagleton puts it in his 1970 work *Exiles* (191, 9). This axiom long
ago became a global cliché. 'We have learnt from Europe that a writer or
artist lives on the fringe of society', Chinua Achebe wrote in 1965,
'wearing a beard and peculiar dress and generally behaving in a strange,
unpredictable way' (40–1).

The pose of marginality remains easy to parody, nonetheless it confers
a certain type of authority. As historians such as George Stocking and
literary critics such as James Buzard have noted, the distance a modernist

---

1 Levenson uses this term to describe Forster. As Cucullu observes, Forster encouraged this rhetoric
himself in, among other places, his *Commonplace Book*, where he notes 'I don't belong
automatically' (49; Cucullu 19).

keeps from his or her fellows resembles the detachment cultivated by professionals in disciplines like anthropology (Stocking, 'Ethnographer's'; Buzard, 'Mass-Observation'). As it does for social scientific observation, the descriptive power modernism associates with literature inheres in one's separateness from what one observes. In modernist literature as opposed to anthropology, however, the writer is not simply a stranger but also pointedly strange. As Achebe characterizes him, he appears less detached – like the scientist in the bush – than deranged – like a madman on the loose.

The association of artistry with mental illness and, indeed, with illness in general is a modernist cliché too, if a sometimes controversial one. In the most notorious example, Virginia Woolf's oft-debated sickness, we find the two tropes working in tandem, as illness isolates her from the larger world and appears a means for making available hidden resources of creativity. 'I believe these illnesses are in my case – how shall I express it? – partly mystical', she wrote in her 1930 diary. 'Something happens in my mind . . . It becomes chrysalis. I lie quite torpid, often with acute physical pain . . . Then suddenly something springs . . . I then begin to make up my story whatever it is; ideas rush in me' (3: 287). The burden of explaining modernism's outsider posture entails making sense of the role that illness plays in it.

To be sure, modernism inherited tropes of physical suffering and social alienation from its forebears in romantic and Victorian fiction. I am arguing that it reworked them in a distinctive fashion to bind exile to illness, and in so doing, distinguished its version of the author-function. Modernism presented authorship as a profession for men and women whose dysfunctions and distempers made them unfit for life in the mainstream and, thus, uniquely qualified to explain and even champion subcultural, peripheral, and niche market activities opposed to the standardization of English literature, language, and culture. The project of constructing a coherent authorial stance seemed so urgent to the modernists themselves because it distinguished them not only from their literary predecessors but also within a field of professions competing to reinvent the notion of English at a moment of geopolitical upheaval. How these professions collabourated despite and through their differences becomes my focus in subsequent chapters. Here I show how modernism dealt with its intradisciplinary inheritance to define literary authorship as a distinct brand of expertise.[2]

---

2 As Bourdieu contends, when writers in the later decades of the nineteenth century set out to
  'invent, against established position and their occupants, everything necessary to define [a revised

No figure better illustrates how modernism empowered itself through the language of illness and marginality than Joseph Conrad. Conrad's letters offer the definitive guide for linking the style and quality of literary work with a distinctive persona. They provide a day-by-day embellishment of the sort of author-function that helped bring modernism into being. As Conrad describes his arduous and often painful labour to friends, editors, and other privileged readers, he cultivates discursive habits that we find reprised in Woolf, Lawrence, Joyce, Forster, among the various modernists whose production has been seen through the lens of personal suffering.[3] Doubly marginalized, suffering for their art and exiled to the cultural periphery, this was the dominant pose of modernist artistry.[4]

notion of literature]', they started with 'the unprecedented social personage who is the modern writer or artist, a full-time professional, dedicated to one's work in a total and exclusive manner' (*Rules* 76–7). By concentrating on modernist authorship, therefore, I begin at modernism's conceptual beginning.

3 For decades, arguments over Woolf have turned on the status of her mental health. Bell detects a 'pathography' of psychological illness (2: 195). J. Marcus rebuts Bell by discovering a vigorous public voice rather than a weak and retiring patient. In approaching this debate, London is absolutely indispensable. Dalsimer argues, 'At times she railed against her illness, felt frustrated and impeded by it, and at other times she felt it was essential to her. She returned to the question again and again, contradicting herself without coming to a resolution. Was her illness a terrible obstacle to her art, or was it the necessary condition for it?' (188). And Woolf herself wrote in her letters, 'As an experience, madness is terrific I can assure you, and not to be sniffed at; and in its lava I still find most of the things I write about. It shoots out of one everything shaped, final, not in mere driblets, as sanity does. And the six months – not three – that I lay in bed taught me a good deal about what is called oneself. Indeed I was almost crippled when I came back to the world, unable to move a foot in terror, after that discipline. Think – not one moment's freedom from doctor discipline – perfectly strange – conventional men; "you shant read this" and "you shant write a word" and "you shall lie still and drink milk" – for six months.' (4: 180). Readers of Lawrence often depict his 1916 collapse as the landmark event that inaugurated the era of his greatest work. Maddox tells us that while Lawrence lay paralyzed on his left side, with a burning chest and a trembling stomach, he suddenly found himself 'full of ideas and too ill to write them down' (221–2). When he was finally able to do so, according to Sagar, these scribbled notes became his masterpiece *Women in Love* (152). On this method of literary production, see also Herzinger 101–2. Physical and mental illness are not the only kinds of suffering, however. Fletcher's analysis of how 'Forster erases himself as a sexual subject' establishes another, rather different model. See also Dellamora. Norris notes that Joyce criticism often validates that author's work by reiterating a 'romantic plot of the heroic artist saving art's power to transcend' the 'degradations' associated with life in an unfriendly 'modern world' (6). And, in a less traumatic vein, Spacks finds evidence that '[b]oredom provides the initiating pretext in [Stein's] career . . . Looking back, a woman who believes she has suffered boredom declares her suffering the instrument of change' and the key to her distinctive style (243–4).

4 Eagleton warns, 'It is important not to vulgarise the notions of exile and expatriation to some simple model of "outsider", with its banal imagery of a fixed ontological gap between isolated artist and inauthentic society' (219). Surely not, and it is crucial to remember that Conrad was a Pole living in England, a literal exile rather than a figurative one. Even so, one wants to consider the spectrum of affiliations between modernist literary practice and marginality.

There is no getting around Conrad's status as an exile within English fiction. His lot as a Pole living in England is habitually linked to the stories of uprooting and isolation he tells in his fiction. Few scholars would disagree with the sentiment offered by Geoffrey Galt Harpham that 'a foreignness . . . informs and infects such disparate Conradian phenomena as his heroes, his political ideas, his plots, his 'universality', his settings, even some of his stylistic exotica' (*One of Us* 13).[5] An outsider in more ways than one, he wrote fiction that has proven notoriously difficult to place in the standard literary history and hierarchy. His work always ends up in the middle, between high and low, between Victorian and modern. As Ian Watt describes him, Conrad constitutes a bridge between nineteenth- and twentieth-century tendencies. He leans towards the 'solidarities of human experience . . . much commoner among the Romantics and the Victorians' even as he is also inclined to a typically modernist interest in 'alienation and exile' (32). Fredric Jameson characterizes Conrad as straddling a 'strategic fault line' between high and low, his place singularly 'unstable', 'his work unclassifiable . . . floating uncertainly somewhere in between [that of] Proust and Robert Louis Stevenson' (*Political Unconscious* 206).

By taking Conrad as a case study in the construction of modernist authorship, this chapter draws on scholarly and critical commentary that has long treated modernism in the context of professionalism. Leonard Diepeveen cites nearly 150 sources before 1950 alone that connected modernist aesthetic innovation to the notion of literature as a professional pursuit (262n9). More recently, scholars have articulated this change to alterations in the transatlantic literary marketplace of the turn of the century. Thomas Strychacz, for instance, sees as emblematic Henry James's conception of a market 'subdivided as a chess-board, with each little square confessing only to its own *kind* of accessibility' (21). Such an account suggests that modernism shaped the market that was also shaping

---

5 Conrad surely exemplifies Kenner's insight that, 'about 1895, innovative books commence to be written by people who've had to learn the written idiom' (52). In some accounts, Conrad's work appears best read as part of a salutary immigrant's tale, with his canonization the ultimate triumph of assimilation. An early version of this story appears in the memoirs of Lady Ottoline Morrell, which contain the confession, 'It seemed difficult to believe that this charming gentleman with . . . the unmistakably foreign look . . . was . . . such a master of English prose' (142). Other commentators portray Conrad as more of an insurgent. Precisely because English was not his first language, he was able to do more with it than any native. According to Najder, Conrad found English 'softly pliable because not hardened in schematic patterns of words and ideas inculcated since childhood' (116). For commentary on both of these accounts, both of which have a long and substantial history see Harpham's excellent analysis of Conrad's critical reputation (*One of Us* 142–3).

it. Insofar as readers of modernism thought of themselves as reading an elevated sort of fiction, they likely understood modernist novels to circulate in a manner distinct from 'ordinary' books. Such buyers belonged to what Lawrence Rainey calls modernist circuits of 'patronage, collecting, speculation, and investment' (*Institutions* 3). This scholarship identifies the kinship between modernist writing and contemporary expertise, but leaves less satisfactorily answered the question of how exactly a particular sort of literary market came to be identified with a particular author-function. I explain that thinking of novel-writing as a service is what created the paradoxical demand to connect fiction to the figure who composes it, while at the same time to treat writing as a learned skill rather than an aspect of individual genius.

The first section of the chapter delineates the type of service Conrad described himself as providing, an editorial sort of work centring on the rewriting of older textual material. This description could not help but distinguish his writing from the spontaneous creation associated with romantic stereotypes of authorship, and I take it as an opportunity to elabourate on the difference. The second section furthers this discussion by explaining what suffering means in the modernist literary marketplace. I suggest how changes in author-function related to more general economic shifts with the help of the economist Jagdish Bhagwati's theory of a 'disembodiment effect' that accompanies the commodification of professional services. Bhagwati's theory helps me to describe Conrad's descriptions of bodily suffering as part of the process of participating in the literary market, rather than as evidence of resistance to commodity culture or as the effects of a punishment exacted by the commercial book trade. Finally, the last section of the chapter argues that by revising the rhetoric of authorship Conrad's letters also strove to redefine the notion of readership. By imagining an audience as international as the settings for his fiction, Conrad tended to dislodge the association between reading and national belonging (elaborated most famously by Benedict Anderson) and instead associated readership with niche marketing. Jameson reminds us that the modernists behaved as if they knew 'no identifiable public ("I write for myself and for strangers", Gertrude Stein famously said)' (*Singular Modernity* 199). This stands to reason: a marginalized author could only expect a marginalized readership. If by the time Stein was writing such a fate was almost expected, Conrad's notion of his audience models that expectation. I conclude with a consideration of the transnational group of 'strangers' to whom Conrad addressed his published prose.

MODERNIST ART WORK

Conrad's letters portray a figure who works to transform popular material into art, who crosses over from high to low and back again in a never-ending search for raw material. They define the work of writing as a salvage operation, an act of textual rescue that led not only into the depths of mass culture but also to the jungles and desert islands of the tropics.[6] They portray the author as a bit of an explorer, an expert with an exotic lifestyle that, curiously enough, never requires him to leave his desk. Not that he could leave it, for the side effect of Conrad's adventurous labour was considerable pain. For him, writing brought on the gout. Gout so profoundly affected Conrad's writing practice that the letters describe it is as essential. To make a full diagnosis of this approach to composition, it will be best to start with the most familiar description of his method, which appears in the Preface to *The Nigger of the 'Narcissus'*.

The stringency of Conrad's labour is easily detected: '[I]t is only complete, unswerving devotion to the perfect blending of form and substance', he explains, 'only through an unremitting, never-discouraged care for the shape and ring of sentences that . . . the light of magic suggestiveness may be brought to play for an evanescent instant over the commonplace surface of words: of the old, old words, worn thin, defaced by ages of careless usage' ('Preface' xlix). Conrad did not create texts so much as import, edit, and elevate them. He rewrites more than he writes. And what he writes is notable less for its inherent novelty than for the new twist that it puts on generic convention. In a 1902 letter to the publisher William Blackwood, he explains that '*Youth* . . . (which I delight to know you like so well), exists only in virtue of my fidelity to the idea and the method. The favourable critics of that story, [Arthur] Q[uiller-Couch] amongst others remarked with a sort of surprise "This after all is a story for boys yet–" Exactly. Out of the material of a boys' story I've made *Youth*' (*Letters* 2: 417). For Conrad writing entails revising and thereby estranging the raw matter of adventure fiction with its stereotypic missionaries, treasure hunters, and naïve ship chandlers.

6　J. Clifford situates Conrad's salvage work in an early twentieth-century discourse of ethnography (*Predicament* 107–9; 112–13). For an analysis of how the idea of rescue structures the plots of Conrad's Malay novels, see GoGwilt, *Invention*. On Conrad and rewriting, see Bongie. On the implications of his notion of revision for our understanding of narrative form, see Fried, 'Almayer's' and 'Painting'.

The trope of writing as revision appears in the work of other modernists as well. Notably so in Eliot, who describes the 'business of the poet' as one of recycling and transformation. To write 'is not to find new emotions', he argues, 'but to use the ordinary ones and, in working them up into poetry, to express feelings which are not in actual emotions at all' ('Tradition and the Individual Talent' 43). He enjoins the writer to 'be *difficult* . . . to dislocate if necessary, language into his meaning' ('Metaphysical Poets' 65). Gregory Jay explains that Eliot consistently distinguished between an elevated form of writing that revised literary traditions and a debased mode that simply repeated them (34). A. D. Moody contends, furthermore, that Eliot's very 'inventiveness was mainly a matter of reworking existing poetic forms, and discovering new possibilities in them' (23). Beyond Conrad and Eliot, James Joyce, Henry James, and Stein are among the modernists to consider composition in a related fashion.[7]

Roland Barthes contends that such emphasis on revision was central to a post-1850 shift in the evaluation of literary quality. In this period of modernism's emergence, '[l]abour replaces genius as a value', Barthes indicates; 'there is a kind of ostentation in claiming to labour long and lovingly over the form of one's work' (63). To conceive of writing in this way, Barthes argues, is tantamount to treating the writer as a 'craftsman . . . who roughs out, cuts, polishes and sets his form exactly as a jeweler extracts art from his material, devoting to his work regular hours of solitary effort' (62–3).[8] It is not difficult to find an emphasis on strenuous labour in Conrad's published and epistolary descriptions of 'the worker in prose' ('Preface' xlix). Indeed, according to Harpham, 'Conrad's work qualifies as 'modernist' partly because of the sheer effort his pages cost him, a labour that indicates a dedication to craft, the exercise of discipline

---

7 Joyce's novels toyed with similar ideas, as P. Lewis's interpretation of the lines that conclude *A Portrait of the Artist as a Young Man* suggests: 'Stephen imagines . . . [his future writing as] not an absolutely original creation but a transformation' (1–2). Thomas observes that the very opposition between revision and creation becomes blurred in this novel's conclusion. 'Stephen announces that he intends to "forge" the uncreated conscience of his race. He chooses in *forge* a word that indicates both invention and imitation, authorship and fraudulence, authenticity and counterfeit' (265). Henry James famously revised his own work to create the New York Edition, which he calls the 're-accepted, re-tasted, exquisitely re-assimilated and re-enjoyed' version of his writing (18). Of the numerous analyses of this project, Horne provides a place to start. And in just one more example of writing as revision, Stein identifies 'Beginning again and again' as the sine qua non of composition (516).

8 Barthes continues, 'Writers like Gautier (past master in Belles-Lettres), Flaubert (grinding away at his sentences at Croisset), Valéry (in his room at the crack of dawn) or Gide (standing at his desk like a carpenter at his bench) form a kind of guild' (63).

and skill in the construction of aesthetic form' (*One of Us* 145). Innovative though this notion of writing as an arduous discipline may have been, it led to a new problem. No matter how desirable the acknowledgement of strenuous labour, no self-respecting modernist (in the English tradition at least) wished to be mistaken for an ordinary tradesman.[9]

To show that the work was both demanding and elevated, a writer needed to reveal the nuts and bolts of authorship without making it seem like a job anyone with the right tools could perform. To demonstrate his particular skill, Conrad occasionally took the liberty of rewriting his friends' prose. One example of this rather uncouth tactic may be found in an exchange between Conrad and Sir Hugh Clifford, a colonial governor and the author of several well-received volumes on life in the tropics. In 1898, the editor of the literary weekly *Academy* contracted Conrad to review Clifford's *Studies in Brown Humanity*. The appreciation that resulted describes the text as full of 'sympathy' for its characters, 'Umat, the punkah-puller' and 'the coolie, Lim Teng Wah' (*Notes* 60–1). It hastens to add, however, that Clifford's *Studies* was not a work of art. '[T]o apply artistic standards to this book would be a fundamental error', Conrad cautions. '[A]rt veils part of the truth of life to make the rest appear more splendid, inspiring, or sinister. And this book is only truth, interesting and futile, truth unadorned, simple and straightforward' (*Notes* 60). Content does not matter, Conrad contends, nearly as much as presentation. In this respect Clifford's work is wanting.

In the months following the appearance of the *Academy* review, letters were exchanged, and the colonial governor paid Conrad a visit at his home in Kent. When Clifford's next book came out in 1899, he made a point of mailing his acquaintance a copy. This volume, called *In a Corner of Asia*, focused on Clifford's Malay subjects. Conrad acknowledged receipt in a letter featuring a backhanded compliment that again denigrated Clifford's style.

Of course the matter is admirable – the knowledge, the feeling, the sympathy; it is sure to win perfect and full recognition. It is all sterling metal; a thing of absolute value. There can be no question of it not only for those who know but even for those who approach the book with blank minds on the subject of the race you have, in more than one sense, made your own. And as to the manner – well!

---

9 Menand puts it this way: 'By the end of the century, then . . . the terms of the problem had become clear: putting the literary vocation on a respectable standing among occupations, in order to prevent it from seeming . . . outmoded and slightly absurd, risked sacrificing all the advantages derived from the general perception of its essential *difference* from respectable kinds of work' (117).

I know you are not a seeker after mere expression and I beg leave to offer only one remark. You do not leave enough to the imagination. (*Letters* 2: 200)

With the suggestion that Clifford has taken possession of the 'race . . . in more than one sense,' Conrad gestures toward the colonial appointment that provided his friend with his subject matter and gave him the time to write. Conrad hints, further, that imperialism also has smoothed the way for the consumption of Clifford's prose. His official status authorized his study of native life, and granted his book a value matched only by the universally recognizable pound sterling. Needless to say, Conrad's own writing lacked similar authority and had no such currency. Despite its obvious advantages, Conrad questions the ultimate worth of Clifford's text. In the last line of this passage from his letter, he chiasmatically reverses the logic of Clifford's claim to the 'subject of the race [he has] made [his] own', and thus makes a claim of *his* own.

According to Conrad, Clifford's text presumes that it has all of the facts under control and, further, that those facts refer to a world outside language. Conrad identifies a crucial flaw in Clifford's reasoning. Writers who believe that their work refers straightforwardly to the world mistake the power of the word. They fail to realize that 'the *whole* of the truth lies in the presentation' (*Letters* 2: 200). With this linguistic turn, Conrad reverses the implicit hierarchy of subject 'matter' over what he ironically calls 'mere expression' (*Letters* 2: 200). The real subject of writing, he asserts, is just writing. 'The things "as they are" exist in words . . . [that] should be handled with care, lest the picture, the image of truth abiding in facts should become distorted – or blurred' (*Letters* 2: 200).

To ensure that Clifford understands he has been trumped, Conrad proposes to revise several lines from *In a Corner of Asia*. He selects a passage symptomatic of Clifford's abuse of language: 'When the whole horror of his position forced itself with an agony of realization upon his frightened mind, Pa' Tûa for a space lost his reason' (*Letters* 2: 201). For Conrad, these lines exemplify a lazy style. 'In this sentence the reader is borne down by the full expression . . . The word *frightened* is fatal . . . [It] is totally inadequate to express the true state of that man's mind' (2: 201). In order to convey what Pa' Tûa feels, a more sophisticated, and more roundabout, technique must be used. First, Conrad counsels, excise the word 'frightened'. Second, refuse to interpret for the reader: 'The imagination of the reader should be left free to arouse his feeling' (2: 201). The slippage of the word 'his' in this sentence – Does 'his feeling' refer to Pa' Tûa or to the reader? – only reinforces Conrad's argument. The appropriate language should be evocative without strictly delimiting Pa' Tûa's fright. Conrad expects his reader to detect fear without being handed the word 'frightened'. He wants a reader who will interpret what a text leaves open or unsaid. He asks his reader, we might say, to behave like a writer. And he envisions prose that will solicit a reader's interest in the nature of writing qua writing. What matters is not Pa' Tûa per se, but rather the stylistic decisions involved in portraying his fear.

Having explained the rationale behind his proposed revision, Conrad goes ahead and rewrites the text. Here is his version: 'When the whole truth of his position forced itself upon his mind, Pa' Tûa for a space lost his reason' (*Letters* 2: 201). 'This is truth', Conrad raves. 'And look how finely it goes on with a perfectly legitimate effect':

When the whole truth of the horror of his position forced itself upon his mind, Pa' Tûa for a space lost his reason. He screamed aloud, and the hollow of the rocks took up his cries; the bats awoke in thousands and joined the band that rustled and squeaked above the man etc. etc. (2: 201)

When he rewrites Clifford's prose, Conrad makes it more productive. With the rustles and squeaks of those thousands of bats, Pa' Tûa's fright bursts from the page. This revision provides an object lesson in the efficacy of what Edward Said calls Conrad's 'minimal but hauntingly reverberating phrases' (*World* 96). The newly improved version is redolent with the 'oppressive mysteriousness' and inexactitude that so famously annoyed F. R. Leavis and that makes Conrad's writing easily identifiable (*Great Tradition* 209). In revising Clifford's lines, Conrad makes them his own.

Through this example of textual appropriation, the letters suggest that Conradian prose is simply writing that has been worked over by Conrad. According to this logic, Joseph Conrad does not write texts per se: he 'Conrads' them. He supplements them with an unmistakable style. We may thus interpret the crucial argument from the Preface to *The Nigger of the 'Narcissus'* as saying that Conrad takes writing for his own when he revises it to bring 'magic suggestiveness' to 'old words', themes, and stories that have been 'defaced by ages of careless usage' (xlix). Authorship hinges less on originality and innate creativity than it does on demonstrated skill in the manipulation of language and the keen sense of literary history necessary to avoid cliché.

When he describes authorship as an editorial activity involving extensive revision and rewriting, Conrad decisively departs from the romantic author-function associated with what Frank Kermode famously described as the creation of pristine, 'utterly original' literary objects (44).[10] As critics ranging from Kermode to Robert Kaufman have shown, modernism and romanticism share an interest in autonomy. Both credit 'aesthetic suspension' for providing a sense of freedom that 'allows for concentration on the problem of [artistic] construction (of imagining and making the form)' (Kaufman 721). The difference remains, though, in how these movements conceived of the work involved in such construction.[11] The 'angelicism of the romantic representation of the artist', as Pierre Bourdieu puts it, could never abide overt reference to the excruciating labour that modernists like Eliot and Conrad are at pains to display (*Rules* 149). Modernist writers and literary critics habitually unveil the very 'handling, configuration, and manipulation' of literary raw material that the romantics and their readers just as habitually occlude (Kaufman 715).

It is axiomatic that authorial attribution results from a complex operation, the precise rules of which change from period to period. Indeed, Michel Foucault's foundational essay 'What is an Author?' can only hint at the wide variety of procedures for defining author-functions over time and across genres. Such variety reflects the history of reading practice, Foucault asserts, since those 'aspects of an individual, which we designate as an author . . . are projections . . . of our way of handling texts: in the comparisons we make, the traits we extract as pertinent, the continuities we assign, or the exclusions we practice' (127). Stereotype tends to dominate our habits, Foucault concludes, often against the force of material evidence. No one who has glimpsed the heavily worked

---

10 In his 1957 classic, *The Romantic Image,* Kermode describes modernist and romanticists alike as creators of 'aesthetic monads', organic texts 'independent of intention, and of any form of ethical utility' (44). For an opinionated account of the importance of this book to modernist literary scholarship, see O'Hara, who describes Kermode's project as a 'corrective of the polemical, self-serving, anti-Romantic views of T. S. Eliot and the first generation of modernist critics, such as the American New Critics and the Leavisite *Scrutiny* group' (368).

11 Another, very different argument for distinguishing between modernist and romantic literary work is that of T. Armstrong. He describes modernist literature as a prosthesis or 'cultural extension', which certainly resonates with Conrad's declaration that what he 'is trying to achieve is, by the power of the written word, to make you hear, to make you feel . . . before all, to make you *see*' (Armstrong 89, 'Preface' xlix). Considerable scholarly energy has been spent contextualizing this sentence to an extent greater than I am able within the confines of this chapter. The dominant critical strain links Conrad's emphasis on sight to impressionism. See Watt, for a foundational example. A list of intriguing more recent discussions of literary impressionism ought to include Banfield and Fried.

manuscript pages attributed to William Wordsworth would ever imagine an author who had done anything but laboured long and hard on his verse. Yet scholars and general readers cannot ignore Wordsworth's thesis in the Preface to the *Lyrical Ballads* that 'all good poetry is the spontaneous overflow of powerful feelings', and may even be inclined to emphasize it at the expense of his corollary assertion, 'poems to which any value can be attached, were never produced . . . but by a man who . . . had also thought long and deeply' (62). Conventional understanding of the romantic ideology of authorship, observes K. K. Ruthven, has as its 'operative terms' such concepts as 'solitary geniuses and unique texts', whose circulation depends in part on our capacity to ignore contradictory elements of romanticism's self-presentation (91). Just as the sustained intellectual energy Wordsworth describes receives less attention than his spontaneous overflow of emotion, so too the collaborative practice that appears to have been integral to the romantic process of writing remains less interesting to us than the notion of individual creative genius. 'Romantic practice condoned various kinds of collaboration', Ruthven reminds us (91). Evidence of this is easily found in the Preface to the *Lyrical Ballads*, whose 1802 edition begins with reference to the 'friend' who assisted its composition – it was Coleridge – and the various readers whose comments helped shape Wordsworth's aesthetic argument. No doubt ignoring these components of authorship affects how readers approach the poetry. But more importantly for the purposes of this chapter, it affects how readers interpret the author-function itself as it was conceived at the time.

Scholars have noted a similar confusion in modernist practice, which likewise privileged both individualism and the merits of collaboration. Levenson observes that while 'Romantic notions of the solitary creator' persisted in the modernist period, 'Pound, Lewis, and their confederates learned from Marinetti the benefit of a collective war-cry' (*Genealogy* 136). Modernist collectivities were not open to just anyone, however. In her study of manifestoes and the movements they announced, Janet Lyon explains that the revolutionary rhetoric of a journal like *BLAST* pertained most pointedly to the activities of a 'select and self-limiting group' (128). Lewis and others acted as gate keepers restricting the potentially welcoming 'we' of manifesto rhetoric to the more narrow confines of a like-minded 'school', which could involve significant numbers but in Pound's description was more likely to mean just 'two or three young men [who] agree, more or less, to call certain things good' (quoted in Lyon 134). If the school could become the place where good art was recognized as such, that would justify an emphasis on collective practice. Groups of modern-ist writers and critics working together might side-step the mass market and designate the value of literary work on their own.

This is precisely what the professional organizations that Perkin ana-lyzes tried to do. Trade unions and disciplinary associations are larger-scale institutions for 'closing the market . . . [by] control[ing] entry, training and qualification, and seek[ing] a monopoly of the name and the practice' of a particular kind of work (*Rise* 378). Modernism relied on a variety of tactics to enact such a 'strategy of closure', Strychacz observes. '[I]f a body of formal knowledge underpins a professional's power within a mass society, then the idiom of modernist writing – arcane allusion, juxtaposition, opaque writing, indeterminacy, and so on' has precisely the same function (27).[12] By emphasizing these attributes, novelists and poets took advantage of professional ideology to lend new meaning to literary practice whose social value was less than readily apparent.[13]

Characterizing writing as editorial salvage clearly distinguished mod-ernism's craft from that of romanticism. But in order to securely attach this labour to an individual writer, modernism needed to give him a character as identifiable as his writing. Some modernists appear to have approached this problem by revising an authorial stereotype associated with romanticism, the pose of the suffering artist. Kermode explains, '[T]he artist who is vouchsafed th[e] power of . . . [generating] that "epiphany" which is the Joycean equivalent of Pater's "vision" – has to pay a heavy price in suffering, to risk his immortal soul, and to be alone,

---

12 Modernist practice did more than parallel efforts to distinguish and elevate professional work in other disciplines. T. Armstrong shows that writers like Pound borrowed terminology and conceptual tools from several fields. Pound owed to science the notion that the human body was a sort of 'man-machine' and that the senses were regulatory mechanisms that modernist literature might influence and equip with new tools (89). From Darwinian and Freudian thought modernist writers poached the idea that 'a substrata of primitive material' was atavistically percolating away within the self and, further, that writing could address it (3). Conrad imagined his prose 'reach[ed] the secret spring of responsive emotions', while others such as André Breton contemplated the capacity of automatic writing to reveal the repressed but 'actual functioning of thought' (Conrad, 'Preface' xlix; quoted in T. Armstrong 202). Modernism's appropriations enabled it to portray literary expertise as akin to that in other specialized disciplines and to assert that the author was not unlike 'a scientist, physician or surgeon' (T. Armstrong 89).

13 They solved an intradisciplinary problem that Menand characterizes as an opportunistic response to the ideology of professionalism. Since professionalism exerted pressure 'on a way of conceiving of literature that had become customary since Romanticism', he contends, '[I]nsofar as literature was understood generally to be an activity pursued by individual artists answering solely to the dictates of their own genius and producing objects whose value was to a significant degree a function of their originality . . . it became necessary to find new ways of describing the proper practice of literature and the definitive characteristics of the worthy literary vocation' (99–100).

"not even separate from all others but to have not even one friend"' (2). Suffering and marginality go together, Kermode contends. Conrad agrees, although the suffering he describes and the marginality it engenders differ from the transcendent model Kermode invokes.

When Doubleday brought out Conrad's uniform edition in the 1920s, it acted to satisfy consumer appetite for authorial detail by soliciting a new preface for each volume. These 'Author's Notes' varied in content and length, but frequently offered a glimpse of Conrad's writing habits that complemented the account appearing in the letters. The note for *Nostromo* plays up the difficulty of composition by portraying Conrad knocking about the house, struggling to come up with ideas. '[I]t seemed somehow that there was nothing more in the world to write about', he laments, 'This so strangely negative but disturbing mood lasted some little time' (31). A stray anecdote catches his imagination soon enough, and he is off 'on a distant and toilsome journey into a land full of intrigues and revolutions. But it had to be done' (31). Writing is a rigorous adventure: '[M]y sojourn on the continent of Latin America lasted for two years . . . [which included] many intervals of renewed hesitation, lest I should lose myself in the ever-enlarging vistas opening before me as I progressed deeper in my knowledge of the country' (31). The style of this note echoes the cover copy on the dust jacket of the novel's first edition, which proclaimed *Nostromo* 'a moving tale of high adventure – of revolution, romance, hidden treasure, and a hero of the most vivid personality' (quoted in Batchelor 131). By reproducing that rhetoric in his commentary, Conrad implies that the real hero of the piece is none other than the author himself.

Far from undermining such a mythic narrative of authorship, the tales of physical and psychological trauma contained in the letters suggested that literary production was every bit as perilous as tramping through the jungle. This author's note secures that suggestion by exporting Conrad's deskwork into a landscape more in keeping with the exotic settings of his fiction and with the distant horizons of his earlier life as a sailor. Scholarly readers have long collaborated in this conflation by treating authorship as an extension of Conrad's time in the periphery. None other than Leavis established the critical habit in his *Great Tradition*, which describes Conrad's writing as combining stylized prose and immigrant experience (211). Unlike the romantic stereotype, the modernist suffers not because he is a genius but because he engages in adventurous and risky labour. Suffering indicates a diligence and strenuous effort that sets the writer apart. For a more elabourate account of this operation we can return to the letters and the descriptions of suffering they detail.

SELLING ART

By all accounts, Conrad was never truly well. Even as a child, he struggled with disease. As he grew older, gout, a metabolic condition characterized by painful inflammation of the joints, began to overshadow his other maladies. During one especially severe attack in 1891, Conrad's hands swelled so dramatically that his doctor sent him to Geneva for a special 'water-mountain cure' (Karl 311). This crisis occurred while he was hard at work on his first novel, *Almayer's Folly*. From this moment forward Conrad's letters link attacks of gout with the writing of fiction. It accompanies inspiration – 'Gout. Brought on by – by – by agitation, exasperation, botheration – You know; those things you laugh at and bite your thumbs at – O! Lord! And I write! I write! I write! I write! Certainly. Write quick' – and is part and parcel of writer's block as well – 'When I face that fatal manuscript it seems to me that I have forgotten how to think – worse! how to write . . . I knock around blindly . . . till I am positively, physically sick' (*Letters* 2: 176; 1: 296–7). It is the writer's constant companion – 'I got up and went down again some four distinct times since that time; having nevertheless managed to do some 13 thousand words – the last paper of the Mirror of the Sea vol.' (3: 287). And ultimately a metaphor for writing itself – 'a short story of about 5.000 words . . . like a fell disease got me under' (1: 298). All of which leads Conrad to conclude, in a letter to John Galsworthy in April 1906, that 'perhaps . . . the hard, atrocious, agonizing days are simply part of my *method* of work, a decreed necessity of my production' (3: 327).

Biographers and critics have echoed this thesis. Frederick Karl argues that Conrad 'could not work effectively unless he were close to breakdown, on the edge of psychic disorders, ill in body and in mind' (527–8). Many of Conrad's early scholarly boosters, among them Albert Guerard and Thomas Moser, make suffering a barometer of his aesthetic accomplishment. The result can be somewhat puzzling, as Watt observes: 'Some biographies, of which that by his wife, Jessie Conrad, was the first, and that by Bernard Meyer is the fullest, make this side of Conrad's personality dominant; and although one certainly cannot blame them for not explaining Conrad's genius – who could? – one is left wondering how the psychologically crippled valetudinarian they present could have managed to survive past the age of sixty-six, and produce some twenty volumes of fiction' (25). John Batchelor sets out to solve this problem by separating Conrad the writer of the letters from Conrad the author of the novels: 'the hysterical, attention-seeking and dependent part of Conrad's personality displayed in the letters was split off, I believe, from the artist' (45). This answer is a little too neat. Rather than insisting that the different Conrads remain distinct, we might well ask how their collabouration defines an author-function. Such an approach would be consonant with Foucault's insight that modern authors are defined in part through the scission of multiple voices ('What is an Author?' 129).

We can ask how the various versions of Conrad collabourate by returning to the 1899 letter that contains the writing lesson I cite above. It wraps up with an acknowledgement of Clifford's recent visit – 'Our meeting – Your visit here – mark an epoch in my life' – and an apology for the messiness of an 'interlined letter', which Conrad blames on his work: 'It's past midnight and I had a rough time with MS all day' (*Letters* 2: 202). Fatigue leads to interlining, but one could equally observe that interlining leads to fatigue. Revising Clifford is not a break from writing, but more of the same. Conrad compares the two acts when he confesses that the Clifford sentences he edited are not so different from sentences of his own:

[I]t is the sort of thing I write twenty times a day and (with the fear of overtaking fate behind me) spend half my nights in taking out of my work – upon which depends the daily bread of the house: (literally – from day to day); not to mention (I dare hardly think of it) the future of my child, of those nearest and dearest to me, between whom and the bleakest want there is only my pen – as long as life lasts. And I can sell all I write – as much as I write! (2: 201)

Continuity between composing letters and novels connects the writer who suffers in the correspondence with the author who crafts 'Heart of Darkness'. But even more important is the market context this passage provides for both activities. Conrad is not a recluse writing for posterity but a husband and father who needs to live off his prose. What he writes must be sold, and he is not afraid to explain to his friends that his efforts are not going well. We may treat such explanation as part of the letters' marketing campaign.

Whether it was meant to function this way or not, Conrad's letter to Clifford worked as a sales pitch. Clifford and Conrad stayed in touch. Conrad sent him *Lord Jim* the following year; Clifford returned the favour with his *Bushwhacking and Other Sketches* in 1902; and Clifford warmly reviewed Conrad's collection *Youth* in the *Spectator*. The big payoff came in 1909, when Clifford persuaded the editor of the *New York Herald* to serialize *Chance*. The book went on to be Conrad's first bestseller. Though documenting his suffering did not in and of itself allow Conrad to cultivate relationships that would yield such results, the consistency with which he describes it for Clifford is too much to ignore. The very letter thanking him for wooing the *Herald* opens with 'the confused recollections of a nightmare' and 'the usual (but not very severe) illness' during 'the time I was involved in one of my 40,000-word "short stories"' (4: 451). Such references were typical. Said summarizes what nearly all of Conrad's correspondents could expect to encounter: 'Loneliness, darkness, the necessity of writing, imprisonment: these are the pressures upon the writer as he writes, and there is scarcely any I have read who seems so profligate in his complaining' (*World* 93). Not so profligate as all that, for with each complaint Conrad presented another reader with the opportunity to invest in his work.

Though it may not seem like it, this letter was as much a professionalizing gesture as Conrad's description of writing as a service. The context of economic history and theory helps to explain why. As the historians P. J. Cain and A. G. Hopkins contend, the service sector has always been treated by economists as a multifarious entity involving such widely various activities as shipping, insurance, and education. As a result, the term service professional has never been a very exact one. As for services themselves, Cain and Hopkins lament that '[n]o satisfactory definition . . . has yet been devised' (1: 20).[14] The best they know appears in the research of economist Jagdish Bhagwati, who calls services activities that 'splinter' from the production of goods (*Wealth* 93). In a market of any size, Bhagwati explains, production requires ancillary services to deliver, advertise, and sell commodities. Companies need specialists who will keep the books and insure the workers, conduct research and development, and so forth. Services are defined as well by their tendency towards specialization and the transformation of production. At the macro level, the rise of the service sector in greater Britain facilitated the growth of export economies the world over. Economists from Rudolf Hilferding forward have observed that the emergence of financial services altered domestic

---

14 The economic sense of the term dates to Adam Smith, whose suggestion that they 'perish in the very instant of their performance' Cain and Hopkins find less than entirely clarifying (1: 20). Marx had little time for services. He associates them with the transitional stage of mercantile and merchant's capital and describes them as an expression of simple use value 'which does not increase capital; rather, capital consumes itself in it' (*Grundrisse* 272). Lee follows the development of services in his economic history of Great Britain, and notes that 'The small amount of attention paid to the service sector is one of the curiosities of the historiography of British economic development' (*British Economy* 98).

economy as well. At the micro level, Bhagwati explains that the process of splintering goes both ways, not only goods into services but also services into goods (*Wealth* 93). An advertising campaign designed for a particular product can in turn affect what happens on an assembly line, while research into smaller computer chips can change the production of certain hi-tech goods. As far as literature is concerned, such critics as Chris Vanden Bosche, Peter Keating, Mark Morrison, and Lawrence Rainey among others show that the increasing importance of literary agents and copyright attorneys, specialized book sellers and niche journal editors reconfigured the production and consumption of fiction in the late Victorian and modernist periods. Considering the writer as a service provider, therefore, makes him one of many in the wing of the market focused on books.

Literary production and consumption were not always so conceived, of course. Mark Rose shows that eighteenth-century authorship employed the vocabulary of landed capital in an attempt to elevate literary labour and solidify rights of textual ownership. Rose directs us to the example of Joseph Addison, who said of one author, 'his Brain, which was his Estate, had as regular and different Produce as other Men's land' (40). Litigants in nineteenth-century debates over copyright revisited this simultaneously aristocratic and organic rhetoric. William Dougal Christie imagined 'a class of men holding hereditary estates, not in broad lands, but in books' (quoted in Bossche 60). Such a characterization gave writing an 'aura of gentility' with which to challenge the Taylorizing tendencies of commercial publishers (Bossche 60).[15] Other participants in the book business were less antagonistic towards the Victorian mass market. When the author and publisher Charles Dickens helped make serialization popular in the 1830s, he gave the novel greater visibility and created a whole new set of conditions for novel writing. Mary Poovey shows that part-issue publication figured the author as just 'one instance of . . . [the] labour' required to put out a book (104; see also Bossche 52–3). Publishers attempted to force novelists to write on schedule, to compose their words in evenly distributed portions, and to plot their narratives so that each chapter's conclusion would also function as an advertisement for the next instalment.[16]

---

15 On late Victorian copyright, see also Feltes and Keating.
16 Wicke observes that Dickens's version of the author was tailor-made for a moment in literary history when advertising became the de facto 'literature of capitalism' (*Advertising Fictions* 20).

This was the market that Conrad confronted. To get his work read, Conrad needed to persuade editors to bend the rules to accommodate his redefinition of writing. This entailed persuading them to acknowledge that his work might be worth supporting even if it was antagonistic to the protocols governing serial publication. He never wrote on time, for instance. His stories did not break neatly into regularized chunks. Their chapters neither began nor ended in a manner that would prove familiar to a reader of Dickens. Conrad needed help to sell such fiction. He needed intermediaries within the trade who could explain not only that his writing was good but also that he was changing the meaning of writing for the better. Only those who recognized the difference of Conrad's method could do this. Not that they needed to be able to describe his service using that technical term, but they had to recognize that his work was different and be able to argue that the difference was worth cultivating.[17]

To say this is to reiterate a point Bourdieu has made routine, namely, that as much as artists trade in paintings and novels and poems, they also trade in recognition. Where education, specialized skill sets, and other forms of human capital are absolutely necessary to success as a lawyer, financier, or other professional, they only matter if they are recognized as valuable in the first place. Specialized training and expertise in and of themselves mean little unless society sees one's specialty as useful or otherwise important. In order for experience in a field to be seen as valuable, the labour that takes place within that field as a whole has to be recognized as worthwhile. Such recognition underwrites the capitalization of any skill or form of knowledge.[18] What is true for the field is also true of the individual.[19] Without making the mistake of a completely

---

17 'To change the values of resources requires more than individual actions', Lin notes 'it needs the mobilization of other actors who make similar demands' (32).

18 Lin's definition of human capital is clarifying: 'Human capital, unlike physical capital, is the value added to a labourer when the labourer acquires knowledge, skills, and other assets useful to the employer or firm in the production and exchange process . . . the value embedded in the labourers themselves' (9). If these assets or skills or knowledges are not recognized as useful, it follows, possessing them is worth nothing at all.

19 For Lin, there is an intimate connection between being recognized and getting paid. '[R]eputation', he explains, 'is a functional calculus of the worth of public awareness in social networks in terms of its value representation, recognition' (150). Converting this value into the economic form of capital, i.e. money, involves different mechanisms in every field. But Bourdieu discerns a shared logic behind all of them. He argues that the symbolic capital of recognition behaves like a 'credit, but in the broadest sense, a kind of advance, a credence' given by other participants in the field who, if the credit is truly valuable, are themselves recognized by the field at large (Bourdieu, *Logic* 120; Lin 151–3).

instrumental reading, we can interpret Conrad's letters as attempts to manage this process. He strives not only for recognition, but also to convert that symbolic capital, that 'veritable credit', into 'long term, "economic" profits' (Bourdieu, *Rules* 142).[20]

The problem of how to ensure that symbolic and economic returns benefit the writer and not simply his novels and their publisher is one permutation of a fundamental issue confronting service professionals of all sorts. According to Perkin, one of the paradoxes of efforts at professional standardization is a continued reliance on highly personalized labour. The value accorded to intellectual labour frequently relies on the worker's reputation, and this despite the necessity that many fields see their work as depersonalized or disinterested. Even though the nineteenth century saw the emergence of qualifying examinations, review boards, and other presumably objective means for evaluating the relative merit of expert work in Britain, still Perkin notes the 'professional *had* to assert the high quality and scarcity value of the service he provided or forgo the status and rewards that went with it. And since that service took a personal form it could not be detached from the superior person who provided it' (*Rise* 390).[21] In order to succeed as an attorney, for example, it is not enough to go to the right school and to pass the bar exam. One also needs to act the part. Slight permutations in manner can matter a good deal. As Magali Sarfatti Larson notes, professional labour frequently appears 'inextricably bound to the person and the personality of [its] producer' (14). Often enough, what distinguishes specialists working in the same field – what makes one doctor different from another, for instance – is the personal flair they bring to the job. Eliot Friedson explains further, 'Most professions produce intangible goods. Their product, in other words, is only formally alienable and is inextricably bound to the person and the personality of the producers' (32).[22] Or should remain

---

20 His solicitations may be said to constitute evidence for Bourdieu's theory that 'only those who know how to reckon and deal with the "economic" constraints inscribed in [the art market] are able fully to reap symbolic and even "economic" profits on their symbolic investments' (*Rules* 149).

21 Perkin considers this personal investment the source of professional elitism and, even, of interdisciplinary rivalry: 'This indeed was the Achilles' heel of professionalism, through which entered the spears of individual arrogance, collective condescension towards the laity, and mutual disdain between the different professions' (*Rise* 390).

22 Thus, 'the producers themselves have to be produced if their products or commodities are to be given a distinctive form' (32). Aguirre provides a literary gloss on this dynamic: 'To speak of a "Dickensian" novel or a "Tennysonian" lyric is thus to name the quality that makes each writer unique' (572).

inextricably bound: establishing the logic that ties producer to product is among the most crucial steps in any field's self-definition. It is exactly what the author-function and the techniques of attribution Foucault studies in 'What is an Author?' are designed to guarantee. The fact that these techniques change, and that they have altered in the century since Conrad began writing, is indication that their smooth functioning cannot be assumed.

Perhaps the most famous modernist version of the paradoxical attempt to link impersonal expertise to a personality appears in Eliot's essays on artistic production. Eliot is surely the strongest proponent in the English canon of the text's autonomy from its author. His pointed description of composition as 'a continual extinction of personality' leaves no doubt that his poems stand alone ('Tradition and the Individual Talent' 40). And yet in the same manifesto Eliot offers a caveat. '[O]f course', he allows, 'only those who have personality and emotions know what it means to want to escape from these things' (43). Such contradiction leads Colleen Lamos to conclude that Eliot's impersonality thesis is 'designed to fail, and the artist's or critic's mask of self-abnegation seems to invite exposure of the seething and possibly seedy demands of the personality beneath' (24).[23] It is not unreasonable to imagine that contemplating the 'intensity of the artistic process' might lead one to speculate on the intensity of the artist himself ('Tradition' 41).

Bhagwati elevates this predicament into an economic principle. He theorizes that a 'disembodiment effect' is usual when goods such as novels or other works of art 'splinter' off from the services involved in producing them:

. . . the services, initially embodied in the person providing them (for example, Placido Domingo singing at the Metropolitan), and requiring the physical presence of the provider of the services at the time of use, are disembodied as a result of technical change and encapsulated into what we call goods (such as the invention which brings Placido Domingo via records – that is, goods – into our homes) . . . [This] goods-from-services splintering process, reflecting the

23 'The success of Eliot's theory', Lamos continues, 'may reside not in the efficacy of its prohibition but in the sense of a temptation barely escaped and of overwhelming desires scarcely contained' (24). This is a reading with a tradition; Ward observes that Eliot's Ben Jonson essay published the same month as 'Tradition and the Individual Talent' speaks of transfusing personality into poetry. 'All of this', Ward concludes, 'modifies the notion of impersonality radically; it suggests an idea which is almost opposite to the idea as it has been generally understood' (55). It is not surprising, therefore, that biographically informed readings of Eliot remain popular. Vendler, who remains one of Eliot's and modernism's most influential and popular readers, treats his early poetry as an effort 'to give voice to the qualities warring within him' (84).

disembodiment effect, generally leaves behind a residue of service activities which are technically unprogressive and generally labour intensive. (*Wealth* 93)[24]

Because artists find themselves on the labour-intensive side of the bargain, their share of the profits could actually decrease if their services prove acceptable for the mass market. Placido Domingo may get rich from his CD sales, of course, but one suspects his record company has the potential for greater profit than he does. The discrepancy between the gains seen by service professionals and commodity producers may be even wider in a case like Conrad's, where the total amount of revenue involved is so much smaller.

Since what Bhagwati theorizes is a structural condition, it seems unlikely any single artist could find a way around it. And, indeed, Conrad's letters do not read like an attempt to resist the process of disembodiment so much as a gambit to accommodate and manage it. They consistently lead readers from the novels to the scene of their writing. They clear a trail from commodity to service, from 'Heart of Darkness' back to Joseph Conrad. In so doing, they reembody the texts. We can observe this process in a sequence of letters detailing the completion and publication of *Nostromo*. In the author's note to that text, Conrad describes the book as 'the most anxiously mediated of [his] longer novels' (*Nostromo* 29). His letters contain a more extensive report. They depict the final days of composition in gory detail, and give an evocative depiction of the moment when Conrad's writing practice splinters off a finished commodity.

There are two versions of the events leading up to *Nostromo*'s completion. One appears in a series of short letters to James Pinker, who was among the first literary agents in London, and whose client list over the years included Ford Madox Ford, Henry James, D. H. Lawrence, and H. G. Wells in addition to Conrad. The notes to Pinker reproduce the familiar fits and starts of Conrad's writing method. The first, dated 24 August, includes a promise that he will finish *Nostromo* in two days time. He asks for a 'check in advance', because 'I haven't the price of railway fare in the house' (*Letters* 3: 156). Two days pass and Conrad posts another letter to say that he is not yet done. He has had a sore tooth, which 'made him unfit to work', but he guarantees that copy will be in the mail the

---

24 Berman employs a similar metaphor to describe the poor returns early modernists saw for their art. '[B]ecause they are personally involved in their work', he explains, they are veritably 'sell[ing] themselves piecemeal' when they manage to find buyers (117–18).

next morning, a Saturday (3: 156–7). Saturday comes and goes, as does Sunday, and the next letter Conrad sends is dated the 31st, which would be a Wednesday.[25] Conrad explains, 'I could not resist the temptation of a Sunday intervening and kept the MS to work at it a little more' (3: 157). 'I may just as well thank you for this work being finished', he remarks rather pitifully, 'for thanks are due to you undeniably. And if I don't say more it isn't that I grudge you the words but because I am tired – done up' (3: 158). These letters surely make Conrad into a victim of the book-production process. In finishing his novel, he expends the scant resources in his possession, his words and his health. To make matters worse, he soon learns that the publisher has treated his manuscript in a decidedly slipshod manner. 'I am disgusted with the slovenliness, meanness of the book's get up', Conrad complains to Pinker as he reviews his advance copies, 'the horrid misprints, the crooked lines, the dropped punctuation marks. By Jove a fourth of the page slants! I've never seen anything like this! It's painful!' (3: 171–2).

Conrad found the reviews painful too when they appeared a week after the book's 14 October 1904 publication, although a glance at them will help to confirm that contemporary readers were entirely capable of imagining the arduous means of the novel's production. Karl sums up the negative notices in publications ranging from the *Daily Telegraph* to the *Spectator* as the misunderstandings of reviewers who 'tended to judge the novel by the standards of popular fiction' (569). The unnamed commentator in the *Times Literary Supplement* gives Conrad a little more credence than this, but not much. 'We do not object to an author's finding his way by first losing it, or at any rate by first trying many others – probably it is the safest means – but we do object to being taken with him on the search', the reviewer remarks. 'In other words, we think that the publication of this book as it stands is an artistic mistake' (quoted in Karl 569). Such critique puts meat on the bones of the more general complaint that Conrad had failed to write popular fiction according to previously accepted standards. At the same time, the difficulty of his work has the merit of inviting this reviewer to contemplate the experience of the author, whom he imagines struggling to write. What distinguishes *Nostromo* from the other books on the market is that it turns our attention to the writer's practice. It does so, moreover, regardless of whether one

25 In their editorial notes, Karl and Davies produce evidence to suggest that in fact the day was Tuesday, early, around 4 o'clock in the morning.

actually likes the book. It is as if Conrad's variety of commodified writing never fully splinters away from its producer. Good and bad reviews alike agreed that the novel could not help but invoke suffering. To wit, Karl cites the review by John Buchan, which cautioned that *Nostromo* was 'not a book which the casual reader will appreciate. The sequence of events has to be sought painfully through the mazes of irrelevancy with which the author tries to mislead us. But it is a book which will well repay those who give it the close attention it deserves' (quoted in Karl 570). Here is a review that treats the reader as a writer like Conrad himself, confronting a text that demands a thorough going over and meticulous revision before it can make narrative sense.

While the letters to Pinker lead inexorably to *Nostromo*'s decline into shoddily produced under-admired commodification, another set of letters anticipates something more like Buchan's appreciation of the service involved in both writing and reading. This competing account of *Nostromo*'s composition, publication, and reception begins in a letter to Galsworthy, which opens with Conrad's declaration that the novel is 'finished! Finished on the 30th in Hope's house in Stanford in Essex, where I had to take off my brain that seemed to turn to water' (*Letters* 3: 158). The correlation of two events – the completion of the novel and the liquefaction of the author – captures precisely the disembodiment effect Bhagwati associates with the splintering of a service such as writing into a commodity like *Nostromo*. The rest of the letter expands on this process. It portrays Conrad polishing off his novel while his body comes apart at the seams.

The first bit to go is a tooth. 'On the 27th had to wire for dentist (couldn't leave the work) who came at 2 and dragged at the infernal thing which seemed rooted in my very soul. The horror came away at last, leaving however one root in the gum. Then he grubbed for *that* till I le[a]pt out of the chair' (3: 158). Conrad uses 'horror', one half of what is easily his most famous published line, to darkly comedic effect. He thus invokes the rhetorical force of the narrative often hailed as his masterpiece, 'Heart of Darkness', to describe a sore tooth. He develops such suggestive hyperbole, giving his writing environment an atmosphere not unlike that he ascribed to upriver regions of the Congo.

At 11.30 something happened – what it is I don't know. I was writing, and raised my eyes to look at the clock. The next thing I know I was sitting (not lying) sitting on the concrete outside the door. When I crawled in I found it was nearly one. I managed to get upstairs and said to Jessie: We must be off to-morrow. (3: 158)

After Conrad loses consciousness, his body takes on a life of its own. Such a development is more usual than it might seem. Doppelgangers are remarkably common in commentary on authorship. Foucault describes the 'I' narrator as a 'second self' ('What is an Author?' 129).[26] Tim Armstrong refers us to Robert Louis Stevenson who 'during illness . . . felt his experience split into that of two selves, "myself" and "the other fellow"' (190). What makes this experience so jarring is the feeling that someone other than the writer is doing the writing. In addition to Stevenson, one might refer to Eliot, the intense productivity that accompanied his retreat to Lausanne in 1921, and the poet's later reflection on the relationship between sickness and composition. In 1933's *The Use of Poetry and the Use of Criticism*, Eliot speculates,

> some forms of ill-health, debility or anemia, may (if other circumstances are favourable) produce an efflux of poetry . . . though . . . the material has obviously been incubating within the poet, and cannot be suspected of being a present from a friendly or impertinent demon. (*Selected Prose* 88)

Eliot presents composition as deeply embodied at the very moments when it seems most profoundly alienating. The practice remains intimate even when it seems most estranged, when we might mistake it as being under the control of someone or something else.[27]

The letter to Galsworthy about *Nostromo* reveals Conrad's similar disavowal of alienation. According to the letter, the morning after his body ambles away from his desk, Conrad charges out of the house with his wife in tow, off to visit his friend G. F. W. Hope. He is clearly not himself. Even the driver notes that he looks off. 'I sat by the man's side like a corpse . . . [He] said to me You look ill sir; shall I stop?' Conrad is in control neither of his faculties nor of his synaptic functions. His recollection of events is uneven. He recalls the occasional detail – 'Sittingbourne I remember as a brandy and soda.' – but the rest is a blur. Frederick Karl and Laurence Davies suggest in their notes to the letters that Conrad has even mistaken the day of this voyage.

Just as he threatens to collapse altogether, a stranger appears at the roadside. He is clearly a labourer, and he is in nearly as wretched

---

26 'It would be as false to seek the author in relation to the actual writer as to the fictional narrator', Foucault argues; 'the "author-function" arises out of their scission – in the division and distance of the two' (129).

27 T. Armstrong contextualizes such examples in terms of early twentieth-century experimentation in automatic writing, but we might equally explain them in light of literary economics.

condition as Conrad. Even before, that is, the writer's car hits him: 'In Chatham, street crowded, packed. Going dead slow knocked down a man – old chap, apparently a bricklayer. Crowd around cursing and howling.' The accident has a remarkably salutary effect, on Conrad at least. He gives up a seat to the elderly victim and surfs all the way to the emergency room on the running board as the automobile careens through the hostile mob. 'Helped him to my front seat and I standing on the step got him to the hospital in 10 minutes. No harm. Only shaken. Saw him all comfy in bed for the rest of the day' (3: 159). It is as if Conrad transfers his catatonic condition to this startled old man. He literally puts the bricklayer in his place, slumped over in the passenger seat. As part of the trade he acquires what amounts to a new lease on life. In a matter of minutes he is hoisting himself up on running boards rather than sitting corpselike.

After pausing at the hospital, Conrad speeds on to his friend's house. He remains curiously rejuvenated. He eats food and, for the first time in over a week, '*tasted it too*' (3: 159). In his biography, Karl notes that this letter describes 'something close to that disordering of the senses we associate with synesthesia' (565). In its later paragraphs, however, any lingering dissociation clears up as Conrad settles back into his body and, even better, back into his work. After a good night's sleep, he sits down at a desk and finishes *Nostromo*. Sated, he sleeps again and then writes to Galsworthy. 'Wasn't sure I would survive', he confesses, 'But I have survived extremely well . . . I am quite recovered and ready for work again' (3: 159). One act remains, however, before Conrad is willing to declare victory. He awaits Galsworthy's recognition. 'There is wanting to the finish of this undertaking the sanction of your presence and voice', he writes in conclusion. 'Drop me a line. Come down if you can!' (3: 159).

This request holds the secret to Conrad's success. If the letter to Galsworthy imagines a more positive outcome to *Nostromo*'s completion than the letters to Pinker, recognition is the reason why. Where Pinker can only offer botched publication and symptomatic reviews, Galsworthy and his fellow literati can offer a network of like-minded and reasonably well-connected intellectuals, the symbolic capital recognition by such a network can provide, and ultimately the promise of a certain reputation among a larger readership. This is the way the service economy of literature works, according to Conrad's letters. Galsworthy and other friendly readers offer the possibility that Conrad might earn recognition for the quality of the work that goes into his writing, recognition that could mitigate against unsympathetic reviews and poor sales. Conrad's case suggests that reputation can offset such losses and eventually reverse them. An author with a good reputation and soft sales can stick around, find new publishers, and even write a bestseller in the end. At the very least, he has the possibility of generating a back list and the sort of modest interest that, at a middling publisher, can be enough to stay in print.

The letters that follow the one to Galsworthy reveal Conrad endeavouring to receive recognition from members of a growing circle. He shares his tale with R. B. Cunningham Graham, Ford, Edward Garnett, Wells, and others, invoking for each of them the 'half-delirious state', 'two blank hours . . . on the concrete', and ghastly tooth extraction – 'It broke!' (3: 165–6). Each correspondent responds to Conrad's request for acknowledgement – 'I receive magnificent letters', he reports (3: 178). Cunningham Graham's note in particular brings the pink back to his cheeks: 'Your letter was indeed worth having and I blush deeply as I re-read it', he gushes (3: 175).

Renewed health signifies recognition and the promise of economic compensation, but not right away. In a belated acknowledgement, Arnold Bennett reminds us that Conrad was not appealing to the masses. '[P]eople are so blind', he exclaims, 'and so infernally obstinate in complaining because a book is not something that an author never intended it to be. Only other creative artists can understand a creative artist' (Stape and Knowles 87). Bennett splits the market in two. On the one hand lies the mob, on the other a smaller but more discerning and, therefore, more likely group in which to find recognition. '[I]f one could but convey to you the *passionate* comprehension which some of us have of your work', he stresses, 'I think the effect on your health would be good' (Stape and Knowles 87). Privilege the positive response of the elevated few, this letter recommends, pay attention to the artists who recognize the service you have provided, and you may deem yourself successful regardless of sales figures. This is how the economy described in the letters works: be clear about the pain and suffering involved in writing, elaborate upon the disembodiment effect entailed in commodification, and recognition will be the reward.

THE WORLDLY NOVELIST

Though letters from supportive writers and columnists grew more numerous over the course of Conrad's career, it proved no easy task to convert the symbolic capital they delivered into currency he could use to support his family. Conrad certainly tried to make the case for the economic value of his work with various publishers. His correspondence with editors at Blackwood's links matters of aesthetics and marketing as it explains how to value his expert work. The strongest polemic appears in response to an attack from George Blackwood, a junior editor at the house, who complained not only about the rate at which Conrad wrote but also the pace at which his stories moved. George focused on a tale entitled, appropriately enough, 'The End of the Tether', which his uncle the senior editor William Blackwood planned to run serially before including in a short-story collection. After paging through the first instalment George opined that, 'as far as [it] goes at present' – some 14,000 words – 'one can hardly say one has got into the story yet' (Conrad, *Letters to Blackwood* 148). If this were true, if 14,000 words represented only the beginning of the narrative, then George was right to be worried. Conrad had a bad habit of starting stories that turned out to be books. *Lord Jim*, for instance, began life humbly as a piece entitled 'Jim: A Sketch'.[28] To make matters worse, George reminded Conrad that 'Tether' was late.

Conrad responded with a rousing defence addressed, notably, not to the lowly nephew but to uncle William. A meaty letter dated 31 May 1902 refers to his gout and other sundry ailments to demonstrate his commitment. 'You may believe me implicitly when I say that I never work in a self satisfied elation', Conrad notes tersely, 'I am conscious of having pursued with pain and labour a calm conception of a definite ideal' (*Collected Letters* 2: 416). He acknowledges that he has struggled to find a readership, but protests that an audience will come when his work begins to be credited as art.

I would . . . recall Wagner the musician and Rodin the Sculptor who both had to starve a little in their day – and Whistler the painter who made Ruskin the critic foam at the mouth with scorn and indignation . . . They had to suffer for being 'new.' And I too hope to find my place in the rear of my betters . . . This is my creed. Time will show. (2: 418)

By designating Wagner and Rodin and Whistler as his predecessors, Conrad places himself among artistic talent of a pointedly cosmopolitan cast. He does so with a sweeping gesture that makes suffering the governing condition for important aesthetic production worldwide. Artists starve because they work outside the mainstream. If every new

---

28 In the case of 'Tether', at least, Blackwood ultimately got what he had contracted for. The narrative remained a story, albeit a long one.

and worthwhile artist begins in a marginal position, it stands to reason that marginality is a clue that Conrad's work too is great.

Conrad tried out this syllogistic rhetoric on all his publishers, not only Blackwood's. In 1913, he wrote a long letter to Alfred Knopf, then an editor at Doubleday. '[A] writer may be taken up as an investment', he explained. 'An investment must be attended to, it must be nursed – if one believes in it' (*Collected Letters* 5: 258). As with all speculation, Conrad implies, writers worthy of investment may be a bargain so long as their work remains obscure; but such an investment also commits the investor to nurse the writer along. Investment was not simply a metaphor for Conrad. In 1911, the American collector John Quinn began snapping up his manuscripts and other literary ephemera with an eye to their eventual resale (Karl 702). A decade later the market for such goods was sufficiently established that the famed Paris bookshop and small press Shakespeare and Co. could issue *Ulysses* in a highly profitable collector's edition. Rainey recounts that a scarce seven weeks after the book had been published, copies were being sold and resold for as much as 350 times the sticker price (*Institutions* 69). 'Participants followed the vertiginous success of the first edition with the intensity of stockbrokers' (*Institutions* 70). The market for modernist fiction had begun to mimic the market for modernist art. Instead of selling disposable volumes at train station bookstalls, select editions could sell at auction. Bookcases could be thought of as displays akin to the walls of Gertrude Stein's famous Paris flat, which were hung floor to ceiling with paintings from the starving exiles who would soon be known as modernist masters.

What Conrad may or may not have known is that William Blackwood had once thought of him as an investment. In an 1899 memo, one of Blackwood's advisors writes to assure the publisher that he is 'doing all that is possible, and successfully I think, to secure Conrad as our author solely for the future' (*Letters to Blackwood* 44). Even earlier, in September 1898, Blackwood himself informed Conrad that he agreed his work ought to be treated differently from that of a Victorian novelist writing for a popular audience. 'I have always looked upon the writing of fiction as something not to be bounded altogether by time or space', he wrote, 'notwithstanding my old friend Anthony Trollope who went to a desk as a shoemaker goes to his last' (29). By 1902, however, Blackwood seems to have lost faith that supporting Conrad would ever pay. In a note dated 3 June, he cut Conrad off. Even as he did so, however, Blackwood confirmed that investment was the proper term for describing their fiduciary relationship. '[I do not] feel justified', he explained, 'in risking another big sum which we do not see our way to realize from the copyrights you offer for a very long time to come' (*Letters to Blackwood* 156). The question, it seems, was not whether Conrad ought to be thought of as an investment, but whether he ought to be thought of as a good one.

Though he may have looked like a long shot in 1898, by 1913 Conrad was a sure thing. *Chance* had gone into its serial run in the *New York Herald,* and his earlier novels were still in print. In correspondence from this period, Conrad writes from a position of strength. In one letter, he goes so far as to chastise Knopf and Doubleday for not picking him up sooner. 'Mr. Doubleday might have had all my books up to date in his hands if he had cared', Conrad observes. 'Other people bought them and I haven't [sic] heard that they have been ruined by it; though I did not give away my work for ten cents a volume, I can assure you. I am not an amateur who plays at it' (*Collected Letters* 5: 257). Though his material conditions may have changed, Conrad still pitched his work the same way. He continued to rely on the trope of suffering to provide evidence of the specialized labour that went into his writing. 'Sixteen years of hard work begins to tell', he remarks on one occasion, and on another mentions that a letter from Knopf finds him 'in bed with a very horrid fit of gout' (5: 258, 368). He continued to portray himself as an outsider, even though his work was beginning to gain recognition. He cautioned Knopf that when it comes to his fiction a publisher 'will have some difficulty to galvanize . . . any sort of popularity' (5: 275).

In these later years, Conrad has reason to believe that the very traits that doomed him with Blackwood's could make him a success with Knopf. Slow production and the scarce output it entails can work in his favour. 'My part will be to write as hard as I can', he affirms in a letter from August 1913, as he was just starting to compose *Victory.* 'And I am not likely to overwhelm you . . . you know I don't shake these things out [of] my sleeve. So you must make the best of what comes along – obtain the full effect from the rare products' (5: 269). Conrad convinced Knopf to reprint his memoir *A Personal Record,* the 'story of his first book and of his first contact with the sea' as well as to publish a scholarly volume about him by a 'young literary friend of mine, Richard Curle' (5: 259). When he feels Curle has been mistreated by Knopf, furthermore, he gives the editor a good dressing down: 'Both Mr. Conrad as subject and Mr. Curle as writer deserve better treatment' (5: 274). He continues: 'You don't seem to realize that a book about Conrad *will* get published anyhow' (5: 274). Conrad has not changed in these later letters – he is still a gout-ridden Polish immigrant who writes convoluted fictions at an excruciatingly slow pace – but the recognition he has been accruing has begun to convert into hard currency. When he invites a publisher to invest in him now, he sets the terms.

Never one to miss an opportunity to capitalize on success, Conrad decided to renegotiate his old contract with Blackwood's, which had written to suggest 'the inclusion of Lord Jim in our 1/- Editions might be a successful undertaking' (*Letters to Blackwood* 192). Conrad agreed to a reissue, on the grounds that the novel was increasingly difficult to find. But he also contended that Blackwood's still misunderstood his work. Cheap editions were for popular fiction; his demanded different treatment. 'I have been hearing for some time now that the booksellers tell people *Lord Jim* is out of print', Conrad agrees, '[but] I would much prefer a new edition at 6/- leaving the Democracy of the book-stalls to cut its teeth on something softer' (*Letters to Blackwood* 193). In the book market, as in the art trade, price can be an indicator of quality. The way to target readers prepared to appreciate what goes into making *Lord Jim* is to hike the cost of the book. By linking taste to price, Conrad imagines a marketplace defined less by mass leanings than subcultural niches. This is a market conceived not as an amorphous thing guided by an invisible hand but as a knowable and therefore manipulable organization of demographics. In this conception, aesthetics and economics are not enemies. They are complementary diagnostic matrices for analyzing and satisfying consumer behaviour.

As much as such a market implied new ways of consuming literature, it implied new ways of understanding readership. In a literary marketplace as expansive as that of the visual arts, it was impossible to think of consumers as an imagined community commensurate with the nation. One could think in terms of smaller niches, but one could also imagine a niche stretched across nations, which was Conrad's inclination. Just as he took his literary predecessors from the pantheon of cosmopolitan art, he imagined his readers as an international bunch. He claimed in a letter to Blackwood's that his writing appealed 'to such widely different personalities as W. H. Henley and Bernard Shaw – H. G. Wells and professor Yrgö Hirn of the Finland University – to Maurice Greiffenhagen a painter and to the skipper of a Persian Gulf steamer who wrote to the papers of my "Typhoon" – to the Ed. of PMM to a charming old lady in Winchester' (*Collected Letters* 2: 416). The eclecticism of this lot testifies to Conrad's difficulty in attracting an immediately identifiable readership, and provides a good approximation of the reach his work would eventually acquire.

Conrad's account of his audience – with its Finnish reader and Polish writer, its Persian Gulf skipper and its 'charming old lady' from Winchester – uncouples the production and consumption of English fiction from any clear cut association with the British nation. It forsakes the novel's history as a tool for bonding often far-flung 'fellow-readers, [all] connected through print, [into] the embryo of the nationally imagined community' (B. Anderson 44). And draws instead on the competing history of English fiction as a medium with international appeal. Conrad demonstrates that English readers need not be British men and women. He shows, further, that reading novels in English does not make readers any less foreign. Yrgö Hirn was an English-reading Finn, not so different in this way from Conrad the English-writing Pole. Each reader on the list occupies a simultaneously cosmopolitan and localized position. If such a contradictory posture was unfamiliar at the beginning of the twentieth century, Stuart Hall describes it as commonplace in the postcolonial era, when English has been localized and hybridized into 'Anglo-Japanese, Anglo-French, Anglo-German, or Anglo-English' (179).

Cosmopolitan though his readership may have been, Conrad made clear that it remained subject to stringent strategies of closure. His list is hierarchically structured according to demonstrated excellence in, precisely, the reading and writing of English literature. Thus Henley, editor of the *New Review*, like Wells and Shaw, demands mention by name.[29] Mark Morrison considers the formation of 'counter-public[s]' a highlight of early modernism (515).[30] Surely this was so, and as Conrad's list suggests they had the potential to be far flung. Eliot theorizes the literary audience similarly: 'The [recent] authors who . . . write for a small public are not writing for a more cultivated *class*, but for a heterogeneous number of peculiar individuals of various classes – for a kind of elite' ('On the Place and Function of the Clerisy' 242). Elitism and cosmopolitanism were not incommensurate. The creation of a cultivated but disparate audience for Conrad's fiction was helped along by collectors in the Americas and Asia, as well as biographers and editors on nearly every continent. G. Jean-Aubry published a collection of Conrad's correspondence in 1926. Curle

29 Yrgö Hirn was the husband of Karin Hirn, who translated Conrad's *Tales of Unrest* into Swedish, while Greiffenhagen illustrated many of Conrad's books and stories (see *Letters* 2: 416n1).
30 Thus Morrison's account of Ford's *English Review*, with its 'unorthodox literature (such as Lewis's stories) and not only its other literary pieces, but also the non-literary contributions (such as letters to the editor regarding farming issues)' reveals one of the major early journals of modernism to be every bit as eclectic as the early modernist audience produced by Conrad's list (525).

did the same two years later. The proliferation of similar efforts served a readership interested not only in particular novels but also in the minutia of modernist authorship.

As this case study of Conrad's letters has endeavoured to show, the modernist dictate to write from the margins functions as shorthand for more sweeping change in the literary market. To generate such a dispersed and sophisticated readership meant revising authorship as well. Suffering connoted the marginality of the artist, in as much as Conrad and others made it speak the arduous labour necessary to generate art. And in so doing it called up an author determined to make apparent the ardour of his writing. Suffering in solitude, out of the glare of the mass market, entailed more than voluntary exile and a 'denial of the economy', to employ Bourdieu's formulation (*Field* 50). It was the essential first step in generating a market niche whose relative autonomy might enable writers and their confederates to use the rules of literary economics to their advantage.

The key to this revision was ensuring that suffering connoted the quality of one's labour rather than an aspect of one's person. What modernism offered its audience was less individual genius in the romantic mode than hard won expertise. Conrad's gout provided his epistolary interlocutors with a glimpse inside his workroom, not his soul. It confirmed that he laboured long and hard to produce even the shortest of fictions. The very letters themselves with their crossed out lines and edited paragraphs confirmed the difficulty of Conrad's method of composition. They confirmed the editorial nature of his labour as well, which would also be apparent to the reader attentive to the ways his novels reimagined habitual fictional settings and plots. Documenting suffering made apparent the difference of his labour, his emphasis on the salvage and elevation of narratives and even whole genres that had previously been considered more pedestrian than aesthetically interesting. In the letters, gout becomes the sign of expert service work, the gruelling labour of transforming imperial adventures – 'stor[ies] for boys', as Conrad put it (*Letters* 2: 417) – into what would in time be recognized as some of the earliest modernist fictions.

To be ill was not to be weak, since it provided Conrad with the means to ensure that his interlocutors noticed the special quality of his work. When considered as part of the logic of service economics, furthermore, Conrad's gout suggests an effort to manage the disembodiment effect that Bhagwati describes as the accompaniment of commodification. As Conrad's books splinter off into the marketplace, his suffering directs attention back to his labour, as the correspondence surrounding the publication of *Nostromo* ably demonstrates. With well-placed accomplices and allies, the letters help us to see, documenting the pain of writing can bring recognition of one's expertise that might, in the end, lead to the growth of a highly particularized but still potentially substantial niche of dedicated readers. As Conrad's letters portray it, such a niche might span the globe. The insistence with which 'Heart of Darkness' appears on university syllabi worldwide bears out the prescience of this dream. For his pains, Conrad found himself part of a cosmopolitan community that could include not only multifarious readers of difficult English fiction but also fellow exiles and invalids like Eliot, Joyce, and Woolf – the usual suspects, in short, of the modernist canon.

CHAPTER 2

Sentimental administration

> Squatting with towel in hand on the crumbling veranda. Excellent
> setting for a novel. But what about the plot?
>
> Bronislaw Malinowski, *Diary* 211

Modernism's outsider status could not keep it from influencing thought
in a wide range of disciplines. Fictions including 'Heart of Darkness' and
Lady Chatterley's Lover long have served as points of reference in debate on
topics ranging from the politics of empire to the history of sexuality.
According to many early twentieth-century writers, exile from the mainstream was precisely what made literature of lasting impact possible.
'The advantages incident to this removal are many', Wyndham Lewis
commented in 1927. '. . . being in solitary schism, with no obligations at
the moment towards party or individual colleague, I can resume my
opinion of the society I have just left, and its characteristics which else
might remain without serious unpartisan criticism' (23–4). Scholars have
often reiterated this appraisal. Edward Said, for instance, contends that
the detachment maintained by Joseph Conrad facilitated both the form
and content of his novels: 'Never the wholly incorporated and fully
acculturated Englishman, Conrad therefore preserved an ironic distance
in each of his works' (*Culture and Imperialism* 25). Remaining aloof from
English culture enabled terse questioning of British imperialism, while
Conrad's legendary irony permitted 'readers to imagine something other
than an Africa carved up into dozens of European colonies, even if, for his
own part, he had little notion of what that Africa might be' (*Culture and
Imperialism* 26).

Ironic detachment is only half the story, however. While modernism
may have developed a finely tuned rhetoric of distance, it did not neglect
the surprisingly complementary idiom of sympathy. We may be used to
thinking of these two modes as contradictory but Amanda Anderson
contends that they were frequent fellow travellers. She discovers calls for

'disinterestedness and sympathy' side by side in a variety of writings (15). According to Christopher Herbert, such a rhetorical combination is the hallmark of modern ethnography, and he traces it back to the mid-nineteenth-century work of Harriet Martineau. '[She] articulates the principles of fieldwork subjectivity in precisely the language in which they will frequently be invoked by twentieth-century writers, [and] makes clear that the prized attitude of "sympathy" can in fact only be defined as a kind of psychological emptying, a voluntary creation of a vacuum into which the ideas and affective forces of a foreign people can rush' (154). Though Herbert focuses on Martineau in order to establish her unacknowledged importance within the history of anthropology, her arguments represented just one impetus behind what in the era of modernism was a broadly interdisciplinary effort to combine detachment and sympathy.

Among colonial administrators, interest in this combination was provoked by and also helped to provoke a sense that interaction between colonizer and colonized was changing. Early twentieth-century documents show administrators treating contact between District Officers and their subalterns as generating new interpersonal relationships as well as an administrative dynamic. Such treatment entailed a reconception of Britain's overseas subjects as well as the posture that officers should take towards them. Relating to colonized subjects as people necessitated sympathy, while administering a population required a more detached approach. Combining these two was especially challenging in bureaucracies just beginning to form in the Gold Coast, Nigeria, and Kenya, where governance increasingly appeared to depend on close cooperation between Europeans and Africans. Britain recruited locals to do administrative work. In so doing, it invited questions about the ethical foundation of colonial rule. An English-speaking African population well versed in the languages of culture, nation, and human rights challenged Britons who had become used to treating such vernaculars as their special possession. Administrators turned to sympathy in order to make sense of this development. They behaved as if focusing on the intimate feelings between individual Europeans and Africans might allow them to extrapolate a theory for understanding how to deal with a colonial population expert in an Anglicized idiom of ethics and morality. They supposed a new set of narratives about interpersonal relationships might help generate the sort of distance required to generate a revised model of governance.

A whiff of scandal provided anthropology with strong incentive to become more sympathetic. Scientific detachment acquired a bad reputation from incidents such as one involving the naturalist James Jameson, who sponsored a cannibalistic spectacle while he was posted to the rear camp of Henry Stanley's 1877 expedition to central Africa. Jameson allegedly paid six handkerchiefs to have a young woman consumed in his presence, an event he preserved in both sketch and detailed prose description. When accounts of this episode began to circulate, they provoked an outcry against the callousness of one-sidedly disinterested observation. The historian Laura Franey cites an anonymous commentary in an 1890 number of the *Contemporary Review* that asks with dismay 'how any English gentleman could have looked on at the deliberate butchery of a little girl, even a black one, with as much coolness as if it were a scientific experiment' (quoted in Franey 233). The public uproar echoed earlier statements by Francis Galton, the president of the Anthropological Institute, who encouraged his fellows to reconsider their approach to fieldwork:

Foreigners say that we are stiff, and that our naturally narrow powers of sympathy are still further contracted by insular prejudices. Be this as it may, it is certain that the English do not excel in winning the hearts of other nations. They have to broaden their sympathies by the study of mankind as they are, and without prejudice. This is precisely what the Anthropologists of all nations aim at doing, and in consequence succeed in discovering previously unsuspected connections between past and present forms of society, between the mind of the child and of the man, and between the customs, creeds, and institutions of barbarians and of civilized peoples. Anthropology teaches us to sympathise with other races, and to regard them as kinsmen rather than aliens. In this aspect it may be looked upon as a pursuit of no small political value. (337–8)

Galton treats anthropology as a resource for recovering colonial authority that heartless Victorians have undermined. But he also describes it as imported technology that if adopted must make Britons seem a little foreign – less stiff and prejudiced, more emotional, and thus more akin to the people they study. It is worth making the obvious observation that sympathy did not always have such exotic connotations. Martineau did not treat it as an alien capacity. And of course, sentimentality and the desirability of profound fellow feeling have been associated with the English novel since the eighteenth century. What Galton described as an import could be equally thought of as an export. If sympathy were to become the very essence of anthropology, and administrators were to emphasize sentimental ties to the people they governed, Britons would take on an emotional range Galton associated with foreigners while at the same time the colonies would acquire a bit of the flavour readers of English fiction associated with domestic romance.

From his position at the margins, Conrad was perfectly poised to describe this confusion of inside and outside, foreign-seeming sympathy and dyed-in-the-wool English sentimentality. In the first section of this chapter, I show that novels such as *Lord Jim* and *Victory* portrayed an empire populated by emotional adventurers and disinterested subalterns who understood the politics of administration as well (if not better) than their rulers. Sentiment, I argue, was just as important as irony to Conrad's incisive revision of imperial representation. His novels refashioned a habitual conceptual geography by telling love stories set in the colonies and depicting Englishmen more savage than any colonial subject.

Conrad's emphasis on the challenges such revision posed for ethnographic observation sets the stage for Bronislaw Malinowski, whose writing I consider in the middle portion of this chapter. His classics *Argonauts of the Western Pacific* and *The Sexual Life of Savages* pick up where Conrad's novels leave off. His unpublished diaries, meanwhile, make explicit a debt to fiction that remains implicit in the published work. All of these writings treat the love story as the narrative form best suited for elabourating on anthropological method. In these writings, I demonstrate, scientific specialization involves the telling of domestic romances set on tropical isles.

In the last section of the chapter, I show how imperial administrators also appropriated this unlikely logic when they set out to re-imagine their own practice. I refer to the influential writings of Frederick Lugard and other colonial governors and bureaucrats, as I describe specific incidents in Sub-Saharan Africa that reveal how extensively sympathetic language spread in administrative circles. I treat this material in an effort to confirm that modernist innovation was not isolated to the arts. Rather than providing a historical context for my readings of Conrad and Malinowski, therefore, this last section maintains that both participated in a truly interdisciplinary venture to mix literary and rhetorical material previously considered properly English with that customarily associated with the imperial periphery. The agents of this enterprise derived their authority from a capacity to remain above the fray, detached from local events but sympathetic to the lives of those they described and managed. To understand how thoroughly such a campaign renovated the empire, I must turn now to the imperial ideology it sought to displace.

ON THE IMPOSSIBILITY OF GOING NATIVE

'[C]olonial domination', Homi K. Bhabha contends, 'is achieved through a process of disavowal that denies the chaos of its intervention as *Entstellung*, its dislocatory presence in order to preserve the authority of its identity in the teleological narratives of historical and political evolutionism' (111). British colonialism strives to deny that it produces the places it colonizes, this argument asserts, so that it can then promise to undo the damage in the name of development. Such a ruse depends on another, in which the standard of development is an English culture both particular – it comes from England – and universal – making it possible that, as Bhabha notes 'a Polish *émigré*, deeply influenced by Gustave Flaubert, writing about Africa, produces an English classic' (108). Conrad's 'Heart of Darkness' is the classic Bhabha has in mind, of course, but he also attends to another text, a King James testament, which though 'translated into Hindi, propagated by Dutch or native catechists, is still the English book' (108). I am interested in how Bhabha treats these examples from his 1985 essay 'Signs Taken for Wonders', because I am not nearly as convinced as he is that they demonstrate a disavowal of colonial domination. Rather, it seems to me, they articulate a different form of imperial administration.

The English books at issue in 'Signs Taken for Wonders' are the Bible as presented in May 1817 by a young Indian catechist named Anund Messeh to an audience near Delhi, and *An Inquiry into some Points of Seamanship* 'by a man named Tower, Towson – some such name' discovered by Marlow in the second part of 'Heart of Darkness' (Bhabha 102, 104; 'Heart of Darkness' 99). Despite the fact that it belongs to a Russian sailor, Bhabha concludes that Marlow is far from wrong in deducing that both book and book owner 'must be English' (100). They are each products of commercial enterprise that, though it often follows the flag, creates speakers of broken English who are clearly not British. 'Brother sailor', *Inquiry's* owner 'gabbled' when Marlow finally meets him, 'pleasure . . . delight . . . introduce myself . . . Russian . . . son of an arch-priest . . . Government of Tambov . . . What? Tobacco! English tobacco; the excellent English tobacco! Now, that's brotherly. Smoke? Where's a sailor that does not smoke?' (123). This fragmentary soliloquy – with its reference to tobacco grown, bought, and sold under an English imprint to a brotherhood of Anglicized sailors – hints at a fundamental thesis of Conrad's fiction: everything, every person, and every place has been transformed or will eventually be transformed by commerce conducted in English.[1]

Bhabha describes such influence as 'the sign of the productivity of colonial power' and, further, the origin of 'subversion, founded on the undecidability that turns the discursive conditions of dominance into the grounds of intervention' (112). By creating new English speakers, Britain also creates opportunities for subverting colonial authority. The problem that has long troubled colonial scholars, however, is figuring out how to distinguish subversion of British power from collabouration with English culture. For Bhabha, subversion takes the form of an interrogation: 'If the appearance of the English book is read as a production of colonial hybridity, then it no longer simply commands authority. It gives rise to a series of questions of authority' (112–13).[2] Thus the local interlocutors of the Indian catechist Anund Messeh ask, 'how can it be the European book, when we believe that it is God's gift to us?' (103). They refuse to confuse the word of God with the word of the colonizer and, as a result, reveal how colonialism seeks to represent its particular rules as the earthly incarnation of more universal law. In this way, they imperil Britain's ownership of enlightenment and civilization.

Such appropriation prompts queries in return. Bhabha cites those asked by Marlow as he gazes on a 'bit of white worsted round [the] neck' of a dying African man. Although Marlow asks questions he cannot ultimately answer, they serve to focus readers' attention on a 'subversion' that I argue might better be understood as a new administrative problem. To understand what sort of problem we should look more closely at the passage leading up to and including Marlow's examination of the bit of white cloth.

At last I got under the trees. My purpose was to stroll into the shade for a moment; but no sooner within than it seemed to me I had stepped into the gloomy circle of some Inferno . . . Black shapes crouched, lay, sat between the trees leaning against the trunks, clinging to the earth, half coming out, half effaced within the dim light, in all the attitudes of pain, abandonment, and despair . . . The work was going on. The work! And this was the place where some of the helpers had withdrawn to die. They were dying slowly – it was very clear. They were not enemies, they were not criminals, they were nothing earthly

---

1 Simpson puts it this way: 'The fetishized world of the colonial nations has imposed itself upon the far-flung corners of the earth, creating a commerce in the images of its own alienation' (119).

2 He also contends, 'If the effect of colonial power is seen to be the *production* of hybridization rather than the noisy command of colonialist authority or the silent repression of native traditions, then an important change of perspective occurs' (*Location of Culture* 112–13).

now, – nothing but black shadows of disease and starvation, lying confusedly in the greenish gloom. Brought from all the recesses of the coast in all the legality of time contracts, lost in uncongenial surroundings, fed on unfamiliar food, they sickened, became inefficient, and were then allowed to crawl away and rest . . . Then, glancing down, I saw a face near my hand. The black bones reclined at full length with one shoulder against the tree, and slowly the eyelids rose and the sunken eyes looked up at me, enormous and vacant, a kind of blind, white flicker in the depths of the orbs, which died out slowly. The man seemed young – almost a boy – but you know with them it's hard to tell. I found nothing else to do but to offer him one of my good Swede's ship's biscuits I had in my pocket. The fingers closed slowly on it and held – there was no other movement and no other glance. He had tied a bit of white worsted round his neck – Why? Where did he get it? Was it a badge – an ornament – a charm – a propitiatory act? Was there any idea at all connected with it? It looked startling round his black neck, this bit of white thread from beyond the seas. ('Heart of Darkness' 66–7)

When interpreting this scene, we ought to recognize it as a set piece whose formal attributes would have been familiar to readers of fiction at the turn of the twentieth century. This is a perfect example of the sublime representation Audrey Jaffe calls a 'scene of sympathy.' Drawing on examples from the heart of the English novelistic tradition – Dickens, Eliot, Gaskell – Jaffe explains that these scenes generally feature a specta-tor confronted by a collection of suffering figures, a group of peasants, for instance. A crowd gradually distils into a representative individual with whom the spectator experiences a sympathetic connection 'represented as an investment or exchange' (9). Money and sympathy flow in one direc-tion; moral benefit and a sense of self-satisfaction return in the other.[3] Conrad reproduces this scene but instead of urban paupers he presents 'Black shapes' and disembodied limbs.[4] Rather than the clarity of profit-able exchange he offers perplexity: Marlow donates a biscuit, and receives an interpretive dilemma.[5]

---

3 'Sympathy and charity situate the self in a hydraulic relation with other selves', Jaffe writes, 'in which the flow of funds in one direction represents a drain unless balanced by some – usually moral – return' (16).

4 As Suleri explains, imperial prose was rife with sublime descriptions that challenge rather than confirm an observer's capacity for sympathetic response. The immensity of Africa and India, the multifariousness of their inhabitants came to 'signify only the colonizer's pained confrontation with an object to which his cultural and interpretive tools must be inadequate' (31).

5 White notes, 'a primary function of the rhetoric of enigma' throughout Conrad's writing but especially in 'Heart of Darkness' is 'to preserve – indeed to intensify – the "aura" of the art work' (111). By associating sympathy with hermeneutic difficulty, Conrad kills two birds with one stone. He simultaneously distinguishes his version of sympathy from the popular model circulating in

To understand what Conrad means by reworking such a customary aspect of the novel in this way, we might glance at its philosophical precedent. Literary critics have tended to consider David Hume's *Treatise of Human Nature* as the source for the description of sympathy reiterated and revised in English fiction. Hume's sympathy is predicated on an ability to perceive resemblance. '[W]e never remark any passion or principle in others', he asserts, 'of which, in some degree or other, we may not find a parallel in ourselves' (207; see Pinch 35). Once assured that someone else resembles us, sympathy acts as a conduit for 'affections [that] readily pass from one person to another, and beget corresponding movements in every human creature' (368). Such communication confirms the resemblance with which the process began, since the feeling deduced in another is readily reproduced in oneself. 'We might argue, then', comments Catherine Gallagher, 'that Humean sympathy is complete when it dispenses with its original "object", the original sufferer. I sympathize with the sentiments of others by making them mine; and the conditions for such appropriation must be there at the outset: the person who originally feels them must somehow "belong" to me' (*Nobody's Story* 171). This makes the production of sympathy appear solipsistic and, Gallagher argues, the perfect enterprise for a private activity such as the reading of novels, which entails imagining sufferers that can be called forth and dismissed at the will of the reader.[6]

To satisfy such demanding use, fictional characters had to look a certain way. The emphasis on resemblance in Hume's definition of sympathy had a logical counterpart in novelistic theory allowing the reader to deduce the interior feeling of characters by interpreting the signs apparent on their exteriors. 'When I see the *effects* of passion in the voice and gesture of any person', Hume wrote, 'my mind immediately passes from these effects to their causes, and forms such a lively idea of the passion, as is presently converted into the passion itself' (368).[7] Novels taught readers how to perform this interpretive act by mirroring it within

the feminized fictions of domestic romance and distinguishes his account of the complexity of imperial relationships from the popular Victorian adventure fictions.

6 '[A] character came into *fictional* existence most fully when he or she was developed as nobody *in particular*', Gallagher maintains, 'that is, the particularities had to be fully specified to ensure the felt fictionality of the character. A generalized character would too easily take on allegorical or symbolic reference, just as one rendered in mere 'hints' would have been read at the time as a scandalous libel' (*Nobody's story* 175).

7 He continues, 'No passion of another discovers itself immediately to the mind. We are only sensible of its causes or effects. From *these* we infer the passion: And consequently *these* give rise to our sympathy.'

the fiction. Round characters whose detailed surfaces revealed depths of feeling became, as Deidre Lynch shows, 'imaginative resources on which readers drew to make themselves into individuals, to expand their own inner resources of sensibility' (*Economy of Character* 126). Conrad inherited this way of thinking about sympathy as well as the novelistic rules for how to represent it. But in 'Heart of Darkness' he threw an evident wrench into the works when he placed Marlow before a spectacle of fragmented African labourers dying underneath the trees.[8]

The problem for Marlow is that he is unsure about the figures with whom he begins to sympathize. Exploitative labour has distorted them into 'bundles of acute angles . . . scattered in every pose of contorted collapse, as in some picture of a massacre or a pestilence' (67). When read according to the conventions of sympathetic fiction, the inhuman fragmentation of bodily surfaces cannot help but indicate a comparable dehumanization of their interiors. Empire has made Africans into beings whose humanity is in doubt. Nonetheless, Marlow imagines that the barer of the 'white worsted' may have performed a feat of interpretation remarkably similar to his own. He makes a bit of cloth into a talisman of imperial contact by sympathetically imagining the ornamental properties it holds for its wearer. Where Bhabha finds traces of a hybridizing gesture through which Africa made English cloth its own, I see a situation that transforms both 'Africa' and 'England' by making them comparable interpreters of colonial endeavour.

This is not the only time that Marlow finds himself puzzling over the characters he sees on the river.[9] Conrad repeatedly sets scenes that prompt sympathy, but in every case they launch another round of questioning. Near Kurtz's homestead Marlow encounters another mass of 'black limbs'. 'Well, you know, that was the worst of it', he notes, 'this suspicion of their not being inhuman.' (96). '[W]hat thrilled you was just the thought of their humanity – like yours – the thought of your remote kinship with this wild and passionate uproar' (96). Though what he witnesses triggers feelings of sympathy and kinship, Marlow still cannot

---

8 This is not to say that sympathy never leapt across the racial divide. Ellison shows how it gets 'distributed on both sides of . . . interracial encounters' in nineteenth-century American as well as British fictions 'and portioned out to the dying man, or his friend, or both. The whole encounter is charged with the intimate tension of social equality – equality that often registers the struggle to invest narratives of cross-racial imperial relationships with the legitimizing rhetoric that evokes friendship between peers' (98).

9 The questions prompted by Tower/Towson's *Inquiry* take a similar form. The printed text reveals 'a singleness of intention', but when supplemented by the 'cipher' of Russian annotation in its margins the book becomes an 'extravagant mystery' (99).

decide if he discerns a resemblance or not, which makes it impossible for him to fully grasp the hidden passions he senses. He is sure, however, that imperialism is responsible for his difficulties.

Nothing better demonstrates Europe's culpability for the epistemological complexity one finds in the turn-of-the-century jungle than the condition of Marlow's English-speaking African colleagues. At first, he dismisses a uniformed guard 'with a large, white, rascally grin' as 'the product of the new forces at work' and slanders his own helmsman as 'the most unstable kind of fool I had ever seen . . . a dog in a parody of breeches and a feather hat, walking on his hind legs' (64–5, 109). Still, after the helmsman is killed by a spear, Marlow discovers that he misses him. There was between them, he explains, a working relationship. 'He steered for me – I had to look after him, I worried about his deficiencies, and thus a subtle bond had been created, of which I only became aware when it was suddenly broken' (119). Sounding as much like a disconsolate lover as a captain who has lost a member of his crew, Marlow continues, 'And the intimate profundity of that look he gave me when he received his hurt remains to this day in my memory, like a claim of distant kinship affirmed in a supreme moment' (119). In one of the most deeply emotional gestures in the novel, Marlow hugs the helmsman – 'his shoulders were pressed to my breast' – and throws his body overboard – 'Oh! he was heavy, heavy; heavier than any man on earth, I should imagine. Then without more ado I tipped him overboard . . . I saw the body roll over twice before I lost sight of it' (119–20). Having made sympathy into a cipher, Conrad lends it a bit of clarity by suggesting that the most demonstrable feeling between European and African emerges as the result of shared labour. As much as colonialism muddles the sympathetic affiliation between us and them, it also enables a decidedly sentimental bond born of participation in a common venture.

We feel affection for those we work with not because they are like us, but because they are colleagues. Such is the thinking behind Conrad's modification of the Victorian scene of sympathy. The sentimentalization of imperial labour emerges from Marlow's voyage as the most definitive result of Europe's intervention in Africa. Not even the so-named 'cannibals' who travel with him upriver are beyond the reach of such fellow feeling. 'I looked at them as you would on any human being', Marlow reports, 'with a curiosity of their impulses, motives, capacities, weaknesses, when brought to the test of an inexorable physical necessity' (105). The necessity in question is hunger: though they are starving, the cannibals will not feed on Marlow and the rest of his crew. Having dismissed 'superstition, disgust, patience, fear – or some kind of primitive honour' as the cause of the cannibals' evident self-control, Marlow finds himself with 'a mystery greater' than the 'savage clamour' on the river's shore (105). The cannibals' actions must be governed, he concludes, not by any native instinct but by 'restraint', a quality that he associates with dedication to a job (105). Like the rest of the African characters he confronts, the cannibals are less natives than fellow workers.

If such a conclusion obscures the difference between European and African, it clarifies the one distinction that readers of 'Heart of Darkness' could always be sure of, namely that between Kurtz – whose 'impene-trable darkness' exceeds the jungle's own – and Marlow – who may have 'peeped over the edge' and have been tempted to 'go ashore for a howl and a dance' but never does (149, 151, 97). These two characters represent nothing less than the opposition between an older and newer style of imperial management. I am, of course, not the only one to identify Kurtz via his relationship to administration. Michael Levenson describes him as a rogue bureaucrat, while Daniel Bivona calls him a company man who yearns to break free (Levenson 'Value' 395; Bivona 106–7). Kurtz's incom-petence – 'No method at all', as Marlow puts it (138) – best identifies him as part of a generation that may have turned 'a blank space of delightful mystery' into a thoroughly textualized domain 'filled . . . with rivers and lakes and names', but that never figured out how to administer what it had wrought (52). It runs operations manned by 'faithless pilgrims', punctuated by 'objectless blasting', and dominated by 'large and honourable trading company[ies]' that are anything but (76, 64, 104). Conrad's caricatures of Victorian empire builders refer to their African counterparts as 'criminals' and 'enemies' or, in the case of the heads on stakes that greet visitors to Kurtz's station, 'rebels'. 'What would be the next definition I was to hear?' Marlow scoffs. 'Those rebellious heads looked very subdued to me' (132). Disavowal is the not-so-strange bedfel-low of ignorance, as is evidenced by Kurtz's belief that when things go wrong he can just fade away into the jungle. For him, living among Africans means the possibility of going native. For Marlow, the act of going native seems impossible. The very mystery that makes the canni-bals' motivation so interesting also enables him to observe that no clean logic of 'us' and 'them', colonist and native organizes this place. The locals are migrant workers, not aboriginals. The cannibals don't exhibit the gustatory habits that earned them their name but are instead exhausted servants, 'their skins . . . no longer glossy and their muscles no longer hard' (104). In Africa as Marlow sees it there are no natives anymore, only subjects more or less incorporated into a European colonial apparatus.

Before Conrad, H. Rider Haggard was the master manipulator of the going native plot, and 'Heart of Darkness' recycles his favourite tropes in order to distinguish Marlow's vision from that of Kurtz.[10] Haggard's Africa was a seductive temptress, cartographically represented by the treasure map in *King Solomon's Mines* – with its hills named 'Sheba's Breasts' (27) – and dominated by various bewitching women – from the animalistic Gagool, to the white Amazon She, to the alluring Queen sisters of *Allan Quatermain*. As Marianne DeKoven reminds us, the jungle of 'Heart of Darkness' is famously feminized as well. It is forever taking men into its 'bosom' and sucking travellers into a 'somber gap' below walls of 'matted vegetation' (77, 95).[11] We know that Kurtz goes native, moreover, because of the perverse domestic arrangement he settles into with a 'savage and superb' woman 'draped in striped and fringed cloths, treading the earth proudly, with a slight jingle and flash of barbarous ornaments' (135).[12]

If the jungle periphery is feminized in 'Heart of Darkness', so is the European centre. After Kurtz, the most pronounced disavowal of Empire's dislocatory presence comes from women such as his Intended and Marlow's 'excellent aunt', whose reverie about 'emissary[ies] of light' is interrupted by her nephew's impertinent reminder that imperial missions are 'run for profit' (59). Though men do the work, women are Empire's gatekeepers. At the Company's European office, 'guarding the door of Darkness' sit the 'Old knitter[s] of black wool', while in the jungle stands the 'barbarous and superb woman' (57, 146). As she stretches 'tragically her bare arms', so too the Intended reaches out, clad in the black of mourning, an 'eloquent phantom . . . resembling in this gesture [the] other one . . . bedecked with powerless charms, stretching bare

---

10 On the generic elements and various permutations of the 'gone native' plot, see Torgovnick, *Gone primitive.*

11 Conrad never lost his taste for such descriptive language. One finds it in *Lord Jim* as well, where the village of Patusan lies at the base of 'two steep hills very close together . . . separated by what looks like a deep fissure [or] cleavage' (163).

12 In Haggard, love in the Empire is only possible once an elaborate and well-documented ethnography has outed the natives as closet Europeans. In *Allan Quatermain*, for instance, the 1887 sequel to *King Solomon's Mines*, Sir Henry is able to fall for the Queen Nylepcha only once her people, the Zu-Vendi, have been shown to descend from the Phoenicians, and the same cradle of European humanity that helped produce the English (149, 156). Through editorial notes and the speculations of its narrator, Haggard's novel elaborates an ethnography for the Zu-Vendi that portrays them as outsiders in Africa and, even, white (139).

brown arms over the glitter of the infernal stream' (146, 160). This surfeit of women 'brings us to a curious impasse in the novel's logic', comments Rosemary Marangoly George (86). Various sorts of feminized domesticity awkwardly frame imperial adventure. At novel's end, 'Marlow feels trapped both in the houses of the civilized world, which are presided over by women, and by the wilderness, which is also female' (George 86).

Conrad resolves this dilemma in *Lord Jim* by reforming the perverse domesticity that plagues Kurtz and all of Haggard's heroes. Co-opting the domestic lends certainty to sentimental relationships: Jim acquires a sense of purpose and authority when he falls in love with the half-caste Jewel. Though this is very much a story about Jim's particular fate, Conrad would have us remember that he is but one of a loosely allied network of men guided by their emotions as they strive to reform field stations and commercial outposts. Marlow repeatedly utters the novel's signature phrase for denoting membership in this cosmopolitan collective as he reminds his readers that whatever else they may think of Jim, he will always be 'one of us'.[13] Like many critics, Geoffrey Galt Harpham concludes that the fellowship Marlow describes is residual, that its members possessed a 'nineteenth-century sensibility', and that Jim himself is 'a man whose self-perception is formed by the simple morality of popular fiction, who falls, or leaps, into the ambiguities of the twentieth [century]' ('Conrad's Global Homeland' 32).[14] Stein, one of the elder statesmen of this society, appears to bolster such a reading when he describes Jim as inveterately 'romantic' (*Lord Jim* 160). Sarah Cole's

13 These are sympathetic specialists, captains, traders, and ship chandlers about whom one can say with feeling as Jim does, 'I know he liked me' (140). Typical behaviour involves being 'overcome with emotion' by the drama of Jim's guilty conscience that plays out over the first half of the book, and entranced by the irony that while Jim is still haunted by his actions on board the *Patna*, no one else much cares about what happened when that ship went down (143–4). Marlow represents the group. He knows them all, and knows that every one would have the same positive response to Jim as he did the moment '[m]y eyes met his for the first time' (25). 'He was the kind of fellow you would, on the strength of his looks, leave in charge of the deck', Marlow explains (31–2).

14 Pecora echoes this contention when he describes Conrad's domestic settings as 'noble households' (109). And Moses discovers similarly antiquated residues when he recaptures 'the dissonance . . . originally embodied between the common ordinary name "Jim" and the exalted aristocratic title of "Lord"' (73). He reads Conrad's text as a salvage operation for autocratic authority: 'Jim remains fundamentally a despotic figure . . . [whose] career in Patusan anticipates that of certain authoritarian Asian political leaders, such as Le Kuan Yew of Singapore of Deng Xiaoping of China, who have embarked upon economic liberalization and modernization by means of a paternalistic and nondemocratic method of government' (83). Jameson's influential reading asks us to more or less ignore the content of the novel's recycled themes of 'heroism and courage' in order to grasp what it means to thoroughly abstract and aestheticize them (*Political Unconscious* 209). The true politics of the novel remain buried, he argues, beneath the sediment of the many and various narratives styles and stories with which Conrad plays (214).

revision of critical convention portrays Jim's romanticism as less anachronistic than transitional. It partakes of dated traditions from adventure
fiction, but at the same time aspires 'to create an inclusive domestic space,
whose sanctity is ensured by a regulating system of equalized male
partnerships' (117). What makes that system cutting edge – even as it
continues to rely on older cultural raw material – is its association with
very contemporary notions of specialization.

Romance, sympathy, and sentimentality are hallmarks of expertise in
this book. At the completion of a particularly exciting lepidopterological
expedition, Stein reports, 'my legs became so weak with emotion that I
had to sit on the ground' (155–6). If science immobilizes Stein with the
intense feelings it provokes, the propagation of colonial administration is
likewise an act of love. Stein has a 'characteristically . . . sentimental
motive' for helping Jim, Marlow reports. 'He had a notion of paying off
(in kind I suppose) the old debt . . . [to his] late benefactor', who likewise
helped him establish a place on Empire's fringe (170). When Stein was
young, he punctuated scientific investigation with attempts to manage a
'great noble', or 'great rascal' of the colonial periphery (154). He used to be
married to an exotic 'princess', by whom he had a daughter, but both were
killed by 'infectious fever' and now he lives alone, 'classing, cataloging and
arranging specimens, corresponding with entomologists in Europe', and
managing a 'small fleet of schooners . . . [that] dealt in island produce on a
large scale' (153). Like his benefactor, Jim learns to mediate between places
and peoples, to govern by advising, to manage and to administer territory
he does not own but learns to know.[15]

On his arrival in Patusan, Jim promptly adds Dain Wairis, the son of a
local potentate, to his fellowship of the sea. Marlow describes their
relationship as 'one of those strange, profound, rare friendships between
brown and white, in which the very difference of race seems to draw two
human beings closer by some mystic element of sympathy' (194). Dain
Wairis knows 'how to fight like a white man' and has a 'European mind'
(194–5). He 'captivate[s]' Marlow: 'His – if I may say so – his caustic
placidity, and, at the same time, his intelligent sympathy with Jim's
aspirations, appealed to me' (195). This is clearly an advance on the

---

15 Thus, it seems to me that Pecora only gets Stein half right when he suggests that 'Stein mediates,
rather as the modern anthropologist would, between two cultural economies – modern, utilitarian
West versus traditional, communitarian East – just as he mediates between two narrative
economies, realism and romance' (152). As I argue throughout this chapter, Conrad's fiction – and
especially *Lord Jim* – works hard to undermine precisely this sort of binary thinking.

half-articulated interracial bonding of 'Heart of Darkness'. Resemblance remains a question: Dain Wairis must be neatly whitened before he can join the fellows. But resemblance means something different in a novel that makes such a strong point of describing nearly all of its characters as mongrels of one sort or another. Stein, a Bavarian, acquired his specialized knowledge in Trieste, Tripoli, and various ports in the 'East' (151). Jim may be English – and born in a 'parsonage' even (2) – but his formative experiences all occurred overseas. According to the early Conrad scholar Albert Guérard, the prototype for Jim was the 'ornate and disturbing' eponymous tragic hero of 'Karain: A Memory', another character who struggled to manage a peripheral settlement, 'an insignificant foothold on the earth' (Guérard 91; Conrad, 'Karain' 9, 5).

The area of Patusan itself is far from monolithic. Jim does not so much go native here as move from one cosmopolitan setting – the *Patna* with its Chinese owner and Middle Eastern pilgrims – to another – populated by, among other non-autochthonous groups, 'immigrants from Celebes' and an 'Arab half-breed' (191). Jim finds himself not on an ethnic island, but in the middle of a longstanding contest between multiple factions and shifting alliances.[16] He is but one immigrant among many. Though he reproduces perfectly the sort of domestic arrangement Conrad and Haggard treated as part and parcel of going native, he finds himself in anything but a stock adventure narrative.

Marlow calls it a love story. 'I suppose you think it is a story that you can imagine for yourselves', he comments, anticipating that his audience will prejudge this domestic romance in the jungle. 'We have heard so many such stories, and the majority of us don't believe them to be stories of love at all. For the most part we look upon them as stories of opportunities; episodes of passion at best, or perhaps of youth and temptation' (205). What makes this tale different is the obviously sympathetic Jewel – 'the melancholy figure . . . looking on wistfully, helplessly, with sealed lips' – and the equally sentimental Jim: 'When I tell you . . . you will perceive directly the difference, the individual side of the story. There is in his espousal of memory and affection belonging to another human being something characteristic of his seriousness. He had a conscience, and it was a romantic conscience' (205).

16 Moses provides the most detailed and precise description I have seen of the complicated political history of Patusan. See especially pages 76–80, which make the case that the region is 'a roughly accurate historical representation of . . . what modern political scientists would term "uneven development"'.

Jim's rise to power involves both paramilitary activities reminiscent of *King Solomon's Mines* – he leads the attack against the interloper Sherif Ali's supposedly 'impregnable camp' (196) – and romantic courtship. Jewel joins her beau for 'marital evening walks' and responds with a 'pretty smile' when Jim calls her 'with a . . . homelike, peaceful effect', and she also provides him with ethnographic data (209, 210, 205). 'It seems he had been used to make a confidante of her', Marlow tells us, 'and that she on her part could and did give him a lot of useful hints as to Patusan affairs there is no doubt' (217). It is Jewel who warns of Sherif Ali's attack and who asks, calculating the odds as she contemplates Jim's loaded revolver, 'Can you face four men with this?' (221). Not just a lover, Jewel is also a tactician and the informant who facilitates Jim's ascension. 'The land, the people, the forests were her accomplices' (210–11). With an insider's knowledge at his disposal, Jim establishes a balance of power and clears the way for unfettered trade. His success turns him into a kind of ad hoc political advisor for the region. He becomes known as 'the white man who protected poor people', an Englishman who has entered 'the innermost life of the people' (274, 200).

When he 'leaps . . . into the life of Patusan, into the trust, the love, the confidence of the people', Jim achieves a level of authority that would be the envy of any colonial administrator (284). 'He had regulated so many things in Patusan!' Marlow hyperbolically exclaims. 'Things that would have appeared as much beyond his control as the motions of the moon and the stars' (164). Sentimentality, modelled by affection between men of the sea, extended to Dain Waris, and heightened by romance with Jewel, gives Jim an almost supernatural capacity to reshape the colonial environment. Like any twenty-first-century aid worker, political advisor, or economic consultant, Jim exerts influence from the margins. He clearly relishes his newfound authority, but seems to recognize that in order to retain it he must not be seen as a threat to the leaders in whose name he conducts politics. He must remain somewhat otherworldly, a stranger who lives with the locals and who understands them better for his outsider status. As Conrad's redesigned 'Romance singled Jim for its own', it turns him into something new: a white man who goes native but who shows no signs of the degeneration that typically accompanied such behaviour (210). To the contrary, settling down gives Jim a firmer sense of the 'ideal of conduct' that governs relationships in this place (312).

Sentimentality may be the precondition for his power, but it produces an anti-sentimental backlash as well. The arrival of that 'latter-day buccaneer' Gentleman Brown and his motley crew invites speculation that if Jim represents an imperial avant garde, Europe itself cannot yet appreciate or sanction his sort of administration (263). Brown and company are 'emissaries with whom the world [Jim] had renounced was pursuing him' (289). They are representatives of what Conrad portrays as a rapacious imperial past that does not credit his innovation and is eager to reinscribe older oppositions. 'You have been white once', Brown observes, 'for all your talk of this being your own people and you being one of them' (286). An old-fashioned 'call of race destroys', Cole observes, the 'system of love, friendship, family, and colonial power' (122). It represents a way of understanding the globe out of sync with Jim's effort to make administrating such out of the way places as Patusan interesting and profitable. Because he does not see the world through sentimental glasses, Brown cannot fathom Jim's attachment to this place. Like the other pirates who stalk the South Seas and muse upon rumours of Jim's newfound importance, he does not see the value of Patusan and its inhabitants. He comes to believe that Jim possesses some 'extraordinary gem[stone]' (208). When Brown discovers the truth, he confronts Jim, 'And what the devil do you get for it, what is it you've found here that is so d---d precious?' (286). Jewel may be the ultimate symbol of Conrad's sentimentalization of colonial administration, but her name serves to suggest that the majority of Europeans still associate the islands with the romance of treasure hunts and adventure narratives rather than that of domesticity.

ETHNOGRAPHIC CHARACTER

Among the writers who helped convince Europeans that domestic romance was appropriate for the colonies was the anthropologist Malinowksi. His prose not only evinced a predilection for tales of courtship that rivalled Conrad's own, but also appeared to concur with fictions like 'Heart of Darkness' and *Lord Jim* that the difference between Europeans and non-Europeans was an effect of the methods experts employed to observe their objects of study. Where Conrad tended to represent competing ways of seeing through paired characters – Kurtz and Marlow, Brown and Jim – Malinowksi presented the self-reflexive struggle of a fieldworker awash in the cosmopolitanism of the islands.[17]

---

17 Clifford exhaustively describes Malinowski's debt to Conrad, who he explains not only offered thematic precedence for the ethnographer's description of his life in the bush, but also prefigured the difference between ethnographic field notes – with their glimpses of Kurtzian lascivious

Malinowski conducted his research in places as unabashedly hybrid as the fictional region of Patusan. This is not, I should hasten to note, how his account of life in the Trobriands has generally been understood.[18] It is a critical commonplace that *Argonauts of the Western Pacific* defines culture as the product of internally coherent, mutually reinforcing, local rituals and habits. We would do well, however, to follow Arjun Appadurai and reinterpret Malinowski's seminal volumes as chronicles documenting the fact that local cultures 'do not and cannot take locality as a given' (*Modernity* 180).[19] The islands lack the hyperactive cultural mixing of the modernist metropolis, but they are populated by a host of motley characters who participate in complicated and formative exchanges of people and things.

Early in his posthumous *A Diary in the Strict Sense of the Term*, Malinowski describes the denizens of Mailu, an island just south of Papua in the Coral Sea. These include the 'Whites . . . Hon. R. De Moleyns, nicknamed Dirty Dick – son of a Protestant Irish Lord . . . Alf[red] Greenaway "Arupe" – from Ramsgate or Margate – working-class background . . . Colored. Dimdim (Owani), modern Orestes – killed his own mother when he ran amok' (39). There is a missionary named Saville, several German New Guinea administrators and policemen, the pearl traders Billy Hancock and Rafael Brudo, and an apparently inexhaustible supply of couples, the Shaws, the Riches, the Catts ('very pleasant' [57]), the Higginsons, the Ramsays (59).[20] When he shifts his attention to the Trobriand chain, Malinowski discovers an equally varied crowd featuring the more or less English-speaking informants Igua Pipa, Ahuia Ova (the local constable and zealous Christian convert), the sometimes cheeky Ginger, 'Velavi, Boo, and Utata . . . my "court"', and unnamed others simply called 'the boys' (*Diary* 253, 59). Although imperialism was far from the only force responsible for making the Trobriands so very cosmopolitan, it was an important one. The largest of the islands was

---

violence – and publishable study – in which one discovers a more Marlowian irony and detachment (*Predicament* 92–113).

18 On the cosmopolitanism of Melanesian islands, see Harrison.

19 What we witness in the Trobriands may be one of the world's least acknowledged but most famous 'discrepant cosmopolitanisms', to borrow a phrase from Robbins (194).

20 Not all of the Europeans he meets are so pleasant. Malinowski complains about 'interfering' missionaries and government officials such as the evangelizing Rev. W. J. Saville – against whom he dreams of launching a 'really effective anti-mission campaign' – and the Trobriand Island Resident R. L. Bellamy – who accuses Malinowski of subverting his efforts by, among other sins, disobeying the etiquette of segregated housing (*Sexual Life of Savages* 428; *Diary* 41; Stocking, *After Tylor* 261, and see Malinowski, *Argonauts* 18).

generally thought to be one of the 'best governed and most "civilized" places in the region' (Stocking, *After Tylor* 256).[21]

European commerce coexisted with local pearl trafficking and the regional mode of exchange that most grabbed Malinowski's attention, the 'extensive, inter-tribal' network called the Kula. This was, the anthropologist wrote, 'an extremely big and complex institution, both in its geographical extent, and in the manifoldness of its component pursuits' (*Argonauts* 83). It linked villages in a ring spanning more than 100 miles of ocean and island, situating genealogical and village politics in a broad social organization.[22] Malinowski encouraged his readers to imagine themselves in the outer reaches of this system. 'Perhaps as we read the account of these remote customs there may emerge a feeling of solidarity with the endeavours and ambitions of these natives', he relates (25). 'Perhaps through realising human nature in a shape very distant and foreign to us, we shall have some light shed on our own. In this . . . we shall be justified in feeling . . . that we [too] have gathered some profit from the Kula' (25).

Although it is entirely written out of the fieldwork accounts published during Malinowski's lifetime, the posthumous *Diary* describes fiction as an aid to the development of such sympathetic feeling. In addition to 'Heart of Darkness', the *Diary* records the consumption of Conrad and Ford Maddox Ford's *Romance*, which Malinowski finds 'more spasmodic than interesting', *The Secret Agent*, '[finished] with feeling of disgust', and *Youth*, which he discusses with the local missionary when it causes him to think about Kipling, a 'fine artist (naturally not if compared with Conrad)' (*Diary* 27, 46, 40). Other notable selections include volumes by Dostoevsky, Cooper, Thackeray, and Dumas, whose *Vicomte de Bragelonne* he calls simply 'trash' (63). Of all the fiction mentioned in the *Diary*, domestic romance has the most pronounced effect on the ethnographer. 'Read *Villette*', he records on 9 February 1918, 'has for me the same *charm of quiet fascination as Pride and Prejudice*. Feminine tact, intuition, grasp of *inwardness of things* and longing for life' (200). In

21 'Malinowski's epoch-making fieldwork', Stocking recounts, began in what W. H. R. Rivers considered the 'optimal period . . . a decade after a permanent government station, a decade and a half after the last internal fighting and an abortive attempt at violent resistance to colonial power, two decades after the Methodist Overseas Mission headquarters had been established' (*After Tylor* 255).

22 Through his description of the Kula in *Argonauts of the Western Pacific*, Malinowski showed that local rituals and habits in the island often came from external influence: 'the most important acts of native life', he wrote, are products of a 'sociological mechanism of surpassing size and complexity . . . half commercial, half ceremonial exchange' (513, 510).

his own chronicles of familial existence full of household detail, Malinowski lays claim to these charms.

Stories of Becky Sharp and Jos Sedley from the *Diary* give way in *Argonauts of the Western Pacific* to anecdotes of island '[q]uarrels, jokes, family scenes, events usually trivial, sometimes dramatic but never significant, [which] formed the atmosphere of my daily life as well as theirs' (*Argonauts* 7). During his time in the field, Malinowski remembers, he learned to take 'a personal interest in the gossip and developments of the small village occurrences' (*Argonauts* 7). In *The Sexual Life of Savages*, he approaches the romantic entanglements of his subjects with a confidence on loan from novel-reading, and in a tone not so far from that of the 'truth universally acknowledged' in the opening line of Jane Austen's *Pride and Prejudice* 'that a single man in possession of a good fortune, must be in want of a wife' (51). 'To the average normal person', Malinowski declares, 'attraction by the other sex and the passionate and sentimental episodes which follow are the most significant events in his existence' (*Sexual Life of Savages* 1).

While attending to native domestic life, the ethnographer also contemplates his own. Acclimatizing to the jungle means getting used to the 'strange, sometimes unpleasant' ritual of waking up every morning in a mud hut, he writes in the opening pages of *Argonauts of the Western Pacific* (7). To develop a sympathetic understanding of Trobriand existence, he had to 'see intimate details of family life, of toilet, cooking' and adopt a 'natural course very much in harmony with [the] surroundings' (*Argonauts* 7). Focusing on domestic routine only matters, of course, if one assumes that what goes on in and around the house is essential and that it, as much as action in battle or rhetoric in politics, is what defines a people. Such was the longstanding contention of domestic fiction, and Malinowski relied on a similar thesis in his effort to 'squeeze the full meaning out of . . . physical matter' and 'plunge . . . into the life of the natives' (*Sexual Life of Savages* lxxxi, *Argonauts* 22). This plunge, like Jim's comparable leap into the life of his people, not only granted Malinowski privileged access, but also a '[f]eeling of ownership' which he notes in the *Diary*. 'It is I who will describe them or create them' (140).

Reading does not always so clearly feed Malinowski's research. The pleasure of fiction also distracts him. Books transport him from the heat of the South Seas to the fog of northern neighbourhoods. '[O]nly a few days of . . . [life in the islands] and I was escaping . . . to the company of Thackeray's London snobs', he records. 'I long to be in Hyde Park, in Bloomsbury . . . I even enjoy the advertisements in the London newspapers' (*Diary* 16). This is a trend that must be checked, so the anthropologist puts himself on a literary diet. 'I may read poems and serious things, but I must absolutely avoid trashy novels. And I *should* read ethnographic works' (249). He cannot discipline his uncontrollable urge, however, to 'read, read', and keep on 'reading without letup' (63). Malinowski links this mania to sexual appetite: 'I must never let myself become aware of the fact that other women have bodies, that they copulate. I also resolve to shun the line of least resistance in the matter of novels' (249). As much as fiction facilitates good 'feelings toward the natives', it also sparks 'impure thoughts and lusts' and even Kurtzian rage 'tending to "*Exterminate the brutes*"' (68–9). These responses surprise even the anthropologist himself: 'Woke up at night, full of lecherous thoughts about, *of all the people imaginable*, my landlord's wife! This must stop . . . *c'est un peu trop!*' (165). His fieldwork is a long trial of self-discipline, an ongoing struggle 'to overcome the metaphysical regret of . . . "You'll never fuck them all"' (113–14).

In a more gentle vocabulary, novel buyers had long distinguished between reading practice productive of 'Creative thoughts and filthy thoughts', as Malinowski put it. Needless to say, they also shared his conviction that one ought to 'avoid the latter!' (259). Lynch explains that commentators considered bad reading that which entailed rapid and unthinking consumption. 'Bad readers judged books by their covers' and their interpretations were correspondingly thin (Lynch, *Economy of Character* 149). These were readings and readers driven by the market, which shaped for them a fantasy life charged with sexuality and the 'promiscuous comminglings of commodity exchange' (*Economy of Character* 149). Good reading was comparatively close and attentive. It focused on discovering depth and complexity in characters all the more valuable for their 'modest-looking, plainly dressed' appearance (*Economy of Character* 154). This was reading as an investment that elevated both reader and text. Reading for the details gave new depth to the self, in a process that Malinowski reproduces and displaces from his consumption of novels to his interpretation of Trobriand domesticity. He achieves the self-confidence necessary to further his study by transforming his subjects into round characters.

The *Diary* is a chronicle of Malinowski's struggle to trade bad reading for good. Leafing through his entries, moreover, it becomes clear that textual slumming is not only a persistent element of field existence, but also the kind of transgression that ultimately helps rather than hinders labour.[23] Kipling, whose writing Malinowski dismissed in comparison with Conrad's, focuses the ethnographer's thoughts on religion: 'I [try] synthetically to look at the natives and I also think about the delight we take in mystical, mysterious things (à propos of Kipling and a little bit also my fright): And I restate my theory of religion – or part of it – over again and also that of social psychology' (242).[24] The lustful gaze at the surface of a female body, meanwhile, produces a frenzy of composition. The sight of 'a pretty, finely built girl' leads Malinowski to a conversation and a walk on the beach, while his impulse to 'paw' her takes him back to his scholarship (255). 'Work, excellent . . . everything fine', he comments, 'but I shouldn't have pawed her' (256).[25]

Voyeuristic pleasures lead to methodological insight. It occurs to Malinowski that 'I could learn more by taking part personally' when observing a moonlight dance; 'I like naked human bodies in motion', he muses, 'and at moments, they . . . excited me' (281). Appealing bodies may be the lure, but the goal is an intimacy described in the opening pages of *Argonauts of the Western Pacific*: 'it is good for the Ethnographer sometimes to put aside camera, note book and pencil, and to join in himself in what is going on. He can take part in the natives' games, he can follow them on their visits and walks, sit down and listen and share in their conversations' (21). Given that bad reading seems to prompt good analysis, it becomes possible to understand the *Diary*'s closing line – 'Truly I lack real character' – as a further opportunity for Malinowski to generate depth for his persona and his Trobriand objects of study (298).

The Sexual Life of Savages follows the same trajectory, turning lust into sentiments it portrays as more profound. The vast proportion of this

---

23 As Lynch observes, the elaboration of bad reading serves much the same end for novel readers. Even readers trained in the sort of self-invigilating, careful and slow practice described as good 'could also experience their reading as a support for transgression . . . [or] textual slumming' (*Economy of Character* 149).

24 As Stocking observes, Malinowski's 'erotic impulses both drew him toward and separated him from the Trobrianders' (*After Tylor* 265).

25 Lust leads him to more philosophical insights as well. Malinowski supplemented the notions of Rivers and others who described the power of ritual and orthodoxy in non-European culture by concentrating on his subjects' self-reflexive commentary. 'A man who submits to various customary obligations', he writes in *Argonauts*, 'who follows a traditional course of action, does it impelled by certain motives, to the accompaniment of certain feelings, guided by certain ideas' (22). These responses give room to what Malinowski referred to as 'ethnic peculiarity', a sense of place denied by sweeping depictions of the so-called primitive world (22). The diaries present this innovative approach to local culture as an italicized outline – '*(1) Dogma, orthodox version, theology. (2) Reflex phrases, scholia. etc. (3) The rule and the reality*' (273) – embedded in a narrative of desire – 'I met women at the spring, watched how they drew water. One of them was very attractive, aroused me sensually. I thought how easily I could have a *connection* with her' (273).

book, like the *Diary*, is given over to descriptions of sexual activity that Malinowski well knew European readers would consider prurient. In fact, its foreword imagines they will be every bit as titillated by Trobriand behaviour as he was. 'For pruriency consists in oblique day-dreaming', he lectures, a passing reference perhaps to his own tropical fantasies, 'and not in simple and direct statement' (lxxxiii). Malinowski teaches readers to reproduce his transformation from voyeur to sentimental observer, documenting the annoyances of life in the bush – as the field-worker 'becomes cross and bored with his native instructors' (235) – and eliciting desire by painting mental pictures of scantily clad Trobrianders. '[E]ven for one equipped with European taste and Nordic race prejudices', he assures, it is easy to discover an object of desire in the islands, 'for, within a considerable variety of types, there are to be found men and women with regular delicate features, well-built lithe bodies, clear skins, and . . . personal charm' (242). Not willing to stop at generalities, Malinowski assembles the perfect lover part by bodily part in meticulous descriptions of face and hands, teeth and eyes. Although he is ostensibly explaining what the Trobriander finds desirable, when he reveals that 'Firm, well-developed breasts are admirable in a woman', it is hard not to sense that a line is being blurred (254). Such a feeling is only reinforced by the thorough narration of a young man 'parting the fringe of [his partner's] grass skirt, insert[ing] a finger in her vulva', or repeated references to the most outré practice on the islands, the 'yausa' or seasonal 'orgiastic assaults by women', which the anthropologist regrets he was never able to attend (212, 231–3).

Even at their most explicit, however, descriptions of Trobriander sexual escapades tend to culminate in a transition to sentimental heterosexual narrative. Elaborate representations of child sexuality include 'house-building, and [playing] at family life' (49). The 'bachelors' house', headquarters for sexual licence and freedom, is also a place for 'steering towards marriage, through gradually lengthening and strengthening intimacies' (59). Late night dancing by partially clothed islanders is as transgressive as it is romantic: 'The close bodily contact, the influence of moonlight and shadow, the intoxication of rhythmic movement . . . all tend to relax constraint and give opportunity for an exchange of declarations and for the arrangement of trysts' (202). Malinowski persuades his readers that the Trobrianders, with all of their experimentation and openness, all of their exciting and bizarre sexual habits, are very much like us. 'Love is a passion to the Melanesian as to the European, and torments the mind and body to a greater or lesser extent', he concludes (239).

Malinowski's commitment to the 'institutions which centre round the erotic life' locates his work among that of early twentieth-century sexologists and psychoanalysts (*Sexual Life of Savages* 1). If those theorists helped make sex seem, in Michel Foucault's words, 'the explanation for everything' and if, further, such an emphasis on sex usually meant 'estranging the sentimental', as Suzanne Clark observes, then Malinowski's habit of turning erotic escapade into romantic episode allows us to see how sex and sentimentality could also work together in the new sciences of intimacy (Foucault, *History of sexuality* 78; Clark 1). His 'detailed view of native love-making' in *The Sexual Life of Savages* has as its professed goal the recovery of 'romantic elements and imaginative personal attachments . . . not altogether absent in Trobriand courtship' (281, 341). In the depths of the jungle, he finds 'elements of what we ourselves mean by love' (318).[26]

Such a methodological result had the potential to overhaul relationships between European and native, and Malinowski knew it. In his latter years, he made it his mission to explain how anthropology would change colonialism. Already in his *Diary*, he imagined a memoir entitled 'Value of Ethnographic Studies for the Administration', which would cover several 'Main points' including a detailed explanation of how 'the knowledge of a people's customs allows [one] to be in sympathy with them, and to guide them according to their ideas' (238). In another posthumously published text, *Freedom and Civilization*, he reasons that ethnography could become the key not only to managing far-flung villages but also to generating 'tribe states', nations dedicated to the project of reproducing local culture (329–30). Such homelands would still require the assistance of a professional like himself, however. '[I]n our society', he explained, 'every institution has its intelligent members, its historians, and its archives and documents, whereas in a native society there are none of these' (*Argonauts* 12). The natives may be skilled informants, they may even be very much like us in their desires and domestic habits, but they still require an ethnographer to speak for them, to serve as historian, archivist, librarian, and international advocate.

---

26 Using himself as a representative, he underscores the similarity between European desire and that of the male Trobriander. He presents us with a picture of a woman 'regarded as a beauty' by the natives, and suggests that 'with this opinion the reader will not disagree' (286). When it comes time for such a woman to fall in love, we see her strolling on the sand with one of her fellows, 'picking flowers or scented herbs . . . [before finding] shelter in some nook among the coral rocks' (327–8). Such passages demonstrate what Stocking considers the *sine qua non* of Malinowski's writing, his ability to reduce the distance between European and Trobriander, between exotic and familiar 'while continuing to rely on the appeal of [and the desire for] . . . exoticism' (*After Tylor* 292).

NATIVE ADMINISTRATION

Ensuring that locals from Melanesia to West Africa would remain reliant on European mediators was the project of early twentieth-century colonial administration, a project that only became more difficult the more reliant British Empire became on mediators selected from local populations. Malinowski faced a similar problem on a smaller scale. To describe the 'native's point of view, his relation to life . . . *his* vision of *his* world', he depended on English-speaking informants (*Argonauts* 25). He never learned enough of the vernacular in the places he studied to go it alone. Anthropology as he practised it was a collabourative and sometimes competitive affair.

Although he was on a first name basis with all of his informants, and refers to them as friends, the *Diary* and the published ethnographies also record a catalogue of complaints. Assistants are late for meetings, bargain with varying degrees of insistence before giving over information, tell blatantly contradictory tales, and 'conceal their departures' when they go on walk-about (*Diary* 210, 234). Even as they provide him with the information he needs, they imperil his sense of mastery. On occasion Igua Pipa goes so far as to regale his employer with 'stories in *delightful* Motu, about murders of white men, as well as his fears about what he would do if I died in that way' (*Diary* 73). James Clifford observes that Malinowski's published work is full of material that 'he admittedly did not understand' (*Predicament* 46). In *Argonauts of the Western Pacific* as well as later writing, 'we read page after page of magical spells, none in any essential sense in the ethnographer's words' (*Predicament* 46). Renato Rosaldo describes a similar result in his work with the Ilongots of the Philippine highlands. He worked with informants who 'against pleas to the contrary' responded to questioning with 'the most tedious stories', thus managing the enterprise to such an extent that it becomes difficult to fully distinguish between ethnographic subject and object, writer and translator (*Ilongot* 16).

Ethnographer and informant are not the only participants in this game, moreover. Colonial administrators controlled access to inner regions, soldiers softened up new territory before scientists could move in, and missionaries taught English to potential translators.[27] For Malinowski,

---

27 For accounts of the interplay between these various parties in various imperial outposts, one might begin with the work of Herbert, Mudimbe *Idea of Africa*, Fabian *Out*, or Comaroff and Comaroff.

competition created an opportunity to test the purity of his sympathy against that of the administrator who, 'however much he may sympathize with the natives, is bound to have more sympathy with his wife and children, with his dream of success and constructive enterprise' ('Rationalization' 422).[28] When governors in Africa began to place increased emphasis on fieldworkers trained in methods not so different from Malinowski's own, they argued that no ethnographer had access to a network of informants as comprehensive as that engendered by the colonial apparatus. District Officers and anthropologists traded insults, but they reserved their most pointed barbs for the English speaking, reading, and writing populations from which they drew their adjutants. Tension with 'educated Africans', as they were called, was ongoing but it was also productive. It gave Malinowski the chance to pitch his project of establishing 'tribe states' as a tool for containing the effects of colonialism on local populations. He warned that 'the educated African may be useful as a labourer, clerk or assistant, [but] he also grows into a dangerous competitor' ('Native Education' 484).[29]

Colonial administrators were only too aware of this threat. In Nigeria, Frederick Lugard outlined a programme to counteract a century of missionary and charter company contact that had abetted the rise of a comparatively affluent and mobile population in Lagos and other urban and coastal settlements.[30] He charged District Officers to play the role of the sympathetic expert in the bush, to usurp and undermine the influence of African intellectuals such as Edward Wilmot Blyden, John Payne Jackson – the editor of the *Lagos Weekly Record* – James Johnson, and Mojola Agbebi. From the moment of its inception, Lugard's Indirect Rule vested considerable authority in fieldworkers. In his widely circulated manifesto, *The Dual Mandate in British Tropical Africa*, Lugard described residents 'in touch with native thought and feeling' (194). Not unlike Malinowski, he envisioned a local population 'naturally

28 See Desai, Tidrick, Bivona, and Stocking, *After* for accounts of give and take between Malinowski and colonial administrators.

29 Mudimbe describes Malinowski's applied anthropology as a scheme designed to police 'supposedly aberrant mixtures of the Same and the Other' (*Invention of Africa* 82).

30 As the social historian Tidrick observes, the Indirect Rule system 'was unprecedentedly (for the British) explicit in its assumption of administrative authority in native affairs' (196). 'Indirect Rule with capital letters was born in Northern Nigeria', she writes, 'as a result of Sir Frederick Lugard's compulsion to justify and elabourate in writing his decisions to administer the newly conquered Fulani emirates by installing a British resident at each of the emirate courts' (195). Historians point out that it had been Britain's practice in India and elsewhere to rely on non-European collaborators to give their colonial dictums greater legitimacy (see Afigbo 1–6; Flint 291).

industrious' in farming but unsophisticated in commerce, reliant on European assistants to plug them into regional and international networks of exchange (401).[31] Lugard's administration took responsibility for economic as well as political mediation, displacing African intellectuals and merchants who did such work in the nineteenth century.[32]

In the first decades of the twentieth century, the colonial District Officer acquired a cultish following among imperial commentators and critics, turning him into a bone fide rival to the ethnographer as the champion of colonial populations. E. D. Morel penned *Red Rubber: The Story of the Rubber Slave Trade in the Congo* and *Great Britain and the Congo: The Pillage of the Congo Basin* – among the most famous denunciations of European atrocities in Africa. When he visited Northern Nigeria in 1910, however, he had nothing but praise for the field officer he witnessed at work: 'when one sees that man, living in a leaky mud hut . . . when one sees the marvels accomplished by tact, passionate interest and self-control, with utterly inadequate means, in continuous personal discomfort, short-handed, on poor pay . . . then one feels that . . . the end must be good' (Tidrick 204). As Kathryn Tidrick notes, Indirect Rule 'dramatized, sanctified, and institutionalized the belief that backward races should and could be ruled by force of character rather than by force of arms' (214; see also Bivona 114–15).

Lugard went further even than Malinowski in making the development of personal depth the means and aim of field study. He was among a group of administrators both colonial and domestic who, in the early decades of the twentieth century, helped to turn character into a quality that could be taught, measured, and managed.[33] Lugard's lieutenant Ralph Furse was in charge of evaluating candidates for colonial service from 1919 to 1948. According to him, the vital elements of character included 'powers of initiative and self-reliance, imagination and sympathy,

---

31 According to Lugard, even before he has the benefit of professional advice the typical African tends to labour as if he were born to work in an export economy: 'Though in most districts the pressure of population, which compels hard and continuous work to provide the necessities of life, is absent, you may see him in the very early morning, and even in the heat of the tropical day, hoeing his field sometimes so engrossed that he will hardly pause to look at a passing European with his long train of carriers' (401). Samarin describes how Indirect Rule and ethnographic imperialism in general invented the 'industrious' African at the turn of the century.

32 On Britain's economic priorities in Africa see Zeleza and Adu Boahen.

33 Glover describes the pressures behind a change in the meaning of character this way: 'From the 1880s onward, the assault on the autonomy of the individual subject in fields as various as scientific physiognomy, degenerationism, mental physiology, criminal anthropology and "psychical research" made the classic liberal idea of character as individual self-mastery harder and harder to sustain' (60).

a keen sense of justice, observations and tact in dealing with colleagues and subordinates; good presence, address, and manners' (Kuklick, *Imperial Bureaucrat* 20). Furse contended that these could be produced by completing a 'special course of study' that bred familiarity with and affinity for 'native laws and customs' (Lugard 133).[34]

Like Malinowski, and like Conrad's Jim, Lugard's District Officer acquired authority by coming 'into close touch with the people, and gain[ing] an intimate knowledge of them, and of the personality and characters of the chiefs and elders in every village' (134–5). He did so through what Lugard's successor, the Governor Hugh Clifford, narrates as an extended scene of close and careful reading:

Months, perhaps years, pass before the exile begins to feel that he is winning any grip upon his people . . . Then he gets deep set in a groove and is happy. His fingers are between the leaves of the Book of Human Nature, and his eager eyes are scanning the lines of the chapter which in time he hopes to make his own. The natives about him have learned to look upon him as almost one of their own people. His speech is their speech; he can think as they do; he can feel as they feel, rejoicing in their joys, sorrowing in their pains . . . He never offends their sensibilities, never wounds their self-respect, never sins against any of their innumerable conventions. He has shared their sports, doctored their ills, healed their sick, protected them from oppression, stood their friend in time of need, done them a thousand kindnesses, and has helped their dying through the strait and awful pass of death. Above all he *understands* . . . (H. Clifford 180)

What he understands is the need to shape and nurture local culture, a necessity Clifford and Lugard agree is the result of imperial trade.[35] In Lugard's *Dual Mandate*, as in Conrad and Malinowski's writings, inexpert Victorians have made it 'impossible to maintain the old order'

---

34 As they codified the procedures for qualifying officers, Lugard and Furse ensured the disqualification of those whose knowledge was limited to the classroom by developing testing procedures to weed out the '"bounder", the "prig" and the "bookworm"' and by emphasizing performance in the field above all else (Kuklick, *Imperial Bureaucrat* 139). See Kuklick, *Imperial Bureaucrat* chapter 1 for an extensive review of Lugard's qualifying methods. See Perkin on the role of strategies of qualification in the rise of professional society in general (78–91).

35 Lugard's litany of Victorian abuse echoes 'Heart of Darkness' and Malinowski's prose: 'To-day the young men migrate in hundreds to offer their labour at the mines or elsewhere, and return with strange ideas. Some perhaps have even been overseas from West to East Africa during the war. The produce of the village loom, or dye-pit, or smithy, is discounted by cheap imported goods, and the craftsman's calling is not what it was. Traders, white and black, circulate under the *pax Britannica* among tribes but recently addicted to head-hunting, and bring to them new and strange conceptions. The primitive African is called upon to cope with ideas a thousand years in advance of his mental and social equipment.' (216–17)

and created 'the urgent need . . . to build up a tribal authority with a recognised and legal standing, which may avert social chaos' (217).[36]

To counter claims of pan-African identity, colonial administrators of a formerly homogenous dark continent found themselves arguing against the idea of an African Personality and in favour of local identities they alone could define.[37] As the political scientist Mahmood Mandani puts it, 'the African was containerized, not as a native, but as a tribesman' (22). Administrators made it their business to work through 'a mishmash of ethnic affiliations to create "purer" and clearer tribal identities as the basis for tribal authorities' (Mamdani 81). The implication of such a project, Mandani explains, was that 'tribes are supposed to be in an organized state, each with its own territory, customs, and leadership' (81). If the opposite were true, officials took it on themselves to organize the lives they discovered. In this way, Indirect Rule presented the identification and fixing of custom as a primary and primarily administrative matter.

The historian Sara Berry observes that this campaign gave local culture a malleable quality, which meant that '[c]olonial "inventions" of African tradition served not so much to define the shape of the colonial social order as to provoke a series of debates over the meaning and application of tradition which in turn shaped struggles over authority and access to resources' (328). These battles involved the whole breadth of the black Atlantic and also took place within the hierarchy of the colonial apparatus. Having largely displaced the literate class of coastal and urban traders, Indirect Rule created a new class of clerks and petty

36 Lugard sought to manage the spread of English culture, to 'train a generation able to achieve ideals of its own, without a slavish imitation of Europeans, capable and willing to assume its own definite sphere of public and civic work, and to shape its own future' (425). Sport seemed especially well suited for this enterprise, he concludes, and it appears to have had the added benefit of reproducing a reassuringly familiar class structure: 'In Nigeria we have found that polo was a specially good game for the sons of chiefs and others who could afford it, while for other boys cricket, football, and "athletics" bring the staff and pupils into close touch, and have the best effect in training character' (435).

37 Both Lugard and the Nigerian intellectuals who launched a campaign to define and defend an African essence inherited much from the racial philosophy of African Victorians such as Edward Blyden, although each group put a decidedly different spin on the idea. See Mudimbe, *Invention* on Blyden's influence and see Zachernuk 104–6. Lugard describes international organizations such as the Pan-African Congress and the National Congress of British West Africa similarly, as threats to Indirect Rule's ownership of African authenticity. In response to the efforts of these groups to articulate a sense of Africanness not bounded by the ethnographic categories of tribe and village, Lugard argues that the Pan-African Congress 'could lay no claim to be considered as representative of Africa' because the continent is simply 'too vast a country and with too diversified a population to be represented by any delegation from any particular region' (83–4). As for the National Congress, he grants their importance in colonial politics, but asserts that 'no one in Nigeria outside the coast towns had ever heard of their existence' (84).

bureaucrats.[38] Lugard worried that local recruits were rapidly coming to occupy 'a position of importance out of proportion to their mere numbers. They sit on the Legislative Councils, and make their voices and opinions heard through the medium of their press and in other ways' (79). Obaro Ikime tells of '*kings* losing their sovereignty' under Indirect Rule, 'but as "chiefs" [appointed by the colonial state] increasing their powers over their subjects because the traditional checks and balances to the exercise of their authority were neutralised' (Crowder and Ikime 216).[39] Cadres of new clerks, A. E. Afigbo shows, 'had become so powerful' that they 'had in effect become the village headm[e]n' (124).[40] Clerks, teachers, and others formed professional organizations to put a public face to their concerns, and these organizations eventually came to assume important roles in national politics.[41]

The 1920s and 30s also saw new strains of regional and local political activity expressed in terms colonialism helped to disseminate. In the Gold Coast, a young generation of aspirant intellectuals formed organizations that bore such names as the 'Enthusiastic Literary and Social Club' and required qualifying tests for prospective members (Newell 348). Club members debated the relative merit of Dickens and Eliot, while reproducing a familiar rhetoric of novelistic consumption. '[W]ide reading adds to culture', one wrote in the *African Morning Post*, 'and often makes one a welcome member in refined society'. In recycling such arguments, West African organizations put them to fresh use. As Stephanie Newell recounts, the clubs were made up primarily of 'young scholars . . . working hard to perfect their English literary accomplishments in order to assert their autonomy from existing power elites such as chiefs and elders' (347–8). In Nigeria too, economic, political, and intellectual organization enabled English speakers to work with and against colonial administrative structures.[42]

---

38 Mann shows that in 1880 57 per cent of Nigeria's 'educated Africans' worked as merchants, but as colonialism displaced such traders by 1915 fully a third of the region's elite worked as colonial servants (25).

39 See also Adu Boahen 46–107 and Ohadike.

40 Confronted with this subversion of Indirect Rule's intent, one of Lugard's lieutenants is reported to have remarked, 'the main and to my mind insuperable objection to the Southern Nigeria native courts is that they are not native courts at all', meaning that increased influence of 'Europeanized Africans' made them inauthentic (quoted in Afigbo 122).

41 See, for example, Johnson-Odim and Mba 45–7.

42 '[P]rovincial educated communit[ies] grew local roots but did not sever [their] connections to Lagos and Calabar, . . . [and] the intelligentsia as a whole became better suited than ever before to define Nigeria's situation within the Atlantic horizons of their intellectual world' (Zachernuk 94).

Lugard and others responded by attempting to fine-tune their education system to encourage the production of character while containing any appropriation of English culture. Lugard recognized the 'unlimited demand, not only for subordinates but for doctors and for the Civil Staff' and concluded, further, that the 'progress of Africa would have been impossible were it not for the enormous number of Africans who fill posts in which a knowledge of English, of reading, writing, and arithmetic . . . is required' (442–3). At the same time, Lugard worried that for African students even 'a cursory acquaintance with the evolution of democracy under Cromwell may do more harm than good' (452).[43] Bound to do such damage in order to staff his administration, Lugard had little choice but to treat every crisis and subversion of colonial power as an obligation to deepen the influence of English culture. Two examples of how this philosophy reproduced itself in the field bring me to my conclusion.

In 1929, when Nigerian authorities tried to increase the use of direct taxation in Eastern Nigeria, their efforts sparked what is known as the Women's War. Riots spread through the area as women burnt courts and harassed local officials to protest against the new taxes. Besides drawing the attention of British armed forces – the official casualties included over 100 Africans dead and injured (Isichei 154) – the uprising resulted in two separate Commissions of Enquiry to discover where exactly policy traduced local custom. These committees identified gaping holes in the colony's ethnographic archive and called for 'further enquiry into the social organisation of the inhabitants of the South-Eastern Provinces' (quoted in Lackner 132). At their recommendation, officials conducted village-by-village surveys and wrote up 'Intelligence Reports' based on interviews with various informants (Isichei 155, Ekechi 169). 'By the end of 1934 no less than 199 reports on local groups had been submitted, and in the light of these subsequent reports, the Native Authorities were reorganized to correspond with what were described as live units of government' (Crowder 215). Increased training in ethnography became a requirement for all new recruits assigned to the region. A disastrous event for the Indirect Rule establishment turned out to be an occasion for English speakers – both British and African – to advance their various claims to represent the full complexity of local culture.

---

43 Such material teaches them to expect a greater voice in colonial affairs than Indirect Rule is prepared to grant them. And when they become aware that the state intends to limit their participation, they violently turn against it: 'when the Governor of Lagos was stoned in the streets of the town, the rabble was encouraged to do so by well educated Natives, English trained and clothed' (quoted in Kuklick, *Savage* 206).

My second example of colonialism's ability to reform and extend its hold takes place two decades earlier and on the east coast of the continent. In 1908, Hubert Silberrad, an assistant district commissioner in Nyeri, had an affair with a young woman named Niakazena who, in turn, happened to be the partner of a junior colonial officer named Mgulla. When Mgulla protested, Silberrad defended his actions on the grounds that his liaison followed all the rules of local custom, among them the requirement that he negotiate a payment to the woman's relatives in exchange for her company. Silberrad stressed, however, that 'I had no idea he [Mgulla] had any claim on Niakazena' (quoted in Jacobson 29). Whatever moral or ethical issues were raised by Silberrad's behaviour, his testimony implied that such concerns ought to be addressed in the context of administrative order. Thus Silberrad's chief error was stepping on the toes of a man who might be African but was also a fellow officer. In 1909, Lord Crewe, the Secretary of State for the Colonies, issued a circular that treated the matter in precisely these terms. The document, which became known as the Circular on Concubinage, urged administrators to stop sleeping with local women on the grounds that 'such practices . . . lower us [the British] in the eyes of the natives, and diminish [their] authority' (quoted in Hyam 157). This circular represented a significant revision of conventional practice: during the Victorian era such behaviour was 'tolerated by colonial governments and actively encouraged by some private businesses who recruited only unmarried male Europeans' (Callaway 45–6). It also employed rhetoric on display in Malinowski, as Lord Crewe tied managerial authority to the domestication and sentimentalization of sexuality. Although his indiscriminate use of the term 'native' attempts to fold the junior officer Mgulla back into the general population, such an attempt was truly an exercise in wishful thinking.

Foucault observes that for any 'discipline to exist, there must be the possibility of formulating and of doing so ad infinitum fresh propositions' ('Discourse' 223). Indirect Rule's technique of responding to crises with an increased emphasis on sympathetic understanding and sentimental representation of local culture provides a case in point. From the unlikely scenario of a District Officer ordered to manage an entire province out of a dilapidated hut, to the larger-scale contradiction of an administrative system designed to preserve Africa that runs on the labour of 'European-ised Africans', Indirect Rule generated its own trouble by being as self-reflexive as possible about how it distorted the fabric of local life. In so doing, it generated work for professional employees. If Conrad started the British down this road, Malinowkski helped them to recognize how such an apparently endless reproduction of professional crisis might itself be a form of management. The problem from a British standpoint was that this logic could not remain the property of Europeans alone. Even as Conrad and Malinowksi solidified the expert's hold on the people, they made the sentimentalized native available to the very colonial elite it was designed to displace, to politicians and writers who established their own versions of local culture and their own authority to manage the peoples of Britain's colonies.

CHAPTER 3

Gender, aesthetics, and colonial expertise

We rather feel, than survey . . .

William Gilpin

Before modernist writers could convince readers that their literary efforts featured techniques for reorganizing the world, they had to create a clear sense of the disorder that required such management. They had to portray for their readership the 'immense panorama of futility and anarchy which is contemporary history', as T. S. Eliot described it (*Selected Prose* 177). To this end, they produced what is often called a crisis of colonial understanding. By depicting the dark underside of colonization, and by explaining what happens to European consciousness in the colonies, certain authors made their expertise seem necessary to literate Europeans. For example, I have argued that Joseph Conrad linked Europe's troubles to the sentimentalization of colonial adventure. Narratives such as 'Heart of Darkness' demonstrated both the peril and the possibility inherent in 'intimacy [that] grows quickly out there' by depicting new arrangements between Europeans and their colonial subjects (158).

Conrad's fiction is famously ambivalent about the sentimentality it encourages. Sympathy helps Marlow to become Kurtz's confidant and to describe a complex attachment to his dead helmsman, but belief in sentimental decorum also keeps him from dispelling the Intended's faith in her fiancé's 'generous mind' and 'noble heart' (160). Ambivalence about sentimentality is not restricted to modernist men. One can observe it in *To the Lighthouse*, where the sentimental object *par excellence* is supposedly displaced by a 'triangular purple shape', the figure that marks the place of the absent Mrs Ramsay in Lily Briscoe's painting. What could be less sentimental – or more so? This 'purple shadow,' as Mr Bankes calls it, represents the relationship between mother and child without creating their 'likeness' (52–3). 'There were other senses too in which one might reverence them', Lily shows. 'By a shadow here and a light there, for instance' (52).

By pausing to mull over the way formal abstraction pairs with sentimentality, Woolf reminds us of the habitual opposition between these two. As Suzanne Clark argues, early twentieth-century writing tended to set all forms of aesthetic 'rupture and innovation' against 'the conventional appeals of sentimental language' (1). Woolf's novel suggests, however, that the relationship between modernist form and sentimental content may have been more complex than such rhetoric allows. We find further evidence of that complexity in the third section of *To the Lighthouse*, with the triumph of Lily's 'vision' and the implication that Mrs Ramsay is 'faded and gone'. Success frees the budding artist to 'over-ride her wishes, improve away her limited, old-fashioned ideas', and leave behind her 'mania . . . for marriage' (174–5). Yet because her painting represents Mrs Ramsay, Lily ends by preserving the very sentimental referent she would prefer to disavow. Although this state of affairs certainly does entail a certain antagonism between form and content, far more intractable is the opposition between Lily's abstraction and the stylistic convention it abjures.

These two sorts of antipathy are easily muddled in scholarship that interprets modernist innovation through the lens of gender. As Rita Felski notes, 'critics have drawn attention to a machismo aesthetic characterizing the world of male modernists that is predicated upon an exclusion of everything associated with the feminine' (24). Andreas Huyssens's influential thesis describing the early twentieth-century emergence of a 'great divide' between masculine high art and feminine popular culture contends that such exclusion authorized a sweeping binary opposition cutting across various genres of writing as well as the visual and performing arts. Other arguments track a slippery slope from anti-femininity to outright misogyny. Sandra M. Gilbert and Susan Gubar's monumental *No Man's Land* provides the best case in point with its contention that the 'innovations of the avant garde' were fuelled in large measure by the desire 'to ward off the onslaughts of women' (1: 131). Although ample evidence and sound reasoning bolster these arguments, they remain blunt instruments for dissecting textual examples like Lily's painting or Conrad's adventure.

If we draw the inference from Lily's example that what modernist abstraction opposes most pointedly is a competing aesthetic, we may speculate that modernism's antagonism was less straightforwardly against sentimentality, femininity, or even women per se than against the formal techniques that had become conventionally associated with sentimentality, femininity, and women. If this seems plausible reasoning, then it makes sense to dwell further on the issue of contrasting aesthetics.

Mr Bankes provides us with one opportunity to do so by describing a painting that could not be more differently laid out than Lily's own. 'The largest picture in his drawing room', it exemplifies the form known as picturesque, a mode of representation ably practised by amateur painters at home in their gardens and on their travels through the British Isles and the Empire beyond (53). Mr Bankes's painting is no amateur production, but it is organized like one. It depicts 'cherry trees in blossom on the banks of the Kennet', and from even this fragmentary description we may easily imagine a whole work composed with a foreground of trees in full bloom and a river that flows into the near distance (53).

The picturesque features eminently reproducible rules for domesticating and regularizing any content, goals that were the antithesis of modernist aesthetics and its project of encouraging viewers to see ordinary content in a new way. The reproducibility of the picturesque further allied it with an amateurism contrary to modernism's investment in artistic métier and specialization. Amateurism, domesticity, and sentimentality were not terms exclusively associated with femininity, of course, but in the world of aesthetics they acquired a certain affinity. Scholarship as varied as Naomi Schor's *Reading in Detail* and Sara Suleri's investigation of the picturesque in *The Rhetoric of English India* indicates that over the course of the nineteenth century such terminology became increasingly gendered. It did so not only within the sort of British Isles setting featured in *To the Lighthouse*, but also abroad. As we have already seen, furthermore, modernism's disavowal of femininity was more than a domestic event, as the example of Conrad's ambivalent sentimentality suggests.

In this chapter, I grapple with the geopolitical scale of the relationship between gender and aesthetics during the age of modernism. I begin in the final decade of the nineteenth century and with two techniques of imperial representation that modernism displaced. Picturesque description is one of these. For an extended treatment, I turn to the best-selling travel narrative *A Thousand Miles Up the Nile* by Amelia Edwards. This book merits examination not just for its popularity at the time, but also for the way it contrasts with and complements modernism's ambivalence about sentimentality. Unlike the modernists, Edwards describes the out-reaches of the Empire in sentimental terms designed to make her readers comfortable with alien settings. The methods she employed became so clearly gendered in this period, I explain, that it makes sense to extend to them Suleri's label of the 'feminine picturesque' (75). Edwards's depictions starkly contrast with the other technique of representation that I consider, the scientific abstraction of the Great Trigonometrical Survey of

India, clearly linked with boys' adventure stories and other projects of territorial control understood as masculine. However, neither of these approaches seems to have been a weapon in gender struggle. Rather, the Survey and the picturesque in the *fin de siècle* were part of a largely amicable and eminently productive sexual division of labour: men of science mapped colonial regions while wives, women travellers, and others documented the details of the occupied landscape.

This is the dynamic that modernist writing sought to displace, which we see by consulting a classic of imperial narrative, E. M. Forster's *A Passage to India*. I concentrate on the landscape that appears in the novel's pivotal final scene. This territory resists depiction in either the Survey's terms or in those of the picturesque. I also attend to plot: the story of Adela Quested's declining fortunes is suggestive in its implications for female adventurers in general. Though the novel begins with her interest in the picturesque details of Indian life, by the end she is no longer relevant. Instead of the gendered division of labour featured in colonialism of the late nineteenth century, Forster concludes with a new arrangement that emphasizes the cross-cultural collaboration of two professional men, Cyril Fielding and Dr Aziz. This is an allusive relationship, since it evokes the conspiracy of experts that is the signature of neo-colonial exploitation as much as latter-day empire. Forster's homo-social professionalism may exclude women, but I contend that the openly sentimental bond between Fielding and Aziz implies a feminine referent every bit as significant as that of Mrs Ramsay in Lily's painting. Like Woolf and Conrad, in other words, Forster disavows the influence of a type of discourse Victorian culture had designated feminine, even as his project depends on the incorporation and reconfiguration of that material. Before providing a more detailed account of such disavowal, let me return to the nineteenth-century material that modernism repudiated.

PICTURESQUE IMPERIALISM

The colonial expansion of the Victorian age is often personified in the character Mary Louise Pratt calls the seeing man, 'whose imperial eyes . . . look[ed] out and possess[ed]' Africa and Asia, and who came into being in the early part of the century as England expanded its mission from maritime trade to colonial annexation. Armed with the tools of natural history, ethnography, and cartography, the seeing man's '(lettered, male, European) eye . . . could familiarize new sights immediately upon contact by incorporating them into the language of a system' (Pratt 31).[1] The Great Trigonometrical Survey of India stands as the exemplary scientific enterprise of British colonization. Founded in 1817 by William Lambton and a cadre of surveyors, including the young George Everest, the Survey matched a logic of formal abstraction to a policy of imperial acquisition. 'That the whole of India will be eventually covered with triangles', wrote Everest in 1839, is 'as certain as any future event can be' (quoted in Phillimore ii). Once begun, the Trigonometrical Survey soon captured the imagination of British officials and common British readers alike. In popular accounts, the survey's triangles took on a magical life of their own as they marched across India. '. . . after crossing the hills of Gurwhal', one mid-nineteenth-century commentator narrates, 'the triangles were brought down into the Terai, whence they continued to pass through the deadly tracts of marsh and jungle which fringe the Himalayas' (Markham 105).

As historian Matthew Edney recounts, England used cartography to subsume the 'particular variations and contingencies' it discovered in India 'within a "house of certainty." Each town and district was identified and assigned its own particular location within the fixed and immobile mesh of meridians and parallels. The space of the map was not bounded and limited but was as extensive and as potentially all-encompassing as British power and knowledge could make it' (25). That dialectic of imperial form and local content required surveyors to advance deep into the subcontinent alongside British forces, sketching and 'carrying on . . . [their] plane-tabling under heavy fire' (Black 130). As the military paved the way for science and vice versa, each newly printed map confirmed Britain's ownership of larger and larger portions of Indian territory.[2] The lore of the Survey is also rich with tales of mapmakers striking out

---

1 The totalizing effects of such an archival knowledge should not be underestimated, argues Pratt, who describes the seeing man's 'planetary consciousness' this way: 'One by one the planet's life forms were to be drawn out of the tangled threads of their life surroundings and rewoven into European-based patterns of global unity and order' (31). Britain was not the only European nation to make use of the dialectic between science and economic global expansion, of course, but in the nineteenth century at least, it was the most effective at doing so. 'Seen from the perspective of our own information society', Richards argues further, 'the Victorian archive appears as a prototype for a global system of domination through circulation, and apparatus for controlling territory by producing, distributing, and consuming information about it' (*Imperial Archive* 17).

2 In contemporary descriptions of the Survey's activities, rifle and pencil are often so closely allied that it becomes difficult to tell them apart. When Black notes that in the fall of 1879 in 'Southern Afghanistan some additional geography was obtained', so tight is the cooperation between Army and Survey in his account that one cannot tell whether that 'geography' was obtained by British troops or the surveyors who accompanied them (133).

on their own. In 1883, the Victorian chronicler Charles Black tells us, surveyors in elaborate disguise travelled beyond the official sphere of British influence into the northern territory of Kafiristan. W. W. McNair led this expedition disguised as a '*hakim* or native doctor, for which purpose he shaved his head and stained his face and hands' (Black 149). Though it seems difficult to believe that no one saw through such disguise – Black notes that McNair traveled with '40 people in all, including muleteers, and 15 baggage animals, and among the goods a prismatic and magnetic compass, a boiling-point and aneroid thermometer, and a specially constructed plane-table' (149) – the notion of the Survey as espionage by other means and of the surveyor as a highly specialized spy encouraged British readers to imagine colonization as a kind of great game.[3]

Tales of surveyors bedecked in native garb, ferreting out native secrets helped generate an avid public for the Survey's specialized work. Few texts were more successful at capturing this version of the Survey than Rudyard Kipling's *Kim*. Kim is just the sort of '*liminal* figure', as Edward Said calls him, whose ability to pass as Indian allowed readers of English fiction to imagine themselves in control of the terms of Indian culture (*Culture and Imperialism* 141). The example of Kim, who with a little walnut-juice on his face and neck was so well-disguised that not even his friends could recognize him, enabled readers to think of ethnic distinction as something that could be donned and removed like a costume. Thus conceptualized, ethnicity became an object of study that one became expert in, an object that one might not only learn but also learn how to shape. Once Indian identity became malleable in this way the Great Game was on, with Kim as its ideal player. He is proficient in cartography – 'thou must learn how to make pictures of roads and mountains and rivers', Colonel Creighton teaches him (Kipling, *Kim* 166) – and becomes expert in demography and ethnography as well – Lurgan Sahib has him memorize 'photographs of natives' and build charts of ethnographic difference in addition to mapping India's topographic features (206).[4]

---

3 'Was there ever a native fooled by the blue- or green-eyed Kims and T. E. Lawrences who passed among them as agent observers?' asks Said (*Cultureand Imperialism* 161).

4 Kim's education dovetails with the Survey's own expansion of geography to include ethnography. In the years after the so-called Indian Mutiny, the Survey expanded its archive to account not only for the 'general aspect of the region surveyed, [but also, as Clements Markham wrote in 1878, for] details respecting the cultivation, water supply, inhabitants, tenures, trade routes, and history' (75). To this end, the Indian Colonial Office founded a Statistical Survey in 1869, organized ethnographic surveys, launched the Orthography of Indian Proper Names, and renewed botanical surveys begun in the late eighteenth century. As the *Calcutta Review* put it, these projects would

While geometric abstraction dominated in the official world of the Survey and signified masterful oversight in the popular universe of boys' adventure stories, a substantial number of British observers were more likely to look at the Empire in terms that seemed, by contrast, lavishly detailed and steadfastly local.[5] The art historians Pratapaditya Pal and Vidya Dehejia show that in widely circulated books and portfolios of aquatints and carefully inked drawings the Victorian public encountered a vibrantly coloured and exotically fashioned India that starkly differed from the shadowy world of espionage and cartography associated with the Survey. Artists such as James Ballie Fraser, Thomas Daniell, and Fanny Parks depicted India as a rustic place. In their pictures, British observers discovered a continent rich with the content of local colour, a landscape whose 'vivid green [and] perpetual moisture' revealed a culture 'furrowed by time' (quoted in Pal and Dehejia 44). Their India was composed of expansive mountain ranges, of ancient ruins on wide open plains, and of rivers 'crowded with craft of various descriptions', enhanced by 'the gracefulness of many . . . washing figures' (quoted in Pal and Dehejia 98–9).

So prevalent was this pictorial way of seeing India that the Survey's cartographers felt compelled to denounce it.[6] The rulebook of the British Royal Military College distinguished their specialized approach as 'the

---

'put sinews and flesh on the colossal skeleton' constructed by Great Trigonometrical Survey (quoted in Markham 118). As Bayly notes, 'Traditional India was not a rigid society. It was British rule which made it so, codifying many localised and pragmatic customs into a unified and Brahminised "Hindoo Law" and classing people into immutable castes through the operation of the courts and ethnographical surveys' (156). With these new programmes, British imperialism sought to freeze the human population of India as surely as the Trigonometrical Survey had frozen its landscape.

5 Despite decades of scholarship on the imperial adventures of late-nineteenth-century women like Mary Kingsley, Harriet Martineau, and Florence Nightingale, our understanding of imperial science as masculine is axiomatic even today. The books written by such women, with their slightly more optimistic tone than many of the texts of their male counterparts, are still restricted to the low genres of travelogue and diary, and thus to the margins of imperial history. See Herbert on Martineau's fieldwork techniques (and on the invention of ethnographic culture more generally), Pratt on the way Kingsley's down-in-the-dirt approach anticipates that of modernist ethnography, and Morgan on the advantages women travellers found in categorizing their writing as amateur scientific research. Also instructive is Sánchez-Eppler, who notes that the presence of numerous nineteenth-century travel narratives by women should serve as a reminder that empire-building was never simply a 'reaction against, and a manly alternative to, the bourgeois, feminine home culture of sentimentality and domesticity' (400).

6 And also appropriate it, although only in their spare time. Many officers spent their hours off sketching the landscapes they mapped in the course of their official duties (see Edney 57–63). As one pages through the drawings collected by Pal and Dehejia, and by Archer and Lightbown in their volume, *India Observed*, one cannot help but notice the large number of sketches composed by field officers.

plainest method and stile . . . equally distant from . . . gaudy coloring and miniature elegance as from undistinct roughness' (quoted in Edney 55).[7] For contemporary readers of such a policy statement, the terminology of colour, elegance, and roughness would have been readily identifiable as that of the picturesque. As articulated by its most popular eighteenth-century theorist, the Reverend William Gilpin, the picturesque valued precisely 'the various surfaces of objects . . . [and, moreover,] the *richness* on a surface' (20). Gilpin favoured the very differences among irregular pictorial elements that the cartographers of the Survey were encouraged to render orderly and plain. 'Turn the lawn into a piece of broken ground', Gilpin instructs in the first of his *Three Essays* on the picturesque; 'break the edges of the walk . . . scatter around a few stones, and brushwood; in a word, instead of making the whole *smooth*, make it *rough*; and you make it also *picturesque*' (8). While the plain style of the Survey flattened out texture, the picturesque used 'form, lightness, and proper balance' to give its scenes depth, to divide landscapes into foreground and background, and to create what Gilpin referred to as 'a good composition'. Gilpin's early nineteenth-century accounts of walking tours through South Wales and the Lake District popularized this self-consciously middle-brow aesthetic and helped ensure that it would determine the style of amateur sketchers on tour in Britain and overseas. Though opposed in aesthetics, the picturesque and the Survey were allied in purpose: they both aimed to represent the colonies in recognizably English terms.[8] As the Survey professionalized the work of geography, it left the work of pictorial representation to amateurs, who frequently happened to be women.[9]

Suleri notes that 'British women in the colonized subcontinent [and indeed throughout the Empire] were required to remain on the peripheries of colonization' (75). They were barred from political positions and from most bureaucratic posts as well, but they found other ways to

---

7 Subsuming picturesque landscape within the Survey's geographic logic was a crucial step in the process of professionalizing the Survey's work, as Edney demonstrates. 'Just as natural historians placed each new plant observation within an artificial space of botanical taxonomy', Edney argues, 'so geographers placed each observation of the land into the larger spatial framework. Geography requires an *overview* that subsumes and supersedes the individual *view*' (64).

8 In the aquatints of Anglo-Indian artists, 'one is presented with gray skies, so reminiscent of England', note Pal and Dehejia. 'While the subject matter was novel and exotic, the manner of presentation was familiar' (109).

9 Stafford shows that the scientific and picturesque gazes have a long history of competition and cooperation. She describes them emerging together in the late eighteenth century. Both share a desire to apprehend 'natural objects as lone and strikingly distinct', she comments. '[A] distinctive taste for the singular, for the odd outcropping, the characteristic section of terrain' is not only the hallmark of the picturesque palate but also crucial for the scientific eye (17).

contribute. '[O]ne of the few socially responsible positions available to them was the role of female as amateur ethnographer', Suleri explains. 'They could sketch landscape and capture physiognomy as long as they remained immune to the sociological conclusions of their own data, entering the political domain in order to aestheticize rather than to analyze' (75). As such practice spread in the final decades of the nineteenth century, Anglo-India established what we might call a sexual division of forms. Seeing men were responsible for the abstracting form of the Survey, which rendered localities interchangeable, if not equivalent, while women were left in charge of the local detail that Suleri argues came to be thought of simply as 'the feminine picturesque'.[10] Men and women appropriated Indian territory in their own ways. The Survey took possession of India in its totality, while the women of Anglo-India consumed the subcontinent piece by tiny and highly textured piece. They travelled about India much as English tourists hiked through the Lake Region in search of a visual field whose irregular surface could be captured by pencil.

Instead of English lanes, cottage houses, and cart horses, sketchers portrayed India's mountains and hills, its villages and bazaars, its rundown temples and ancient monuments, and, above all, its curious natives with their colourful attire. In this way, they turned the picturesque into a form capable of competing with science for the right to represent authentic Indian life. As one artist of the picturesque wrote in 1810,

Science has had her adventurers, and philanthropy her achievements: the shores of Asia have been invaded by a race of students with no rapacity but for lettered relics: by naturalists, whose cruelty extends not to one human inhabitant: by philosophers, ambitious only for the extirpation of error, and the diffusion of truth. It remains for the artist to claim his part in these guiltless spoliations, and to transport to Europe the picturesque beauties of these favoured regions. (quoted in Edney 61)

Where the Survey promised an overview, the picturesque offered to capture the essence of the colony, first by reclaiming those sites the Survey had excluded and then by transforming each piece – each mountain range, ancient ruin, and river – into a synecdoche for India that any English viewer could understand. In the same way that Turner's *Picturesque*

---

10 The ambivalent position of Anglo-Indian women within the mechanism of imperialism impacts on their drawings, which, according to Suleri, establish 'lines of contiguity between the position of both Anglo-Indian and Indian women and the degrees of subordination they represent, for even when her writing seeks to enclose the Indian into a picturesque repose, the Anglo-Indian is simultaneously mapping out her own enclosure within such an idiom' (78).

Views in England and Wales 'offered middle-class consumers a way of possessing England (the land) and hence claiming membership in [the British nation]', so books by Emma Roberts and Fanny Parks gave consumers a way of participating in the colonial project without ever leaving their homes (Helsinger 106).

Amelia Edwards was among those whose writing effectively captured for English readers the local colour of the colonial world depicted by picturesque art. Her speciality was rendering the small but telling differences of life abroad, differences that the British colonial government was attempting to subsume and modernize. Edwards owed the success of her 1877 travelogue *A Thousand Miles up the Nile* to her ability to take full advantage of the picturesque's affiliation, paradoxically, both with commodification and with the very kind of authenticity that commodification necessarily destroyed. In addition to her canny use of the picturesque, Edwards had the advantage of a captive audience for her endeavour. She moved in familiar Victorian literary circles, contributing to Dickens's Christmas collections of ghost stories and publishing frequently in the *Saturday Review* and *Household Words*. When she proposed to write about Egypt, then, she did so for the broadest of readerships.[11] Her selection of Egypt was propitious, moreover, since in the 1870s and 80s the Nile Valley was on the minds of a great many Britons. Up river, Britain and France vied to control the Nile's source in the end game of African partition.[12] Back in London, meanwhile, the frenzy for ancient artifacts and a passion for Egyptian style had made anything 'Egypt' a singularly hot commodity.[13] *A Thousand Miles Up the Nile* went through a series of reprints and revisions as Edwards updated her book and kept it in tune with her readerships' exotic obsessions.

A Thousand Miles depicts Edwards sailing conventionally southward up the Nile, towards Nubia and what is now the Sudan, but it also portrays

---

11 Biographical information on Edwards may be found in Birkett. A good summary of Edwards's Egypt trip may be found in Rees, while Levine provides an introduction to her life and writing in general.

12 Good histories of this adventure abound. See, for instance, Lewis's *The Race to Fashoda*. On the economic history of Egypt during this period, see Zeleza (345–54). For a more general political history of the region, see Adu Boahen (34–45). And for an account that places Egypt within Britain's global empire, see Cain and Hopkins (1: 362–8).

13 As colonial politics focused on Egypt, so too did popular culture. Europe, and especially England, developed a taste for Egyptiana and Egyptian-inspired design. One can find it in the obvious places, like the massive Egyptian Court at the 1851 exhibition, and in some less expected locales, such as the stylized waterworks at Kent. On the pervasive influence of Egyptian style, see Curl. See Mitchell, *Colonising Egypt* on Egypt's prominence in the 1851 exhibition.

her increasing impatience with the English appetite for Egyptian things. When she visits the Cairo bazaar, a natural site for conspicuous consumption, she urges her readers not to give in, claiming that one does not need to commodify one's surroundings in order to enjoy them. There is a better way to appreciate the spectacle of the Cairo bazaar: '[I]n order to thoroughly enjoy an overwhelming, ineffaceable first impression of Oriental out-of-doors life, one should begin in Cairo with a day in the native bazaars; neither buying, nor sketching, nor seeking information, but just taking in scene after scene with its manifold combinations of light and shade, colour, costume, and architectural detail' (5). In this passage, Edwards uses her eye for detail to demonstrate a specialized mode of consuming in which no goods are actually exchanged. Similarly, the objects she observes show no traces of the labour that went into generating them, for '[e]very shop-front, every street-corner, every turbaned group is a ready-made picture' (5). Between these ready-made scenes and her singularly unobtrusive style of apperception, Edwards develops a way of seeing and consuming that, in contrast with that of her fellow travellers, seems to leave Egypt completely undisturbed.

Her discretion distinguishes Edwards not only from the surveyor, but also from the ordinary tourists who were overrunning Egypt in the 1870s. Once travel agents incorporated a Nile cruise into their eastern tours in 1869, it became increasingly difficult to explore the region without being part of a crowd (Buzard, *Beaten Track* 323). Edwards recounts that on more than one occasion her party was set upon by salesmen who 'mistook them for the first arrivals of an armada sent upriver by Thomas Cook' (69). Salesmen eagerly satisfied the tourists' rabid desire for Egyptian trinkets, for scarabs, parchments, and even mummies, an appetite that overwhelmed their better sense, Edwards notes, and frequently led them to make ill-advised purchases. After paying an 'enormous price' for a bound corpse that was supposed to be an ancient mummy, for example, two of Edwards's travelling companions discover that they have been had by one of Egypt's less scrupulous vendors. Their mummy begins to stink. '[U]nable to endure the perfume of their ancient Egyptian', Edwards relates, they 'drowned the dear departed at the end of a week' (660).[14]

---

14 The authenticity of such purchases is usually dubious, Edwards reveals when she visits a forger's shop near Thebes. Inside she discovers 'a workman's bench strewn with scarabs, amulets, and votive gods in every stage of progress . . . while a massive fragment of mummy-case in a corner behind the door showed whence came the old sycamore wood for the wooden statuettes' (604).

Edwards explains that commercial compulsion both leads British visitors to mistake the fake Egypt for the real one and threatens to demolish it. In effect, the tourist who snaps up scarabs, parchments, and mummies in Egypt's bazaars conspires with the scientist, whose patterns of appropriating ancient sculpture and carrying off sarcophagi the tourist seems inclined to mimic. If the cartographers of the Survey efface the ancient world by covering it in European maps, the tourist and scientist carry out that rhetorical effacement in material terms.

> Such is the fate of every Egyptian monument, great or small. The tourist carves it with names and dates, and in some instances with caricatures. The student of Egyptology, by taking wet paper 'squeezes,' sponges away every vestige of the[ir] original colour . . . Every day, more inscriptions are mutilated – more tombs are rifled – more paintings and sculptures are defaced . . . When science leads the way, is it wonderful that ignorance should follow? (519–20)[15]

This passage attacks the methodology of scientific observation and, by association, the formalism of the Survey as well.[16] According to Edwards, when the scientist looks out over the Egyptian landscape, he sees only what fits his system. What he excludes – the village too small to register on his maps and the fragmented artifact too damaged to deserve a place in his museum – in fact represents the real Egypt; Egyptian identity lies in just such details.

By locating authenticity in the potsherds and broken bits of sculpture that the Survey discards, Edwards exposes the limits of its formal abstraction. Triangulation cannot render the spirit of India and Egypt, but an approach that highlights details that make manifest the cultural

---

15 Edwards's picturesque gaze adds a new wrinkle to this prototypically *fin de siècle* 'mood of nostalgia' (Rosaldo, *Culture* 68). Such mourning for the authentic world that imperialism destroys figures prominently in modernist texts by authors such as Conrad and in the anthropology of the functionalist school (Rosaldo, *Culture* 81–7, and see Bongie). Because of this, imperial nostalgia has been spoken of as the sign for modernism's intervention into and appropriation of the Empire from its more blithely rapacious Victorian antecedents. Edwards's use of the trope suggests that the origins of imperial nostalgia may be more Victorian and more feminine than heretofore assumed.

16 In the same passage where Edwards decries the 'wholesale pillage' of tourist and scientist, she takes a shot at the museums of Europe: 'The Louvre contains a full-length portrait of Seti I, cut out bodily from the walls of his sepulchre in the Valley of the Tombs of the Kings,' while the 'Museums of Berlin, of Turin, of Florence, are rich in spoils which tell their own lamentable tale' (519). As Edwards well knew, the trade in artifacts was dominated not by these continental organizations but by the British Museum. The Museum's man in Egypt was Wallis Budge, whom the *Egyptian Gazette* tersely identifies as, 'well known as a somewhat unscrupulous collector of antiquities for his museum' (quoted in Fagan 302). On the Museum's alliance with such unscrupulous sorts, see France 174–9.

authenticity of the ancient world can. When she visits the Hall of Pillars at Karnak, Edwards urges us not to dwell on the overwhelming size of the monument but to attend to the distinctions between light and shadow, the variations of colour and proportion that make it picturesque. Science, she tells us, approaches Karnak with measuring stick in hand, trying to discern the secrets of the monument by drawing graphs and charts. 'To describe it [Hypostyle Hall of Seti I], in the sense of building up a recognizable image by means of words, is impossible. The scale is too vast; the effect too tremendous; the sense of one's own dumbness, and littleness, and incapacity, too complete and crushing' (219). Whatever might be gained by such a dizzying relationship with colonial otherness, Edwards reveals that one cannot grasp what makes Egypt truly Egyptian when overpowered with a sense of its sublimity.[17]

She offers the picturesque as a stabilizing antidote to this encounter with the sublime. She composes a picture in her mind and quietly takes possession of the scene.

Yet to look is something, if one can but succeed in remembering; and the Great Hall of Karnak is photographed in some dark corner of my brain for as long as I have memory. I shut my eyes, and see it as if I were there . . . I stand once more among those mighty columns . . . I see them swathed in coiled shadows and broad bands of light. I see them sculptured and painted with shapes of Gods and Kings, with blazonings of royal names, with sacrificial altars, and forms of sacred beasts, and emblems of wisdom and truth. (219)

Naomi Schor refers to such signs of ancient life as 'epic details' capable of animating and 'inspiriting' the inanimate (*Reading* 32). Edwards's narrative is full of such details. When she reduces the hall at Karnak to its rough and crumbling parts, she 'feels . . . [a] sense of awe and wonder' at

---

17 For Gilpin, as for Edwards, the picturesque trumps the sublime as the ultimate of aesthetic effects. Although the picturesque contains an element of the sublime, '*Sublimity alone* cannot make an object *picturesque*', Gilpin warns. 'However grand the mountain, or the rock may be, it has no claim to this epithet, unless its form, its color, or its accompaniments have *some degree of beauty*' (43). Gilpin is arguing with Burke whose use of the sublime enabled a very different sort of imperial perception. As Suleri describes it, Burke's imperial sublime represented India as a space of fear and loathing. For Burke, 'India as a historical reality evokes the horror of sublimity, thus suggesting to the colonizing mind the intimate dynamic it already shares with aesthetic horror; such intimacy provokes the desire to itemize and to list all the properties of the desired object', in the manner of the comprehensive Survey, we might add; 'the list's inherent failure to be anything other than a list causes the operation of sublimity to open into vacuity, displacing desire into the greater longevity of disappointment' (28–9).

the sight of monuments 'watered with the blood and tears of millions'. 'There were times', she recalls furthermore, 'when I should scarcely have been surprised to hear them [the ancients] speak – to see them rise from their painted thrones and come down from the walls' (445). During such moments, Edwards develops a sentimental attachment to the ancient world. This familiarity begins at the level of the detail, and ends with a complex picture of the daily toil and ritual, the ethnographic content of the Egyptian landscape. By privileging an aesthetic of the detail, Edwards transforms the ancient world into an object of our sympathy. She makes it appear comfortable and even familiar by giving concrete form to the very content Victorian science and the Survey rendered distant, typical, and exchangeable.

Above all, it was an ancient and distinctly local way of life that Edwards's details rendered up, Egypt as it was before England came. Perched atop the Great Pyramid, her imperial gaze arranges the monuments of Geezah into foreground and background, light and shadow. She observes,

The ground lies, as it were, immediately under one; and the Necropolis is seen as in a ground-plan . . . We see from this point how each royal pyramid is surrounded by its . . . lesser tombs . . . We see how Cheops and Chephren and Mycerinus lay . . . with his family and nobles around him . . . Recognising how clearly the place is a great cemetery, one marvels at the ingenious theories that turn the pyramids into astronomical observatories, and abstruse standards of measurement. They are the grandest graves in all the world – and they are nothing more. (717–18)

Edwards infuses the Egyptian landscape with ethnographic content. Using the picturesque as her formal guide, she identifies each detail according to its use and in this way gives each element in the view a simultaneously aesthetic and cultural accent.[18] The approach to the Great Pyramid reveals a similar affinity between the picturesque and the ethnographic. As she rides down the road to Geezah, Edwards spies the Pyramids in the distance, while in the foreground 'the brown

18 Of course, her view is no more authentic than that of the Survey. On the contrary, the formal logic of Edwards's vision is one that she repeats as insistently as the abstractions composing the Survey. As Bermingham observes, 'The unique, unconventionally beautiful landscape that [Gilpin and others] encouraged adherents of the picturesque to seek became, when in increasing numbers they sought it, as standardized and predictable as the gardening plans of Brown and Repton, among the most prominent designers of their era' (84).

Fellaheen . . . are cutting the clover' (714–15). 'Villages, shadoofs, herds and flocks . . . succeed each other', she tells her readers, 'and then . . . comes . . . the cavernous ridge of ancient yellow rock, and the Great Pyramid with its shadow-side towards us, darkening the light of day' (714–15). As this carefully organized relationship between village and pyramids suggests, the picturesque allows Edwards to forge a historical link between ancient and modern Egypt in formal terms. Her emphasis on such historical traces clearly distinguishes Edwards's gaze from that of the Survey, which seeks to obliterate the past as it establishes a new map.

Opposed as these descriptions of the Egyptian landscape were to the Survey's geometric abstraction, the two forms of the imperial gaze nonetheless collaborated to support Britain's colonial project: while the picturesque held onto the past, the Survey managed the present. Much as the Survey employed a staff of highly trained cartographers to carry out its labour, so Edwards sought a corps of travellers who would reproduce in detail the very Egypt the Survey sought to efface. To this end, her narrative pauses for a moment of pedagogy. In order to 'compose the stern lines of Egyptian architecture', Edwards explains, one requires but a subject for the foreground, and then 'your picture stands before you ready-made' (379). Finding such subjects is the key to sketching Egypt, as Gilpin would no doubt agree. By sparingly introducing such subjects, he instructs – 'moving objects, as wagons, and boats, as well as cattle, and men' (77) – one may find a way to 'regulate every thing else' and organize the composition (69).[19] Though Edwards agrees that the subject might be anything – 'a camel, a shadoof, a woman with a water-jar upon her head' – her favourites tend to be rural labourers, who speak to her in the language of primitive authenticity (379). 'I believe', Edwards declares, 'that the physique and life of the modern Fellah is almost identical with the physique and life of that ancient Egyptian labourer whom we know so well in the wall-paintings of the tombs' (x).[20]

19 ' . . . nature is most defective in composition', Gilpin writes, 'and *must* be a little assisted' (67). In and of itself, the foreground is 'indeed a mere spot', he tells his readers, '[a]nd yet, tho so little essential in *giving a likeness*, it is more so than any other part in *forming a composition*. It resembles those deep tones in music, which give a value to all the lighter parts; and harmonize the whole' (69).
20 In her eyes, each ritual of the modern Egyptian household recalls an authentic Egyptian past: 'Water is brought to table in the same jars manufactured at the same town as in the days of Cheops and Chephren', she observes, 'and the mouths of the bottles filled in the precisely the same way with fresh leaves and flowers. The cucumber stuffed with minced-meat was a favorite dish in those times of old; and I can testify to its excellence in 1874' (xi).

How the picturesque collaborates with the imperial Survey becomes explicit when Edwards visits Aboo Simbel, a ruin lying just above the Nile's second cataract. Here Edwards comes upon an ancient object that has been damaged by European contact, and takes on the task of restoring it. In so doing, she organizes the surrounding landscape and its inhabitants as an efficient economic model. She demonstrates the practical application of her way of seeing by showing a primitivized population put to work. Her adventure begins when she finds a statue of Ramses the Great, whose head, Edwards claims, was damaged in the 1820s by the Scottish antiquarian Robert Hay while he was conducting research for the British Museum (459). Hay made a plaster cast of Ramses' face, it seems, and when he unpeeled the plaster left behind 'ghastly splotches, which for many years have marred this beautiful face as with the unsightliness of leprosy' (452). To rectify the situation, Edwards has her cook brew gallons of thick coffee, which she then orders the sailors and porters who have accompanied her upriver to spread over Ramses's face. 'Ramses' appetite for coffee was prodigious', Edwards relates: 'Our cook was aghast at the demand made upon his stores. Never before had he been called upon to provide for a guest whose mouth measured three feet and a half in width' (452). This description has the effect of racially coding Ramses. By covering him with a thick coat of burned coffee, Edwards quite literally turns him black. She similarly darkens the workers who assist her, describing them in the most base of racist metaphor, 'chattering and skipping about the scaffolding like monkeys . . . [and crawling] all over the huge head . . . just as the carvers may have swarmed over it in the days when Ramses was king' (450). The consummate bricoleur, she creates a primitivized Egyptian scene through the judicious application of simple coffee. This perversely domesticating gesture demonstrates control every bit as much as the acts of triangulation in which the geographers of the Survey engaged.

In the 1880s, as Edwards was revising the second edition of *A Thousand Miles Up the Nile*, Britain was attempting to transform Egypt from an economic competitor – Egypt's productive capacity was second only to England's in the first half of the nineteenth century, we should remember – into a dependency (Zeleza 354).[21] With this transformation, British

---

21 Zeleza summarizes Egypt's history under British rule as follows: 'In the course of the nineteenth century Egypt had progressively become enmeshed in the world capitalist economy as an exporter of raw materials, primarily cotton, and an importer of manufactured goods and capital. In the process many local political and social institutions broke down, which served only to reinforce the

imperialism itself began to realign the century old relationship between the Survey and the picturesque. In 1878, the economic historian Tiyambe Zeleza recounts, a Briton assumed the post of Egyptian Minister of Finance, and in 1881 Britain seized control of the Egyptian government and began to reshape Egypt's economy into a source of raw materials that would supplement British holdings around the world (354). In order to fit into Britain's world system, Egypt was de-industrialized and its population primitivized in precisely the fashion Edwards prescribes in her travelogue. British administrators aimed to reorganize Egypt into a collective of well-disciplined agricultural workers, a coherent society that, as Timothy Mitchell contends, could be thought of as a nation, a 'community in its entirety' (*Colonising Egypt* 119). Edwards's version of the picturesque provided not only a good sense of how this population might appear – drenched in the blood and sweat that was their ancient heritage – but also a description of how English professional labour might be integrated with the labour of an Egyptian citizenry made over in terms of Europe's agricultural peasantry. Her model established a kind of participant observation, which, through a combination of sympathy and careful attention to ethnographic detail, might guide English managers. Observers with an eye for such detail would be the caretakers of ancient Egypt and, by extension, of contemporary Egypt as well. Edwards staged in aesthetic terms a process of imperial reinvention that the British Foreign Office staged in political and economic terms. She helped readers understand what it would mean to make Egypt dependent on English skill. After all, in her account the most authentically Egyptian qualities could only be seen, and safeguarded from the worst practices of British commerce, by sympathetic feats of picturesque representation. In this way, she made the picturesque available for the modernization programmes of twentieth-century imperial administration and for modernism as well.[22]

---

growing foreign domination of the economy. By 1875 Egypt was virtually bankrupt, perilously indebted to the Anglo-French bondholders. The crisis engendered culminated in the British invasion of 1882' (354).

22 A footnote regarding Edwards's later career: after she returned to London from Egypt, Edwards became an activist for the field of Egyptology, which had not previously been considered a legitimate discipline of study. She helped found its first professional organization, and although she was later expelled from that same organization (for reasons that remain unclear, her erstwhile partners turned on her and forced her out in the late 1880s [Levine xxvi]), she continued to raise money for research. In her will, she left a considerable sum to establish the first British chair in Egyptology, which went to her *protégé*, Flinders Petrie, a man whom Bernal refers to as 'the founder not only of Egyptian but of all modern archeology' (270).

THAT OLD IMPERIAL FEELING

In the decades following the renovation of Egypt, Britain employed its revised imperial philosophy in India as well. During the 1910s and 20s, financial advisors from the City of London and representatives from the Colonial Office sought to open to foreign parties the unilateral trade that had long been the focus of Britain's relationship with its crown jewel. The British government hoped to arrange matters so that its twentieth-century involvement in India would emphasize technological and financial expertise to complement and even displace the activities that had dominated colonization in the region, the extraction of raw materials and the generation of markets for manufactured goods. In its revised plan of operations, Indian entrepreneurs and multinational corporations would provide the capital to develop the subcontinent's economy, and non-English trading partners would become the new consumers of Indian goods (B. Chatterji 15–16).[23] The rise of the professional service industry paved the way for such reform (Cain and Hopkins 2: 193–6), but it was also determined by an intensified Indian anti-colonialism, by Gandhi's emergence as the leader of an 'all-India' nationalist movement, and by the actions of nationwide trade unionism, which demanded more control over India's economic future (Sarkar, *Modern India* 165, 175).[24] Taken together, these forces made an independent India thinkable and even likely, and compelled Britain to reconsider the direction of the colonial state.[25]

Among those responding to the challenge was E. M. Forster, whose *A Passage to India* interrogates imperial expansion by identifying in India a

23 See Tomlinson (113), and Dewey for details on this shift in emphasis. See Chandavarkar, 'Money'on the new centrepiece of Britain's Indian imperial effort, speculative finance (790).

24 B. Chatterji reminds us that through this period of reform, 'the fundamental purpose of imperial policy had not changed' (15). England still sought to control India by controlling its economic growth. It simply pursued that goal by different means. Thus, while specific regions of India experienced dramatic industrial growth after the war, and while this rise in production was coupled with important political changes, India remained dependent on European capital. As Krishnamurty shows, moreover, despite these much-ballyhooed changes, India continued to depend on export agriculture for the bulk of its GDP (548). For more on the political implications of economic reform, see Sarkar, *Modern India* 172–4.

25 The most important official British document in this period of reform was the Government of India Act, which was passed in 1919 and emphasized the development of new 'self-governing institutions' in the subcontinent (Sarkar, *Modern India* 165). The unevenness of such reform, however, became apparent on 10 April 1919, when colonial soldiers fired on and killed hundreds of demonstrators in the city of Amritsar. This incident played out like a Mutiny in miniature, as English soldiers took their revenge for an attack on an Englishwoman the day before the massacre, and served notice that the era of Victorian imperialism was not over just yet (see Das 47–51).

culture that colonialism could not hope to subdue.[26] In so doing, Forster intervened in the ideological field that the Survey and the picturesque had collaborated to produce. The novel offers no better example of how he did so than the memorable horseback-riding scene with which it concludes. The picturesque becomes thoroughly modernist in this scene, losing its association with low culture and becoming a veritable aesthetic complement to Britain's new mode of imperial specialization.

Given that the popularity of Edwards's methodology hinged on its association with femininity, with commodity consumption, and with middle-class leisure, Forster had to rid the picturesque of such gender and class connotations in order to elevate it. He chooses a mountain pass for his purpose. Aziz and Fielding's ride through this pass reproduces every feature of the picturesque but one: there is no woman to witness and describe it. Instead, a landscape as full of detail and as meticulously organized as any Victorian watercolour is the backdrop for a new sort of imperial relationship:

Presently the ground opened into full sunlight and they saw a grassy slope bright with butterflies, also a cobra, which crawled across doing nothing in particular, and disappeared among some custard apple trees. There were round white clouds in the sky, and white pools on the earth; the hills in the distance were purple. The scene was as park-like as England, but did not cease being queer. (317)

Forster divides his setting into back, mid, and foreground as the picturesque dictates, and focuses on the sort of details that aesthetic favours as well. He has not depicted a landscape reminiscent of those generated by the Indian Survey, but this is not to say that his version of the picturesque is habitual either. Not so subtle subversion begins in the opening lines when that cobra appears amidst the custard apples, signal-ling danger of biblical proportions for those who would blithely imagine this a landscape ready for consumption. Like Edwards's Egyptian scenes, Forster's India is 'park-like' and can be rendered according to the formal abstraction that makes it seem comparable to English landscape. And yet, something inassimilable remains. This imperial terrain is 'queer', a term that invites us to query both the nature of the landscape and that of the two conspicuously male observers who look upon it. If India is picturesque but dangerous, we may ask, are these men better qualified

---

26 Parry's recent revisionist reading emphasizes this aspect of *Passage* ('Materiality'). A more sceptical view on Forster's India may be found in Said, *Culture and Imperialism.*

than middle-class women like Edwards to capture both its generic beauty and its distinctly uncanny quality? What is it about them and their relationship that suggests such qualification?

Before answering these questions, it is worth assaying to provide a gloss of the enigmatic term Forster employs to identify the landscape's inassimilable quality, namely, 'queer'. Here and throughout *A Passage to India* the adjective 'queer' signals the novelty Forster brings to imperial representation. It modifies everything from this picturesque scene to the 'queer valley' at the Marabar Caves, from Professor Godbole's 'queer little song' to Fielding's 'queer vague talk', from Aziz's 'psychology' – 'very queer', remarks Superintendent McBryde – to Adela Quested's behaviour – she is at times 'the queer cautious girl' and at others 'the queer honest girl' (149, 133, 169, 24, 249). Scholars agree that this modifier demands careful decoding. We might start by suggesting that Forster appears to have exported to India the habitual early twentieth-century connotation identified by Joseph Bristow. 'Queerness', he explains, 'pointed to those incongruous, uncanny, and peculiar aspects of experience that often left one with a feeling of bewilderment' (91). Charu Malik argues that *A Passage to India* highlights such incongruities to reinforce a critique of the 'monolithic experience' habitual to earlier imperial accounts (224). The result of making such complexity visible, according to Yonatan Touval, is an Indian landscape transformed into 'queer space – if we take "queer" to mean the mapping out, and in the process the demystification, of relations and identities that a hegemony of the normative would rather keep unexamined' (237). Touval explains that as Forster 'opens up such a space' he gives defamiliarization a sexual spin 'in a rhetorical performance that perceptively exposes the insidious collusion between colonial imperialism and Western sexuality' (237).

Although recent criticism tends to agree that Forster links imperial representation to a discourse of sexuality, it is not in accord on the question of how deliberate this linkage may be or exactly how it might guide our interpretation of interaction between Fielding and Aziz. For Malik, 'Forster's awareness' of this conceptual correspondence 'may be traced finally to the marginal vantage point dictated by the author's homosexuality, this enforced "otherness" making urgent to him the dangerous possibility of excluding other experiences in privileging one kind of certainty' (224). According to this critical approach, *A Passage to India* may deserve to be considered part of what Jonathan Dollimore calls that 'obscure, marginal history where race and homosexuality converge' (333). Or we might locate it in what Ashis Nandy describes as the history

of 'unconscious homo-eroticized bonding' chronic among British administrators and their Indian subjects (10). The notion that such bonding was
perhaps not so unconscious is put forward by Elaine Freedgood, who
reads it as a more or less open secret that in many ways facilitated imperial
rule. Christopher Lane questions the obscurity of colonial homoeroticism,
meanwhile, since he finds Forster's novel symptomatic of 'ambivalent
sexual and unconscious fantasies that underpin relations between colonizer
and colonized' (145).

With the exception of an interpretation like Freedgood's, most critical
assessment treats sexuality as disruptive of Britain's colonizing mission.
According to Malik, Forster uses 'sexual ambivalence . . . to show the
ambivalence of colonial authority' (224). For Lane, homoeroticism tests
both imperial rule and 'Forster's anti-imperialism' (165). He argues that
'homosexual desire' shatters Forster's dream of amicable colonial relations
'because it represents the other's difference as violently at odds with the
friendship that homophilia dictates' (165). For Suleri, sex is even more
unsettling, since it is equally damaging to both sides of the colonial power
struggle: 'the disempowerment of a homoerotic gaze is as damaging to the
colonizing psyche as to that of the colonized, and questions the cultural
dichotomies through which both are realized' (136).

These and other scholars have come to interpret the formal characteristics of *A Passage to India* as testimony to sexuality's disruptive effects.
According to this way of reading, the novel's insistent ambiguity, its open
ending, its refusal to provide a definitive account of events at the centre of
the plot, all of these attributes serve as symptoms of uncertainty the novel
shares with the colonial system it portrays. One example of this argument
appears in Lane, who contends that sexual uneasiness makes itself felt as
textual indeterminacy and vice versa, so that the 'gap between the object
and aim of Forster's texts would therefore mark the influence of drives
that turn his representations awry' (149). Colleen Lamos makes a more
general point about the relationship between modernist sexuality and
textuality when she argues that the authority of several of the period's
most celebrated writers is undermined when 'errant identifications and
desires inform and deform their declared aesthetic aims' (5).[27] This
reading contends that the complexity of modernist texts can at least in

---

27 The literature on other modernists and sexuality is voluminous. Valente's edited collection *Quare
Joyce* is a resource on matters of Joycean aesthetics and sexuality, for instance, and Attridge
examines the 'sexual effects' of language in Joyce, especially in *A Portrait of the Artist as a Young
Man* (64).

part be explained through a repressive hypothesis. Modernism's literary and cultural unconscious reveals wayward proclivities that disrupt the authorial mastery characteristically attributed to its most canonical figures. The same argument explains why imperial representation appears so discordant in *A Passage to India*: unsettling desires destabilize the carefully composed surface of the imperial picturesque, making that Victorian landscape disorderly and strange.

I wish to supplement this argument by emphasizing that disorder can also be enabling. The very act of disrupting the picturesque and its accompanying narrative of feminine exploration creates the opportunity for new formal arrangements and new tales to be told about the nature of colonization. I agree with the reigning critical common sense that Forster makes the relationship between Fielding and Aziz bear the full weight of India's colonial past. I demur when it comes to the contention that their friendship represents a disruption of imperial authority. It is better described as representing a change in that authority.

By estranging the picturesque, *A Passage to India* heralds the arrival of a new subject authorized to reproduce it. We will not fail to mistake this transfer of power if we attend to the type of story in which homoerotics plays a part and if we remember that modernists were not the first to take advantage of the triangular narrative structure of homoerotic plotting Eve Kosofsky Sedgwick has made so familiar to us from her foundational *Between Men: English Literature and Male Homosocial Desire*. In the Victorian imperial version of this tale Jenny Sharpe ably describes, triangulation invariably features three players: the European man, the South Asian man, and the vulnerable Englishwoman. In Forster's model, all three characters return, but in a significantly different alignment it will do us well to examine in some detail.

Just as Woolf deliberately undermines Mrs Ramsay's Victorian plotting in *To the Lighthouse*, so Forster commences his revision of the homosocial triangle by providing a genealogy of the Victorian stories tying India to Britain. His genealogy takes shape as each of the novel's three main British characters becomes familiar with Dr Aziz. Forster pairs Aziz first with Mrs Moore, then with Adela Quested, and finally with Cyril Fielding. As we move from couple to couple, the novel traces for us the declining importance of Englishwomen in imperial narrative. It leaves behind the sexual division of labour that coordinated operations between the Survey and the feminine picturesque. In so doing, it establishes a dynamic between Britain and India that is cut to the measure of modernist aesthetics and twentieth-century empire.

Mrs Moore represents a maternal presence in India whose iconicity verges on that of royalty. 'Queen Victoria was different', murmurs Mahmoud Ali early in the novel, and Mrs Moore is different as well (12). Her benevolent display at Aziz's mosque enables what Forster treats as a largely fantastic connection between the two characters, one whose mythic status is confirmed near the end of the story, when a crowd attending Aziz's trial 'Indianizes [Mrs Moore] into Esmiss Esmoor' (225). Mrs Moore's 'sympathy' for Aziz, proved 'by criticizing her fellow-countrywoman to him', gives the appearance of familiarity and causes Aziz to exclaim, 'we are in the same box' (20). Forster's gloss of this remark – he calls it 'cryptic' (20) – read in conjunction with Mrs Moore's translation into 'Esmiss Esmoor', suggests their familiarity is the result of miscommunication, and their convivial but fleeting encounter a symbol of Britain's missed opportunity to truly capture colonial difference.

If Mrs Moore and Aziz express the unfulfilled dream of the Victorian Raj, Adela Quested and Aziz enact its nightmare. Aziz takes on the role of sexual predator while Adela plays the fateful part of innocent abroad. 'I want to see the *real* India', she announces in the novel's opening pages. For her, as for the female traveller she recalls, the real India must appear in the form of the picturesque, complete with a 'pageant of birds in the early morning, brown bodies, white turbans, [and] idols whose flesh was scarlet or blue' (47). Adela professes to know the difference between staged displays – 'I'm tired of seeing picturesque figures pass before me as a frieze', she declares (27) – and the sort of composition that Amelia Edwards would have called authentic. She tells whoever will listen that she wishes to escape the constrained life of the city and get out to the countryside to see 'the force that lies behind colour and movement' (47). Forster refuses to satisfy her desire for this formally arranged authenticity, however, and every scene she comes upon seems 'inferior, and suggested that the countryside was too vast to admit of excellence', except for the Marabar Hills (87).[28] Those hills 'look romantic in certain lights and at suitable distances . . . seen of an evening from the upper verandah of the club', which is where Adela gazes out and develops her craving to visit them (126). As one draws closer, however, the pleasant view decomposes: 'The hues in the east decayed, the hills seemed dimmer though in fact better

---

28 Forster says as much in his novel's first chapter, where he alerts his readers that Chandrapore offers a rather limited selection of views. 'Except for the Marabar Caves – and they are twenty miles off – the city . . . presents nothing extraordinary. Edged rather than washed by the river Ganges, it trails for a couple of miles along the bank, scarcely distinguishable from the rubbish it deposits' (7).

lit, and a profound disappointment entered with the morning breeze'
(137). As picturesqueness fades, Adela's tale mutates into a Mutiny-era
narrative of miscegenation hysteria and retributive violence.[29] Instead of
authenticity, the heroine encounters only assault and insult in the caves.

Adela finds herself, in truth, in a situation Amelia Edwards knew well.
Upon entering the caves, she comes face to face with the sublime. The
caves are 'older than anything in the world' (125). They are impossible to
measure, impossible to see even, for it is pitch dark inside until someone
lights a match. Instead of clarifying matters, light makes Adela's situation
worse, as the polished walls of the cave reflect the flame, and the sound of
the match being struck sets off the infamous echo and the caves resound,
'Boum!' Where Edwards dismissed something like this same threat by
composing a neatly arranged image in her mind, Adela panics. Unlike
Edwards's encounter with sublimity, which triggered the fantasy of
sympathetic, primitivized Egyptian subjects, Adela's experience in the
caves reproduces the Other as a threat.

The Marabar incident serves to defamiliarize the Indian landscape for
the Anglo-Indian population. In the days and weeks following Adela's
'insult' in the caves, '[They] looked out at the palisade of cactuses stabbing
the purple throat of the sky . . . [and] realized that they were thousands of
miles from any scenery that they understood' (180). After employing
Adela to call up the picturesque, Forster undermines her authority. He
takes away all recourse to picturesque authenticity by telling his readers
that Indian landscape is, in truth, nothing like that of England. By
conjuring up an antipathetic India suppressed by the picturesque, Forster
closes off any possibility that Victorian narrative might remedy the
problem at hand. Adela's sentimental vision thus proves as cruelly
obsolete as that of Kurtz's Intended.

A Passage to India divests its female lead not only of her aesthetic
authority, but also of the sensitivity to emotion that accompanied the
Victorian picturesque. '[Y]ou have no real affection for Aziz, or Indians
generally', Fielding scolds Adela (259). 'The first time I saw you, you were
wanting to see India', he tells her, 'not Indians, and it occurred to me: Ah,
that won't take us far. Indians know whether they are liked or not – they
cannot be fooled' (260). Forster's readers learn this lesson when Aziz finds
his final partner, Cyril Fielding, and the novel begins to outline its

---

29 'Read any of the Mutiny records', the Police Superintendent counsels Fielding, 'which, rather
than the Bhagavad Gita, should be your Bible in this country' (169). Sharpe's reading
meticulously examines Forster's reconstruction of the Mutiny story.

ultimate triangular arrangement. Here, the primary attachment is between two men whose relationship is simultaneously erotic – as demonstrated in the novel's notorious collar-stud scene[30] – sentimental, and
ultimately allegorical. India's future, Aziz informs Fielding, rests entirely
'on what we feel' (117). Without it, he asks, 'What is the use of all these
reforms, and Conciliation Committees for Mohurram, and shall we cut
the tazia short or shall we carry it another route, and Councils of Notables
and official parties where the English sneer at our skins?' (117). Where
Amelia Edwards employed sentimentality to make ancient Egypt comfortable and familiar, here the sentimental underscores the sensitivity of
political and cultural negotiation. 'Mr. Fielding', Aziz continues, 'no one
can ever realize how much kindness we Indians need, we do not even
realize it ourselves . . . Kindness, more kindness, and even after that more
kindness. I assure you it is the only hope' (116–17). 'I know', Fielding
replies, 'but institutions and the governments don't' (117). Forster confirms that he has found a successor for the Anglo-Indian woman and the
woman traveller. Having denounced Adela's version of picturesque India
and having surpassed Mrs. Moore in sympathy, Fielding through his
friendship with Aziz can begin reforming imperial relations.

In this way, Forster provides a narrative theory for what Sedgwick calls
'a change of gears' at the beginning of the twentieth century 'by which the
exemplary instance of the sentimental ceases to be a woman per se, but
instead becomes the body of a man who . . . physically dramatizes . . . a
struggle of masculine identity with emotions . . . stereotyped as feminine'
(*Epistemology* 146). Forster may place feminine attributes in a man's body,
but he does so in such a way that he feels free to disavow their feminine
origin. Felski takes this tactic as an opportunity to revise our habitual
understanding of femininity and modernism as inveterate opposites.
'Femininity is now appropriated by the male artist as emblematic of the
modern', she explains, 'rather than standing in opposition to it' (94).
'Feminine traits', meanwhile, 'are defamiliarized, placed in quotation
marks, revealed as free-floating signifiers rather than natural, God-given,
and immutable' (Felski 101). They are not free-floating for long, since
when modernism appropriates traits linked to the feminine it associates
them with expertise. As Felski puts it, 'In this new guise, femininity is
increasingly appropriated as a cipher for the very self-reflexivity and

---

30 In this scene, Aziz assists Fielding in his dressing room by offering to loan him the stud in an offer
that Suleri calls 'a secret gesture of intimacy that barely needs decoding' (138). One is surely
tempted to decode, however, when, the offer accepted, Aziz proceeds to introduce the stud into
the back of Fielding's shirt (see *Passage to India* 64–6).

self-referentiality of poetic language itself' (94). Not just poetic languages, at least as Forster's novel presents it, but specialized vernaculars in general. When he depicts Fielding as an educator whose favoured form of pedagogy involves the 'give-and-take of a private conversation', emotional sensitivity begins to look more like an expert skill than a domestic gift (62). Fielding's professionalism runs deep, to the very core of his being, which means he scarcely distinguishes between his work interactions and the labour involved in beginning and maintaining a friendship. 'I can't be sacked from my job', he explains to Aziz, 'because my job's Education. I believe in teaching people to be individuals, and to understand other individuals. It's the only thing I do believe in' (121). More than anything else, Forster makes clear, Fielding wishes to be identified by the specialized services he provides as a teacher. Thus we mistake him, if we see him simply as an enlightened representative of Britishness. He is, rather, a prototype for a new kind of imperial agent, and his relationship with Aziz is a model for the field of operations in which such a figure might work.

As Forster's plot progresses, however, Fielding learns that there is a limit to his understanding of this form of interaction. Just as 'Anglo-India had caught her [Adela] with a vengeance', so too it redefines Aziz and Fielding as antagonists (197). Once again, Forster borrows from Victorian narrative to help build a context for a new imperial relationship. He describes Aziz and Fielding suffering from the sort of 'idiomatic crisis' that Victor Luftig identifies as endemic to stories of friendship in fiction from the late nineteenth century (95). As in the New Woman fiction Luftig describes, friendship in *A Passage to India* involves level upon level of emotional, erotic, cultural, and political complication. Forster demonstrates the enormous stakes involved in even the most minor of exchanges when Fielding too obviously takes on the patriarchal role of mentor. 'Your emotions never seem in proportion to their objects, Aziz', he chastises his companion (254). Aziz counters, suggesting that Fielding's technique is not subtle enough to maintain the delicate balance required of future colonial relations: 'If you are right, there is no point in any friendship; it all comes down to give and take, or give and return, which is disgusting' (254).[31] In order to establish a less mercantile economy, Forster's formal logic of friendship needs to be adjusted to account for intractable disagreement, the sort produced, in this modernist way of thinking, by deep cultural difference.

31 Lane contends that the problem with Fielding is that he is not sentimental enough. He argues, rightly I think, that Forster's characters often show a 'loyalty to the nation' that prevents them from privileging cross-cultural bonds like the one between Fielding and Aziz (169–70).

Victorian sentimental writing's focus on gender difference made it act carelessly with cultural difference, Adela Quested's narrative appears designed to suggest. Forster and modernism more generally seeks an elaboration of difference seen through an ethnographic lens. So much emphasis is put on culture that, in the novel's penultimate scene, its terms threaten to eclipse those of gender. The difference that matters in this scene lies between village 'worshippers' and the 'four outsiders' who struggle to keep their boats afloat while observing the local ceremony occurring on shore (315). When the vessels carrying Aziz, Fielding, and Mrs Moore's son and daughter collide and capsize in the River Mau, they plunge 'into the warm, shallow water, and r[i]se struggling into a tornado of noise' (315). Forster carefully orchestrates this disorder and surrounds his characters with 'oars, the sacred tray [launched into the river as part of the festival], the letters of Ronny and Adela' (315). In this cluttered stream, whatever differences come between Fielding and his European comrades are subsumed by their status as 'intruders' amidst a 'crowd of Hindus' (316). Dr. Aziz is Indian but hardly a part of the Hindu crowd. Both a Muslim and a professional, he is out of place as well. His presence adds another level of complexity to Forster's already thick ethnographic stew. It also identifies him as an appropriate partner and a worthy antagonist for a European professional.

In the closing lines of *A Passage to India*, Forster leaves his reader face to face with a recalcitrant element of difference that simultaneously triggers and blocks intense erotic desire. As Aziz rides 'against him [Fielding] furiously . . . half-kissing him', the same unbreachable principle of difference is set in a scene paradoxically chaotic and composed. The content of the landscape that Fielding and Aziz traverse is neither domesticated nor familiarized. Indeed, it is accurate to say that landscape refuses to behave as a seamless terrain where English and Indian can exist side by side. Instead, Forster arranges a setting that demonstrates the full extent of Aziz's, and India's, antagonism towards Britain. When Fielding holds Aziz 'affectionately' and pleads, 'Why can't we be friends now? It's what I want. It's what you want', the landscape itself responds by atavistically producing that whole, invisible history of affect that separates the two men:

But the horses didn't want it – they swerved apart; the earth didn't want it, sending up rocks through which riders must pass single file; the temples, the tank, the jail, the palace, the birds, the carrion, the Guest House, that came into view as they issued from the gap and saw Mau beneath: they didn't want it, they said in their hundred voices, 'No, not yet,' and the sky said, 'No, not there.' (322)

Where the British Survey of India had inscribed its own spatial categories on the surface of the Indian subcontinent, Forster's India is governed by subterranean forces that rise up and dictate the movement of European professionals. Where the landscapes of Amelia Edwards's travel narrative collaborated with the scientific gaze of the Survey by homogenizing the contact zone containing colonizer and colonized, Forster's landscape rebels. The scene reverses the effect of domestication and makes commonplace things and people seem suddenly strange – at once very old and utterly new. At the same time, it makes such abstraction appear unique. This is as much Aziz and Fielding's problem as it is India and Britain's. Where the Survey institutionalized abstraction – making it the expression of bureaucratic organization – Forster personalizes it. As much as this landscape symbolizes colonial tension it never stops seeming deeply personal. It is about two professionals exploring the complexity of their relationship as much as it is about the obsolescence of Victorian imperial politics and poetics.

So apparently secure is Forster's formulation and so assured is his narrative, that British authority remains intact despite the resistance it encounters. The novel does not indicate that it might be dangerous to allow Aziz to set the terms of his future with Fielding even as it does indicate that to do so is to imply a future for India as well: '"We may hate one another, but we hate you most. If I don't make you go, Ahmed will, Karim will, if it's fifty-five hundred years we shall get rid of you, yes, we shall drive every blasted Englishman into the sea . . . and then you and I shall be friends"' (322). This speech manifests a mixture of eros and violence that concludes with friendship. Resistance and disruption, Aziz promises, will ultimately lead him and Fielding, India and Britain to reconciliation. In this way, Forster suggests to his readers that whether Britain occupies India or not, whether India becomes independent or not, it cannot help but remain tied to Britain.

This hypothesis depends on Forster's ability to sublate the past, to incorporate it while simultaneously distinguishing his account of Anglo-Indian relations from those associated with the Victorian era. Forster's Englishwoman recalls the Victorian figure whose vulnerability served to justify the intense retributive justice of the so-called Indian Mutiny. Nonetheless, *A Passage to India* pointedly denies her a central place in the relationship between Britain and India figured by Fielding and Aziz. Forster invokes older narrative material with the episode involving Adela Quested and the incident at the Marabar Caves, but he invokes it in order to demonstrate his modernism and his departure from this set-piece scenario of Victorian culture.

Similarly, Forster reworks what Sedgwick describes as the habitual baggage of the triangular narrative, with its 'special connection between male homosocial . . . desire and the structures for maintaining and transmitting patriarchal power' (*Between Men* 25). Because the relationship featured in *A Passage to India* does not hinge on affection for any one woman; because affairs between India and Britain as between Aziz and Fielding are vexed to say the least; and because Fielding's various encounters with Aziz show Forster's Englishman to take scant interest in an India or an Indian masculinity that replicates that of Victorian fiction, it seems clear that Forster is reimagining the power typically engendered by triangulation. Adela Quested remains the third point in Forster's plot, but she is less an object of desire than a reminder of the pernicious Mutiny-era model of fear and desire that bound Indian men, British men, and British women. By using Adela to remind his readers of the past, Forster holds that history responsible for bringing Aziz and Fielding together and, also, for keeping them apart. In this paradoxical manner, Victorian imperialism haunts Forster's leading men as they ride together in the final pages of the novel and discuss the future of their friendship and colonial relations. Like the elements of picturesque landscape he mutates into the atavistic mountain ranges of *A Passage to India*, the homosocial relationship between Aziz and Fielding depends on a feminine referent that must be disavowed. His India resists demarcation and rationalization, to the extent that even the landscape itself rises up and disarranges the compositions associated with both the picturesque and the nineteenth-century Survey.

Even as Forster sublates material from the past, his model homosocial relationship offers a vision of the future.[32] Once we understand how Forster reworks the sentimental and picturesque tradition, it becomes possible to understand this relationship as a marker of new values as much as an attack on old ones. The tight but tortuous bond between Aziz and Fielding represents the best relationship Britain could hope for between itself and its increasingly resistant colony. By figuring animosity as possibility, and the declining power of Anglo-India as the beginning of a new era of détente, Forster uses Aziz and Fielding to keep colonizer and colonized

---

32 Though disavowed, his references nonetheless trigger what Fried dubs, in his study of referentiality and quotation in the paintings of Manet, 'an endlessly regressive sequence of memories of earlier works' that invest 'the present with . . . aura and significance' ('Painting Memories' 521).

together. In this regard, we might even say that Forster's signature phrase, the desperate plea of 'only connect', functions in *A Passage to India* as a subdued version of the Victorian rallying cry, 'Rule Britannia!'

Few moments in the history of Empire are more thoroughly documented and less understood than the period Forster's novel chronicles. Scholars have described in detail how an array of new specialized agents – among them the anthropologist, the psychoanalyst, and the investment banker – displaced a set of more popular characters – the explorer, the adventure hero, and the missionary.[33] *A Passage to India* shows us how modernist fiction made sense of this shift and even encouraged it. By establishing a distinctive form of disorder and by emphasizing cultural difference and the ambivalence of all imperial relationships, Forster invents an imperial object of study suitable for Britain's modern experts. By replacing the confidence, even arrogance of the Survey and its boy spies with 'the extremes of self-consciousness, discontinuity, self-referentiality, and corrosive irony' that Said describes as the hallmarks of twentieth-century fiction, Forster makes imperial narrative more idiosyncratic and personal-seeming than it ever was during its Victorian phase (*Culture and Imperialism* 188).[34] This ironic authority, James Clifford argues further, offered a 'paradigm of ethnographic subjectivity' for anthropologists, colonial officers, and all of Britain's field workers (*Predicament* 100). I made such an argument myself in the preceding chapter. Together, that chapter and this one have contended that modernist defamiliarization served the interests of professionals confronted with the problem of how to manage colonies without thereby assimilating them to some monolithic English culture. In my next chapter, I explain that they were engaged in a complementary salvage operation at home.

33 Kuklick, *Savage* provides a survey of early twentieth-century imperial thought in a range of new professional disciplines. On the inventions of anthropology in particular, Mudimbe is indispensable. For a comprehensive account of turn-of-the-century political writing on empire, see Porter. For a more general history of professionalism and Empire, see Cain and Hopkins.

34 Though critics have tended to use the sentimentality of Forster's motto as grounds for excluding him from the highest of modernist circles, Williams shows that Forster's emphasis on feeling identifies him as a card-carrying member of the 'Bloomsbury fraction'. Raymond Williams sees in the work of the Bloomsburies a 'deep assumption of society as a group of friends and relations'. This assumption, he argues, is compatible with the most disparate of the group's ideas, from 'Freud's generalizations on aggression . . . [to] Bell's "significant form" and "aesthetic ecstasy", or . . . Keynes's ideas of public intervention in the market' ('Bloomsbury Fraction' 167). Forster's sentimentality, therefore, is precisely what guarantees his membership in one of the most exclusive of modernist cliques.

CHAPTER 4

The domestic life of primitivism

Because you see, that is what it is – magic, intoxication. Not 'Love'
at all.
Jean Rhys, Letter to Francis Wyndham, 14 April 1964

While modernist fictions such as *A Passage to India* presented estranging
accounts of Empire, other novels of the era defamiliarized the domestic
realm as well. In truth, modernism treated these domains as more tightly
intertwined than ever before. The close connection between colony and
home was apparent in two familiar modernist narratives about how
everyday existence in the twentieth century differed from that of the
nineteenth century. One of those two stories is the oft-repeated suppos-
ition that the turn of the century saw the reversal of colonization. Such
speculation appeared in coterie and popular fictions alike, and it characteristically involved the intrusion of matter from the far-flung colonies
into the private recesses of the household. The other narrative appeared in
an equally broad range of media and concerned the displacement of
feminine sentimentality by female sexuality. Novels, psychological tracts,
and economic essays described the undoing of heroines by new, unconscious, and largely misunderstood desires that could not help but embarrass and unsettle, even when animating and inspiring, the most composed
of middle-class women.

Given that modernist fiction linked these stories of nation and self
analogically, it makes sense to read each in terms of the other. Indeed, I
argue, they ought to be understood in that dependent relationship.
Although I make my case with references to a host of writings from the
middle of the nineteenth century to the middle of the twentieth, from
Jane Eyre to *Wide Sargasso Sea*, at the centre of this chapter is one book
from the 1920s: D. H. Lawrence's *Women in Love*. This novel has the
singular merit of articulating a geopolitical corollary to the repressive
hypothesis dominant in modernist thinking about domestic relations

and, especially, domestic women. The repression of sexual desire, according to *Women in Love*, indicated a repression of imperial influence as well.

In the world described by Lawrence, if English women seem a bit foreign, that is because they are. According to him, the Victorians noticed such exoticism but repressed it. Nineteenth-century commentators denied any commonality between the woman in the drawing room and the female who inhabited a mud hut. English femininity, as they formulated it, could not resemble its primitive counterpart. *Women in Love* wholly reverses this state of affairs. As the novel would have it, the notion of an English woman or an English culture makes sense only so long as one is willing to acknowledge the category 'English' as an imperial effect.

Such a claim will be familiar to readers of recent scholarship on British literature, which repeats and embellishes Edward Said's argument from *Culture and Imperialism* that Empire 'informs metropolitan cultures in many ways', influencing 'even the minutiae of daily life' (108). Said's contention seeks to overturn the competing claim that core and periphery were and remain so overwhelmingly opposed that to talk of Empire is necessarily to exclude talk of England and vice versa. 'British and colonial identities are staged as radically different', Simon Gigandi observes, but we risk being so transfixed by this staging that we overlook the moments in nearly every imperial-era writing sample treating those identities as 'inherently similar' (2). Primitivism is perhaps the most familiar vernacular in which modernism presented such tension between sameness and difference. Gikandi considers the example of Graham Greene's writing. He explains that works like *Journey Without Maps* 'represent Africa as the mirror in which England must gaze at itself if it is to recover its essential values' (186). Africa is both the model for England's future and the actually existing embodiment of its distanced past.[1]

To argue thus is, as Gikandi observes, to engage in an evolutionary debate. Lawrence weighs in by revising a warning that appeared in mass market and scholarly publications about the point when human beings became over-civilized. Progress was not guaranteed, the argument went, and the very institutions that made British people comfortable tended to

---

1 A similar ambivalence structures primitivism in the visual arts as well. The art historian William Rubin argues both that 'primitivism . . . refers not to the tribal arts in themselves, but to the Western interest in and reaction to them' and also that considerable 'affinities' link these aesthetic histories: 'both modern and tribal artists work in a conceptual, ideographic manner, thus sharing certain problems and possibilities' (25).

make them weak. But degeneration was not inevitable, according to Lawrence. He reasoned that contact with exotic societies had made English culture strong, and that its future lay in capitalizing on a long experience mediating among the world's places, peoples, and things. Instead of ambivalence, he offered his readers conviction that uncovering a repressed but crucial link between home and colony was a promising development. Far from presaging degeneration and national peril, Lawrence portrayed the primitivism of English culture as a sign of renewal.

In order to show how a generational romance like *Women in Love* sought to define an idea of English culture as a substrate for global exchange, I begin by describing the changing commodity culture of imperial Britain. I rely on *Jane Eyre* as an example of Victorian thought about the link between colonial commerce and domestic life. The remainder of the chapter's first section traces the slowly diminishing power of the domestic woman modelled by Jane Eyre. The next section shows how modernism revised the Victorian state of affairs by treating consumption as a more expert activity of connoisseurial appreciation. I explain how connoisseurship fits into the context of professionalism. This is the launching pad for a discussion of how *Women in Love* reimagined domestic romance. I treat Lawrence's revision in light of evolutionary theory. Having considered this broadly historical context, I conclude by examining what primitivism means for imperial geography. Modernist fiction may pose sweeping questions of sexuality and evolution, but Lawrence's novels were not alone in emphasizing the significance of local setting. To show how primitivism could become an aspect of local culture, I turn to Jean Rhys's *Wide Sargasso Sea*.

EXOTIC THINGS

By the turn of the twentieth century, the cosmopolitanism of Britain's imports was no longer a novelty. Consumers would not have been surprised to encounter fine Asian porcelain, bed linens sewn from Egyptian cotton, and oranges from the Levant all prominently displayed in the shops of the local High Street. They faced the problem not of coping with the shock of foreign and strange commodities, but rather of figuring out what it meant that the foreign and strange had become so conventional.

Of the innumerable texts that divine the significance of a home filled with imperial contents, we might begin with an anecdote from Sigmund Freud's essay, 'The Uncanny'. Here we find a table, graven with images of crocodiles that come to life in the wee hours of the morning and slither into a young couple's bedroom. Admittedly, many objects misbehave in Freud's essay, but the crocodile table stands out. Unlike the eyeless dolls, dismembered hands, and supernatural apparitions that also haunt 'The Uncanny', this particular table is tropical in origin. By following its trajectory from swamp to bedroom, we may begin to sense how even the most quotidian of exotic goods remained a potentially disruptive force. Freud paraphrases from a column in the *Strand Magazine*:

In the middle of the isolation of war-time a number of the English *Strand Magazine* fell into my hands; and, among other somewhat redundant matter, I read a story about a young married couple who move into a furnished house in which there is a curiously shaped table with carvings of crocodiles on it. Towards evening an intolerable and very specific smell begins to pervade the house; they stumble over something in the dark; they seem to see a vague form gliding over the stairs – in short, we are given to understand that the presence of the table causes ghostly crocodiles to haunt the place, or that the wooden monsters come to life in the dark, or something of the sort. It was a naïve enough story, but the uncanny feeling it produced was quite remarkable. (244–5)

Just before he relates this tale of a seemingly typical bourgeois domicile infiltrated by the flavour and fauna of the rain forest, Freud tells us that the episode exemplifies what happens 'when a symbol takes over the full functions of the thing it symbolizes' (244). This semiotic explanation is the sum total of his analysis. Though it may seem tangential to the violent confrontation the anecdote details, Freud was not the only theorist to believe that the world of signs and symbols had everything to do with the vexed subject-object relations created by commodity consumption.

In the first volume of *Capital*, Karl Marx describes another table that springs to life. 'It not only stands with its feet on the ground, but, in relation to all other commodities, it stands on its head, and evolves out of its wooden brain grotesque ideas, far more wonderful than if it were to begin dancing of its own free will' (163–4). This behaviour is the result of commodity fetishism, and a definition of value derived by comparing objects with each other rather than by referring to the work that goes into making them.[2] The dancing table exemplifies a tendency to present commodities as 'autonomous figures endowed with a life of their own' (165). Such fetishism 'transforms every product of labour into a social

---

2 'The mysterious character of the commodity form consists', Marx explains, 'in the fact that the commodity reflects the social characteristics of men's own labour as objective characteristics of the products of labour themselves, as the socio-natural properties of these things' (*Capital* 164–5).

hieroglyphic', which it is up to us to decipher (167). Like Freud, Marx privileges a semiotic response to the peculiar animation of commodities. But where Marx only hints at the spell they cast, Freud establishes a categorical distinction between types of commodities by privileging their effects on consumers.

Commodities may enchant us after the fashion of Marx's table.[3] But some of them creep into our dreams, where they become symbols within the unconscious. Freud's emphasis on the 'intolerable' odour produced by the crocodile table implies that such objects appear foreign. They are not only commodity fetishes, but also fetishes in the ethnographic sense. They are things with a life of their own, endowed with thought and meaning in no way contingent on the people who possess or use them. Freud so defines them in order to support a related argument about residues of early man that linger in the modern subject. In our dreams, he contends, the worlds of subject and object cannot be distinguished one from the other.[4] Such fluidity recalls the early moments of child development, as well as the 'magic of art', the fantasies of neurotics, and the animistic religions of certain colonial peoples (*Interpretation of Dreams* 566–7, *Totem and Taboo* 90, 31–4).[5] Europeans of all sorts believe that the boundary between subject and object worlds is unstable but repress that belief, which is why goods become animated in their dreams ('Uncanny' 240, *Interpretation of Dreams* 566).

With this interpretation, Freud converted spatial relations between Europe and its colonies, as well as cultural distinctions between Europeans and the peoples of the larger world, into semiotic components of the unconscious.[6] The uncanny figure of the crocodile table indicated how exotic commodities reminded early twentieth-century Britons of what modern man had once been but could no longer know. Although Freud's analysis disavows any economic implications, we nevertheless may see it as an attempt to resolve the problem posed by Marx when he imagined that

---

3 Bill Brown observes they 'captivate us, fascinate us, compel us to have a relation to them' ('Tyranny' 451).
4 Brown recovers this inflection in Marx's dancing table as well. Its animation enables a 'social relation' between subject and object 'wherein modernity's ontological distinction between human beings and nonhumans makes no sense' ('Tyranny' 451).
5 In 'The Uncanny', as well as in *Totem and Taboo* and *Civilization and its Discontents*, Freud made it increasingly difficult to tell whether this primitive state was a holdover from childhood – 'a piece of infantile mental life that has been superseded', as he put it in *The Interpretation of Dreams* (567) – or an 'animistic state in primitive men, that none of us has passed through . . . without preserving certain residues and traces' ('Uncanny' 240).
6 Fabian describes this denial of 'coevalness' as a chronic feature of ethnographic prose (31).

commodities had begun to think for themselves. Even as we do so, we ought to notice how transforming commodities into symbols enfranchises particular sorts of readers. If treating objects as signs of alienation enables a Marxist style, turning them into residues of primitive belief anticipates a psychoanalytic approach. There are obvious benefits to each technique, but neither will suffice to explain what imports meant to the English mainstream. For this, we must turn from theory to fiction, and specifically to domestic romance. Long before Freud intervened, Victorian common sense stipulated that women provide a buffer between the Empire and the home by organizing the sundry items that found their way from the colonies into store displays and onto pantry shelves. Novels indicated how they might go about doing this.

Nineteenth-century custom 'tended to fix shopping as a female practice', historian Erika Rappaport recounts, which meant a woman's good taste guaranteed that the public differential system of the market would yield the private differential system of the home (180). In holding women responsible for selecting alien objects that would be suitable for display in the parlour, the Victorians did not believe they were placing households at risk. Guided by 'empathies supposedly peculiar to the sex', women seemed especially qualified to mediate between the marketplace and the domestic interior (Riley 46). Department stores laid out like 'an oversized bourgeois home' encouraged their labour with a 'reassuring proliferation of living rooms' stocked with commodities that begged for a woman's touch (Schor, *Bad Objects* 151).[7] Having purchased such items, women required only the most humble of technologies to organize them: 'the box, the cabinet, the cupboard, the seriality of shelves' (Stewart 157).

Arranging objects gave British women a certain authority. Susan Stewart explains that housekeeping was 'a matter of ornamentation and presentation in which the interior is both a model and a projection of self-fashioning' (157). There are few better literary examples of how Victorian women

---

7 Department stores were not the only public collections to encourage and extol the virtues of tasteful arrangement at home. As if appealing for assistance from spectators, 'The Great Exhibition of the Industry of All Nations' presented a scene of 'plenitude and multifariousness [that invited resolution] into a straightforward order' (Richards, *Commodity Culture* 27–8). Coombes notes, further, that by encouraging a synergy between museum and drawing room, and by inviting everyday observers to participate in the organizing of foreign objects, Victorian collections elicited support for imperial commerce as a whole. 'The colonial, national, and international exhibitions . . . were notable for precisely the absence of . . . monolithic structure and an apparent lack of any rigorously imposed control over the viewing space. This semblance of endless choice and unrestricted freedom was an important factor in the effectiveness of these exhibitions in obtaining a broad basis of consent for the imperial project' (112). For more on how department store arrangement interpellated shoppers, see Andrew Miller and Rosalind Williams.

empowered themselves through their domestic collections than the passage in *Jane Eyre* that describes Mrs Fairfax's apartment. It is a 'snug, small room; a round table by a cheerful fire; an arm-chair high-backed and old-fashioned, wherein sat the neatest imaginable little elderly lady . . . nothing in short was wanting . . . there was no grandeur to overwhelm, no stateliness to embarrass' in either apartment or occupant (100). Such evident taste elevates subject and object alike. The unworldly Jane is so impressed that she mistakes Mrs Fairfax for the owner of all Thornfield Hall.

Jane Eyre explains how the skill displayed by a person like Mrs Fairfax could be reproduced. In a gesture not so different from Marx and Freud's semiotic approach to commodities, Brontë treats the appreciation and reproduction of picturesque sketches as a training exercise for the collection of objects.[8] Before she organizes any house, a woman must become an accomplished collector of images. Jane learns to abstract the avian forms she remembers from childhood readings of *Bewick's History of British Birds*, lift them out of their original context, and relocate them in carefully composed drawings of her own. When Rochester asks where these images come from, Jane explains that they emerge '[o]ut of my head', which leads him to imagine her brain as a repository of tastefully arranged objects. 'Has it other furniture of the same kind within?' he inquires (130–1). He may well ask, since Jane demonstrates a knack for interior decorating by walking around the house, sorting and cataloguing its exotic decorations as she goes. 'All of these relics', she recounts, 'bedsteads of a hundred years old; chests . . . with their strange carvings of palm branches and cherubs' heads, like types of the Hebrew ark; rows of venerable chairs . . . stools still more antiquated . . . gave to the third story of Thornfield Hall the aspect of a home of the past' (111). If Rochester's estate is a private museum, Jane is its privileged curator, able to recognize what distinguishes a 'handsome' arrangement of objects even though, as her comments make clear, she knows nothing about such items except how they look together (110).

---

8 Nancy Armstrong shows how Victorian realism taught readers to regard images as privileged representations of the object world. To see the image was to apprehend the object it depicted and at the same time to understand the object world as a more fundamental reality to which images referred. The generalization of this model had the paradoxical effect of making it impossible to see the object world itself, except from a vantage akin to that supplied by images. Distinct from images, 'the real' was also something already seen by them. Image production thus became the first step to organizing and evaluating people, places, and things (*Fiction* 7–28). See also S. Marcus on Jane's special ability to abstract objects and even herself in writing ('Profession').

Brontë points out that strangeness is what makes the attic furniture so fascinating. Recent scholarship can help us to understand why Jane should display an appetite for the unfamiliar. Brontë's heroine appeared at a moment in history when, Lawrence Birken relates, economists were increasingly attentive to consumption. They described a market driven by its shoppers. Marginalist theory turned the classic law of supply and demand on its head: 'desire had replaced productive labor as the origin of value' (Birken 28). Such a gesture enabled the wholesale reconsideration of 'demand [as] a message-sending or production-molding force', placing new and considerable emphasis on the implications of taste in a market economy (Appadurai, *Social Life of Things* 31). In this context, the needs and wants of a largely feminized population of consumers assumed new importance. No longer at the margins of economic life, women shoppers could be described plausibly as organizing a vast system of imperial exchange through their purchases.

It is not wrong to interpret Jane's taste for 'effigies of strange flowers, and stranger birds, and strangest humans beings' as salutary to Britain's overseas trade (109).[9] But even as *Jane Eyre* depicted a heroine eager to perform a service vital to the Empire, Brontë sounded an alarm. Decades before Freud related his crocodile table anecdote from the *Strand Magazine, Jane Eyre* cautioned readers about the effect exotic commodities could have on a body, a warning that appears in the shape of Bertha Mason. Though the narrative of Bertha's downfall remains fragmentary, its arc is unmistakably that of degeneration. She had been attractive enough to lure Rochester into marriage, but since their nuptials her 'pygmy intellect' had been overwhelmed by 'giant propensities' that transformed her into the very antithesis of Jane (323). Enticed by her 'splendidly dressed' appearance during their brief courtship, Rochester eventually found himself married to a woman whose 'vices sprung up fast and rank: they were so strong, only cruelty could check them; and I would not use cruelty', he gravely informs Jane (321; 323) Excessive tastes made her incapable of domestic management; she could not offer Rochester a 'settled household' (322–3).

Though he spares Jane the 'abominable details', Rochester's litany of Bertha's 'intemperate and unchaste' habits, his assertion that 'no professed harlot ever had a fouler vocabulary than she', and his conviction that too

---

9 See David for a thorough reading of Jane's service to the Empire. On the relationship between female authority and imperial ideology, the essay that influences arguments across the board is Spivak, 'Three Women's Texts'.

close contact would leave him vulnerable to the 'contamination of her crimes' all combine to present decadent consumption bred in the tropical environment of the Mason West Indian estate as the accompaniment of sexual perversion (324–5).[10] Bertha's appearance is reminiscent of the 'irregular and unsymmetrical conformation of the head . . . malformation of the external ear . . . tics, [and] grimaces' that Victorian science attributed to sexual dysfunction (Showalter 106). By the time she confronts Jane, a lustful appetite has transformed Bertha into a maniac with a 'discoloured . . . savage face' indistinguishable as 'beast or human' (307, 297). In addition to resembling Britain's sexual dissidents, such an appearance gave Bertha the look attributed to non-European women as Victorian ethnographers photographed them.[11] With their bulging faces and contorted bodies, these figures looked akin to the images of prostitutes circulated by social scientists. As Nancy Armstrong shows, the force of such pictorial representations was to distinguish the 'slim, white, and self-contained figure' of the feminine Englishwoman from figures whose morbidly misshapen features made them seem 'not really women even if they were unmistakably female' (*Fiction* 219). 'Any visual evidence of desire was thus destined to produce fear – not only fear in the body of a woman who aspired to middle-class taste, but fear of resembling other women who did not embody British self-control' (*Fiction* 234–5). By exploiting the connection between sexual excess and racial difference implied by such pictures, Brontë forged a further link between erotic desire, consumer appetite, and the tropical commodities that women had learned to enjoy. Imported goods represented an unacknowledged tie between the primitivism of colonial females and the degenerate lusts of certain European women.

A taste for the tropical, the exotic, and the foreign thus emerges in Brontë's novel as both blessing and curse, the source of a heroine's power as well as the basis for her potential exclusion. The very appetite that enables her to exert influence on the market threatens the femininity that

10 Nature and culture may seem virtually indistinguishable in Rochester's diatribe. He attributes Bertha's madness both to bad genes – the bulk of her immediate family is confined or soon-to-be confined in the asylum (322) – and to a tropical environment that 'physically influenced' him as well (324). We are led to conclude, however, that while Bertha may have been predisposed to degeneration her 'vices' are what truly did her in by his assertion that 'her excesses had prematurely developed the germs of insanity' (323).

11 As Gilman points out, sociology habitually found these features, 'misshapen noses, over-development of the parietal region of the skull, and the appearance of the so-called Darwin's ear', on the bodies of non-European women (243). Sharpe describes Bertha as a woman who 'bears the signs of a plantocracy in the state of decline' (46; see also David 95 and Perera 86).

distinguishes her from peripheral females. When Brontë has Bertha appear dressed in Jane's wedding gown, she not only clarifies the distinction between these two women but also creates grounds for their comparison. Both exhibit a desire for Rochester and the objects his money can buy, but their differing ability to manage such appetite is as clear as Bertha's 'fearful and ghastly' face (297). The image of Bertha incongruously attired in a white gown demonstrates that there is no hiding a loss of self-control and thus reiterates the lessons of popular and scholarly Victorian ethnography, which employed pictorial representation to teach readers how to identify excessive craving with a glance. Fortunately, Jane is a model of the discipline required to cool her love for the 'Tyrian-dyed curtain', 'Parian mantel-piece', and ornaments of 'sparkling Bohemian glass, ruby red' that decorate the Thornfield interior (111). From his first contact with her, Rochester marvels at such control. 'Your pleasures', he notes, 'by your own account, have been few . . . Your garb and manner . . . restricted by rule' (132). To be sure, discipline has scarred Jane, as readers of the novel's opening chapters will conclude, but she shows a keen understanding of why a disciplined appetite is preferable when Rochester offers her a bounty of silk robes and spectacular jewels. Clothe me thus, she warns 'and I shall not be your Jane Eyre any longer, but an ape in a harlequin's jacket' (272).

Maintaining self-control enables Jane not only to manage Rochester's estate, but also to inculcate her discipline in him. Brontë prepares Rochester to receive certain qualities from Jane by stripping him of his land and maiming him in the fire set by Bertha Mason, which leaves him nearly blind. '[P]erhaps it was that circumstance', Jane quietly observes, 'that knit us so very close; for I was then his vision, as I am still his right hand' (475). Through her eyes, Rochester receives a picture of the world whose objects exist in new and normative relation to one another. 'He saw nature', Jane reports, 'he saw books through me; and never did I weary of gazing for his behalf, and of putting into words the effect of field, tree, town, river, cloud sunbeam – of the landscape before us; of the weather round us' (475). As she reproduces her own pedagogical experience, we may imagine that Rochester learns to be guided by the taste that has so handsomely served Jane. It is no accident that as his eyesight recovers, the first objects he sees for himself are the 'glittering adornment' around her neck and the 'pale blue dress' she wears (475–6). He notices the items that make her appearance so neatly understated, the commodities, in short, that reflect and reinforce her power. In this way, *Jane Eyre* lands a decisive blow in the battle between aristocratic wealth and cultural capital that had been waging between the covers of novels since at least the turn of the century. Brontë underscores feminine authority by making it a model for Rochester as well. This does not feminize him, but rather allows him to play the role of good husband. *Jane Eyre* treats a measured appetite as the very essence of a reformed masculinity. Self-control may be modelled by a woman in this novel, but it also redefines what it means to be a man.

By maintaining that the moderate consumption of foreign objects does no harm but is in fact the secret of feminine authority, *Jane Eyre* established a formula for bringing the Empire into the home while containing its influence. As the nineteenth century wore on, however, novelists and social critics alike seemed less inclined to endorse this technique and more likely to portray it as a deliberate disavowal of England's dependence on British commerce. An ever-increasing flow of imports altered dramatically how fiction portrayed relationships among women, their appetites, and the things they consumed.

To wit, Sarah Grand's celebrated 1893 novel *The Heavenly Twins* asks what happens when the primitive comes to seem part and parcel of femininity. *The Heavenly Twins* opens with Evadne Frayling secreting herself away in the library with a collection of scientific tomes (21). Though it recalls the *Bewick's History of British Birds* scene in *Jane Eyre*, Evadne's reading fails to develop her taste in objects, but shocks her with anatomical charts revealing that 'pleasure . . . is the result of the action of living organs' (21). Though located on the inside, the mechanics of desire alter the body's surface. 'Evadne's face recalled somewhat the type of old Egypt', a type simultaneously regal and indicative of those women who could not moderate their excessive appetites (32). Evadne continues to behave in a feminine manner, even though she looks increasingly like a female. Over time, however, deep-seated yearning trumps self-control, female dominates feminine, and Evadne comes to be governed by her cravings. 'My imagination ran away with me', she confesses. 'Instead of indulging in a daydream now and then . . . all my life became absorbed in delicious imaginings' (626–7). Fantastic desires appear an inextricable and inherently unmanageable aspect of personal life. This is not a reiteration of the formula offered by *Jane Eyre*, in which self-control prevented Jane from becoming Bertha. Self-control in *The Heavenly Twins* is simply not available.

In Grand's novel, femininity comes to seem more punitive and regulatory than it ever appeared in Victorian domestic romance. Ann Ardis remarks that New Woman fictions often featured a storyline in which women struggle first to satisfy inchoate and barely expressible longings only to be convinced later on to repress them and conform to a feminine code (51).[12] Women in these turn-of-the-century novels appear terminally 'under construction', according to Joseph Allen Boone (113). Any conclusive sense of self eludes them. They cannot build the comfortingly ordered homes and solidly sympathetic marriages that the heroines of Victorian domestic fiction generated as a matter of course, yet neither are they madwomen to be locked up in an attic. As in *The Heavenly Twins*, heroines move from relationship to relationship until convinced of their inability to contain, satisfy, or even fully articulate desires that seem to demand therapeutic intervention. Reversing the relationship of Jane Eyre to Rochester, Evadne's therapist teaches her moderation. Therapy evolves into courtship, and *The Heavenly Twins* ends with Evadne in her analyst husband's arms, begging him to '[l]et me live on the surface of life . . . And burn the books' (672). Unlike Freud's Dora, perhaps the most infamous of *fin de siècle* heroines, Evadne stays with her doctor, and grants him control over a body whose desires she cannot fathom but is willing enough to repress.

As women lost control of themselves, they also lost control of the places where they had exercised influence. Instead of a domain for women to apply their good taste, the department store appeared yet another sphere for the increase of what Rita Felski terms 'male sovereignty over female desire' (72). The eroticized shopping in Emile Zola's *Au bonheur des dames* is arranged by a manager whose 'entrepreneurial mastery' is equalled only by 'erotic mastery' (Felski 71). His store leaves customers 'breathless and excited, flushed', 'agitated by . . . passion', their 'fingers trembling with desire' and their faces warm with 'sensual joy'. Incited beyond control, 'a pell-mell of ladies arrayed in silk, of poorly dressed middle-class women, and of bare-headed girls' throngs through the store while a 'few men buried beneath the overflow of bosoms [cast] anxious glances'. Female desire appears an insatiable and irrational force in this

---

12 Once writers had located desire within the female subject, women became increasingly defined by such cravings. In his 'Fragment of an Analysis of a Case of Hysteria', Freud presents the ultimate story of a woman whose every expression appears as evidence of inveterate appetite. In Rebecca West's *The Judge*, Ellen Melville's dreams of career and politics – she is a legal clerk and 'a Suffragette, so far as it is possible to be a Suffragette effectively when one is just seventeen' (10) – are no match for her lust for the hunky Richard Yaverland, a wealthy suitor whose bedroom promises to liberate her from the world of work. And Vera Brittain introduces herself in *Testament of Youth* as a woman capable of treating wartime nursing as a kind of foreplay. By cleaning and caring for wounded soldiers, Brittain says she 'came to understand the essential cleanliness, the innate nobility, of sexual love on its physical side' (166).

fiction, Felski notes, which leads one to wonder whether the men who spark it could ever hope to contain it.[13]

If the collapsing distinction between female and femininity challenged and authorized experts to exert new influence over women's bodies and minds, the danger associated with imported goods created opportunities for them to become managers of the domestic sphere as well. Max Nordau's monumental tract *Degeneration* portrayed the interior of the European house as a chaotic array of 'furniture and bric-a-brac . . . dyed in unreal chords of colour', desperately in need of the guiding hand of an interior decorator (11). Instead of providing comfort, everything in the homes Nordau depicts 'aims at exciting the nerves and dazzling the senses' (11). From the same sort of imported materials that Jane Eyre might have used to give Thornfield Hall its soothing ambience, housewives in Nordau's text can only fashion a 'startling' effect as they place 'a gilt-painted couch between buhl-work cabinets and a puckered Chinese table' (10).

Female authors also contributed to the sense that women were no longer capable of organizing a pleasing decorative array. In the third book of *Pilgrimage*, Dorothy Richardson describes the interiors her characters inhabit as 'too full' of uncannily animated objects. 'Things . . . speak', Richardson writes, '[and make a woman] feel like a trespasser . . . breathing in curious odours . . . the strange strong subdued emanation coming from the black grand piano, a mingling of the smell of aromatic wood with the hard raw bitter tang of metal' (448). As Anita Levy notes, Richardson makes 'the house . . . unfit for respectable women' and, in so doing, clears the way for 'domestic managers, nutritionists, teachers, nurses, engineers, and scientists' of all sorts (52, 51).

Professionals even moved in on the historically feminine occupation of consuming. According to Sidney and Beatrice Webb, a common house-wife's standards no longer qualified her to succeed in Britain's markets. The Webbs were among those to lobby for governmental measures to counteract what they characterized as the 'heedlessness of the consuming majority' (201–2). John Maynard Keynes found it necessary to make women better shoppers. Writing in the popular press he hectored 'patriotic housewives [to] sally out to-morrow . . . and go to the wonderful

---

13 Zola was not the only novelist to entertain this question. Radclyffe Hall's *The Well of Loneliness* confirms that aberrant patterns of spending lead to alternative forms of sexuality, and that such habits are more easily stoked than stopped. Hall's heroine Stephen is an inveterate shopper. If sexology and psychoanalysis authorize her desire, Stephen's trouble managing it 'provides a stark illustration of how limited the medical model actually was', writes Halberstam (96).

sales that are everywhere advertised. You will do yourselves good' (*Essays in Persuasion* 152). Keynes's fellow theorist Hazel Kyrk, meanwhile, imagined consumers with so little control over their appetites that they did not understand what they wanted 'in such a way that [they could] select it with exactitude when it [was] displayed in the market' (120). Experts were necessary, the political scientist J. A. Hobson concurred, to assist in evaluating the multifarious goods with which the public was daily confronted. Only professional guidance would enable consumers to 'cease to demand more, and begin to demand better commodities, more delicate, highly finished and harmonious' (375–6).

Such commentary made clear that women of good taste could no longer mediate the relationship between the differential system of market and house. Things appeared too inscrutable, home decorating too demanding, and the appetite that drove consumption too dangerous for women blessed only with a feminine sensibility. In this way, turn-of-the-century narratives chronicling the decline of domestic heroines created the opportunity, the necessity even, for a new kind of consumer to discriminate among the commodities that cluttered the global marketplace.

CONNOISSEURSHIP AND CONNOISSEURS

Modernism identified various failings of women who made nineteenth-century domestic arrangements. Beyond their readily apparent sins of mawkish sentimentality and excessive fondness for picturesque composition, Victorian women were far too easily swayed by middlebrow fashion. Felski finds 'Women's lack of aesthetic distancing' at the heart of modernism's critique (87). In the modernist revision of consumption, intellect tempers appetite and allows the disciplined shopper to resist impulse purchases. The ideal consumer craves objects that stimulate thought, cause puzzlement, and demand careful appreciation. In the modernist aesthetic, the curious, surprising, and strange become valued for the way they make one notice something worthy of potentially intense contemplation. Sometimes novels treat strangeness as a property that becomes intelligible when the object is considered as a thing in itself.[14] Just as frequently the context in which one encounters an object determines meaning and interest. Fascination derives from the object's juxtaposition with adjacent objects in a shop window, its orientation on

---

14 Mao, Brown ('Secret Life'), Banfield, and others document how such an approach dovetails with modernist philosophy.

a full pantry shelf, or its position amidst the décor on a parlour wall. A suggestive comparative field can alter the meaning of everyday objects as well as pieces of art or haute couture. Such fields are not self-generating: they require a guiding hand. Like *Jane Eyre*, modernist fiction links consumption to display. But because modernism credits different sorts of people for organizing its collations, these could not be more different from those privileged in the nineteenth century.

Ulysses contains numerous arrays of commodities whose combination encourages interpretation. Jennifer Wicke directs us to one in the 'Circe' chapter, which is ushered onto the stage by Leopold Bloom. As he plays the role of 'the world's greatest reformer', the 'future chief magistrate' of 'Bloomusalem', Bloom disseminates a cornucopia of splendid objects to his admiring public (15: 1459, 15: 1372, 15: 1547). The list of goods distributed is too long to quote in full, but includes everything from 'Maundy money' to 'loaves and fishes', 'rubber preservatives in sealed envelopes tied with gold thread' to 'cheap reprints of the World's Twelve Worst Books: Froggy and Fritz (politic), Care of the Baby (infantalic)' (15: 1569–85). This is clearly a collection that demands close reading. But where to begin? With the sacrilegious synergy of 'loaves and fishes' and 'Froggy and Fritz'? By organizing subcategories (trashy books, candies and sweets)? Regardless of what readers ultimately do with these objects, Wicke urges us to note that we feel impelled to do *something* with them. Joyce entices us into making 'distinctions, ever shifting' about what objects 'it makes sense to envision in relation to one another, which . . . give off sparks of elective affinity, which . . . look different given what rests on the shelf above or below' ('Appreciation' 398). Even as it provides one context for observing these objects, *Ulysses* encourages us to dream up another.

We cannot help but notice that changing the context in which we perceive them changes these objects in the process. Bloom's version of loaves and fishes is related to without being the same as the New Testament incarnation. According to Bill Brown, lifting an object out of its habitual pattern of exchange and placing it in another is always a transformative experience. It has the tendency to convert objects into more substantial, complexly meaningful things. 'Producing a thing – effecting thingness – depends', Brown argues, 'on a fetishistic overvaluation or misappropriation, on an irregular if not unreasonable reobjectification . . . that dislodges the object from the circuits through which it is what it typically is. Thingness is precipitated as a kind of misuse value' ('Secret Life' 1–2). Regular patterns of consumption conceal thingness.

Misappropriation – distributing loaves and fishes along with rubber preservatives certainly qualifies – gives us a hint of that excess.

Modernist fiction experimented with this process, Brown explains, and Woolf in particular did so repeatedly. *Jacob's Room* stands out for elucidating the thingness of things. This novel is filled with out of place objects. Even commodities for sale are akimbo. The clothing shop window that Fanny eyes is arranged in such a manner that it may prove difficult to imagine using the apparel on display for any usual purpose:

[T]he parts of a woman were shown separate. In the left hand was her skirt. Twining round a pole in the middle was a feather boa. Ranged like the heads of malefactors on Temple Bar were hats . . . And on the carpet were her feet – pointed gold, or patent leather slashed with scarlet. (118)

Dismembered mannequins cannot keep these garments from tempting the consumers who 'feast upon' them (118). Misappropriating things may be marketable, it seems. Indeed Brown argues, with the exception of certain utilitarian devices, we like to imagine that our objects are things. A tendency towards thingness makes objects seem more likely to become part of our lives. Without such metonymic potential, there would be little emotional heft to what is surely *Jacob's Room*'s most powerful scene: the finale wherein Jacob's mother gives voice to her grief by holding out a pair of her son's shoes and asking the rhetorical question, 'What am I to do with these?' (173).

Modernism obviously held no monopoly on idiosyncratic displays and collections, but in privileging the excessive quality of things it did articulate a way of evaluating arrangements that differed from nineteenth-century methods. *Jane Eyre* privileges such qualities as 'quaintness' and 'hush', which Jane discovers amongst the exotic objects that populate Thornfield Hall's attic (109). She compliments Mrs Fairfax's apartment, meanwhile, for its 'demure' and 'snug' feeling, the 'beau-ideal of domestic comfort' (100). In contrast, modernist compositions privileged discomfort.

Consider the formula the art critic Peter Schjeldahl details in the museum house Dr Albert Barnes began to fill in 1925. Founded in Lower Merion Township just outside Philadelphia, the Barnes Foundation has long been thought one of the world's most significant private collections. Like its Victorian precedents the Barnes house joins consumption to display: guided by John Dewey, Barnes collected in order to inculcate in his visitors a particular relationship with objects. Not just art works, it is crucial to observe, but objects of all sorts find themselves arranged in the Barnes's rooms. The result is not calming. Displays in this house are 'startling' and 'striking'. Objects placed adjacent have 'exacerbating effects' on one another.[15] This is desirable, according to Schjeldahl, who relishes every 'thunderclap of audacities, each shattering some conventional expectation' (202). '[A]rrangements that appear chaotic' yield 'aesthetic rapture' and encourage rapt attention (202). 'Scanning this array as if it were a rune', Schjeldahl writes, 'I felt momentarily possessed of a secret that might save the world, on the impossible condition that I could understand it' (203).

Like the objects disseminated by Bloom in *Ulysses* and the garments on display in *Jacob's Room*, paintings in the Barnes become more interesting when provocatively arranged. Matisse's *Le Bonheur de Vivre* may be 'the single most consequential modern painting before "Les Demoiselles d'Avignon"', but if you haven't seen it at the Barnes 'you have no idea' how stunning it really is (Schjeldahl 203). The same effects of combination transform driftwood, armchairs, and a panoply of other items including 'hundreds of School of Paris modern paintings' and 'enough andirons to outfit an andiron museum' (202). Engaging though this smorgasbord may be, it is not for everyone. The Barnes seems designed less for the 'plain people' whose 'experience' of art Dewey wished to cultivate than for experts already in the know. 'Using the Barnes for introductory teaching is like starting a basic arithmetic course with calculus' Schjeldahl observes; 'it's more apt to daunt naive minds than to develop them' (203).

In truth, this collection may teach us less about art than about its architect. Everything Schjeldahl sees appears to him 'pre-considered, pre-loved' by the man who owned it (203).[16] This simultaneously intellectual and intimate bond between collection and collector serves as a reminder that modernist consumption produced a new consuming subject. Schjeldahl gives this figure a name when he notes of the Barnes that 'the over-all level of connoisseurship is sublime, though riddled with

---

15 Things are all so expressive it is a wonder they do not jump off the wall. Art and everyday goods are juxtaposed in ways occasionally 'crudely jokey (two unusually wide wooden chairs beneath two massive Renoir nudes)' and always 'mysterious' (202).

16 Marking goods in this way is one of collecting's primary goals according to Matty Alperton, who writes, 'Like any serious art collector, I have always felt that it was the responsibility of collectors to . . . respect the art in their care . . . By respecting the art, I refer, of course, to displaying it to best advantage [which itself entails making] your collection part of your life. Live with it, look at it, fondle it' (quoted in Price 77).

idiosyncrasies' (202). The quirky and smart consumer whose displays turn objects into things is none other than a connoisseur.

Sally Price explains that the early decades of the twentieth century saw the emergence of a new breed of consumers who described their method as a blend of ' "Discrimination" [that] allows us to distinguish flavors of variable merit; "restraint" [that] adds a consideration for the feelings of others' (10). Though these special qualities echo the careful judgment and sentimentality considered the cultural property of Jane Eyre and her sisters, connoisseurs like Barnes employed them to exacerbate rather than domesticate the exotic and excessive features of consumer goods and art works alike. Connoisseurship accentuated the alien atmosphere that *fin de siècle* critics like Nordau argued had taken hold of the household and its occupants.

Connoisseurs were surely elite, but like other experts they drew their authority not from primogeniture or from wealth but from demonstrated skill. Whether understood as learned or innate – and Price observes that both theories were prominent (17–21) – the highly developed taste of the connoisseur is enough to distinguish him. Sean Latham captures something of this reasoning in the early Oscar Wilde, who 'desire[d] to form his own paradoxical nobility, one founded not in bloodlines or tradition but in the transitory discipline of fashion' (39).[17] It is not, of course, as if class is entirely unrelated to connoisseurship. But as Pierre Bourdieu's famously ambitious cross-section of French society *Distinction* demonstrates, no tripartite class structure will suffice to describe the social stratification entailed by taste. Though connoisseurship is generally bestowed on the 'privileged classes of bourgeois society', the ways such experts distinguish themselves from their brethren makes them appear as different from the run-of-the-mill bourgeois as he is from any mill-worker or lord (*Distinction* 169). In this the connoisseur is kissing cousin to the professional, although he is likely to lack the gainful employment of an expert in economics or medicine. He possesses an aesthetic expertise that does not neatly fit into but nearly always overlaps with circuits of capital accumulation.

In addition to supplementing class and altering consumption, the connoisseur's intervention reconfigures production. He partakes of what Douglas Mao calls the general modernist tendency to conceive 'production as a test of meaning' (21). Origin, vintage, terroir, the tell-tale marks

17 The late Wilde took a different approach according to Gagnier and Nunokawa and denounced 'mere taste' (Gagnier 164; Nunokawa 82).

of convention in some items and the indication of individual creativity in others, all of these components feature prominently in connoisseurial appreciation. Because the connoisseur is the one who draws our attention to such identifiable traits and derivations, these are properties he discovers in an object as much as they are aspects of manufacturing. The novelty that Barnes brings forth from the objects in his collection – andirons as well as paintings – transforms them, supplementing when not entirely displacing any meaning connected to their moment of creation.

There is something alchemical in the effect that a connoisseur has on the objects he touches. Price calls it a '"mystique" that envelops the communion between the world's great art and the world's great connoisseurs' and she finds that it 'intensifies in the case of Primitive Art' (90). Communing with exotic goods reveals a bond between consumer and thing that is simultaneously intimate and global in scale. Nelson Rockefeller epitomizes this as an empathetic 'response to strong feelings'. 'It was not a conscious intellectual effort on my part, or a matter of discipline', he reflects. '[P]rimitive art never seemed strange to me' (quoted in Price 90–1). That such work seems strange to most people but not to Rockefeller implies there may be something strange about him. Primitive objects are 'against everything', as Pablo Picasso put it, but comprehensive antagonism can be a breath of fresh air to the man who declares 'I, too, I am against everything' (quoted in Errington 75). Affinity in antipathy makes Picasso, Rockefeller, and their brethren stand out, and it also provides them with their *métier*. They strove to create a place within modern culture for that which it had tended to exclude. Connoisseurs created space for the *unheimlich* within Europe and North America – in museums, galleries, and private collections – and laboured to prevent it from losing its alien feel.

For an example, we may turn to yet another scene of reading that recalls the *Bewick's History of British Birds* chapter from *Jane Eyre*. In Lawrence's *Women in Love*, Rupert carefully copies the outlines of a 'Chinese drawing of geese' (88). As it did for Jane, reproducing images provides Rupert with a special understanding of things. Instead of teaching him to arrange them in pacifying domestic collections, however, drawing sketches helps Rupert to place goods in a global taxonomy. The quality of his copy combined with the 'skill and vividness' of his technique allow him to grasp what it means to be Chinese, to 'know what centers they live from – what they perceive and feel . . . the curious bitter stinging heat of a goose's blood, entering their own blood like an inoculation of corruptive fire – fire of the cold-burning mud – the lotus mystery' (89). Rupert's sketch abstracts the object from the domestic context in which he finds it, Hermione's boudoir, and drenches it with the 'alien, menacing, and virtually unutterable' qualities that William Rubin infamously identified as the essence of primitive art (259).

Rupert reproduces the habitual connoisseurial paradox of associating sensual immediacy with symbolic abstraction. Just as an oenophile's elevated palate allows him to locate a bottle of Bordeaux on an imaginary map of regional *terroir*, so Rupert's sensitivity to objects like the Chinese drawing allows him to place it within an archive that, in addition to the Chinese 'lotus mystery', also includes the 'putrescent mystery of sun-rays' associated with sub-Saharan Africans and the 'ice-destructive knowledge' belonging to northern Europeans (89, 254). Idiosyncratic but eminently reproducible, Rupert's world system has an analogue in almost every Lawrence novel. It may be compared to the equally idiosyncratic catalogues of cultural essence readers could have encountered in the work of Oswald Spengler or James Frazer.[18] The writer Amit Chaudhuri distinguishes Lawrence's catalogues from those of *The Golden Bough* and T. S. Eliot's 'The Waste Land', however. Where such works use modern methods to compensate for a 'disintegrated past' and fashion a new universalism, Chaudhuri contends, Lawrence evinces zero romance for lost unity. His is a 'romance of lost difference', whose strangeness fiction offers to preserve as such (133).

With such romance in mind we might linger over Lawrence's emphasis on the 'utterly sensual' quality of objects, a phrase that recalls the language of 'sensuous form' found in Walter Pater as well as the art-historical category of the 'Antique'.[19] According to Shelly Errington, 'antique' was a privileged term among early twentieth-century artists and art collectors. Things identified as 'antique' were said to be products of 'sensitive "artists" working in "traditional" modes for "traditional" religious functions, untouched by the market, by filthy lucre, by the restless forward movement of history . . . that will eventually destroy it' (71). Privileged as marketable commodities precisely for their provenance outside the market, 'antique' things might better be regarded as joint products of artists and of the connoisseurs who authenticated them. As it does in the

18 On Lawrence and Spengler, see Shaffer. On 'blood-consciousness', Lawrence, and Frazer, see P. Marcus. And see Lawrence's own essayistic description of global cultures in 'Fantasia' 166.
19 On Pater's aesthetics, see Adams. For Pater, Greek art offered equivalent rewards as Lawrence's primitive. It granted a glimpse of those 'deepest thoughts concerning the conditions of . . . physical and spiritual life' that modernity represses (see Munich 77–8).

Barnes collection, in *Women in Love* the ability to discover an 'antique' says as much about the discoverer as it does about the discovery. Only by displaying a 'feel' for things could Rupert's 'rare faculty of having an instinct for quality' allow him to be recognized as a person of singular taste (Price 11, 21).

Though few Europeans could lay claim to such skill, Lawrence maintained that non-Europeans never forgot how to sense the primitive aspect of things. Commerce outside Europe is different, he reported. It is more about the mixing and meeting of various cultures than the sale and purchase of objects. In 'Mornings in Mexico', he describes a market in which money changes hands, as do goods, but '[o]nly that which is utterly intangible, matters. The contact, the spark of exchange' (52). 'In this transaction', Chaudhuri glosses, 'the relationship between signifier and signified, commodity and value, no longer remains all-important: other things take its place, such as "human contact" and the atmosphere of the market' (141). People feel a connective electricity coursing through even the most banal of commodities, and Lawrence wants his readers to share this relationship with his Mexican shoppers, to feel through the goods they purchase the rich and strange lives of others. If only Europeans could come to appreciate that even the boots on one's feet 'are . . . saturated with . . . magnetism [and] vital activity' ('Fantasia' 164).

In asking his readers to alter their relationship to things, Lawrence encouraged them to collapse the distinction between European consumption and non-European production that Brontë and her fellow Victorians put in place. *Women in Love* demonstrates that appetite changes a person. The exoticism of imported things lets us feel what others feel and, in this exchange, makes us alien to ourselves. Tropical objects are Rupert's 'soul's intimates' (253). With 'thousands of years of purely sensual, purely unspiritual knowledge' behind them, they 'knew what he himself did not know' (253). Paradoxically alien and familiar at the same time, such things testify to 'some kind of miracle', as Fredric Jameson calls it, which makes items 'radically other, whose very being is that which we are not . . . human enough to reflect the human beings perceiving them' (*Sartre* 84). Lawrence treats this as a reciprocal relationship: Rupert's appearance confirms his affinity for exotic things. Sitting before a fire, he is 'motionless and ageless, like some crouching idol, some image of a deathly religion' (196).

There is much of interest in Lawrence's version of consumption, with its account of the strangely primitive connoisseur and with its tendency towards the construction of global catalogues of primitive essence. But it would be wrong to behave as if the set pieces of consumption, appreciation, and display that punctuate *Women in Love* stand alone. Instead, we must acknowledge that they acquire their greatest significance when read in the context of Lawrence's revision of domestic romance.

SEXED UP DOMESTICITY

Lawrence confirms his novel's difference from Victorian domestic fiction by threatening the distinction between feminine and female it worked so hard to secure. *Women in Love* repeats every step of *Jane Eyre*'s cautionary tale, demonstrating how appetite can change a young woman like Ursula Brangwen into a base and lustful female. As Lawrence tells it, however, this story is not about degeneration so much as regeneration. According to *Jane Eyre*, sexual desire and consumer appetite go hand in hand. An immoderate craving for things leads to unchaste behaviour. *Women in Love* agrees, but applauds such behaviour. When the most ordinary of shopping excursions – popping into a store to acquire 'bread, and cheese, and raisins, and apples' – triggers Rupert's 'reality . . . subtle, potent, indiscoverable', Ursula senses that her amour has a bit of the savage about him (319).[20] This does not trouble her, but instead causes a 'strange uplift of elation' (319). Just as his appreciation for exotic objects makes apparent his exoticism, so too gazing upon Rupert's 'dark, subtle reality' brings out the beast in Ursula: 'She too was dark and fulfilled' (319). This exchange could not be more richly complicated, and yet it occurs in the midst of a shopping venture that is thoroughly banal. At the same instant that Ursula is realizing her inner darkness, Rupert is 'throwing some packages into the car' (319). Primitivism and domesticity may appear strange bedfellows, but over the course of his novel Lawrence explains that they are entirely complementary.

The same can be said for love and lust. In Lawrence's lexicon, sex is 'delicate, vulnerable, [and] vital' ('State of Funk' 67). It elicits a 'proper awe of the body's strange experience' that allows early twentieth-century Britons to experience alienation as pleasure ('A Propos' 93). If we have

---

20 Lawrence's adaptation of what the Victorian novel considered a feminine scene of shopping had significant consequences for the category of masculinity, but we would be wrong to summarize these effects as feminization. Femininity and masculinity prove no steadier guides in *Women in Love* than in Brontë's fiction. Where Rochester's education in the conclusion of *Jane Eyre* suggested the revision of the masculine subject, Rupert's appropriation implied a further redefinition not only of masculinity, but also femininity, domesticity, and the techniques of symbolic manipulation that tied these all together in nineteenth-century fiction.

been educated to think otherwise, Lawrence is sure that Victorian fiction is to blame, as it made sex a 'dirty little secret', dirty because secret, and precious for the very same reason ('Pornography' 77). '*Jane Eyre* verges towards pornography', he reports, because such novels treat sex as dirty and worth hiding, and thus turn it into 'a kind of hidden sore or inflammation which, when rubbed or scratched, gives off sharp thrills that seem delicious' ('Pornography' 74, 77). In asking women to contain their desire, Victorian fiction demanded that they think of sex as a physical experience that must be mastered and controlled like any other bodily function. For Lawrence, in contrast, sex is a therapeutic release, the ritualized expression of a vibrantly mongrel humanity.

To understand how sex takes on such meaning, it will be best to observe Rupert and Ursula in action:

She stood in the old yard of the inn . . . Above, she could see the first stars. What was it all? This was no actual world, it was the dream-world of one's childhood . . . The world had become unreal . . . They sat together in a little parlour by the fire . . . And she was drawn to him strangely, as in a spell. Kneeling on the hearth-rug before him, she put her arms round his loins, and put her face against his thighs . . . Unconsciously, with her sensitive finger-tips, she was tracing the back of his thighs, following some mysterious life-flow there. She had discovered something . . . a strange reality of his being, the very stuff of being, there in the straight downflow of the thighs . . . She closed her hands over the full, rounded body of his loins, as he stooped over her, she seemed to touch the quick of the mystery of darkness that was bodily him (312–14)

Several elements in this passage bear comment. First, this scene shows that, unlike his Victorian predecessors, Lawrence was not convinced that the truth of a person was visible on his skin. In contrast to *Jane Eyre*, which made clear that excessive consumption produced changes on the surface of the body, Rupert's self appears as an essence that cannot be seen with the eyes but must be felt with the fingertips.[21] When she touches him

---

21 This is far from the only instance where Lawrence displaces visuality, as L. R. Williams notes in directing us to 'Fantasia of the Unconscious', with its dismissal of sight as 'the least sensual of all the senses' ('Fantasia' 102). In *Lady Chatterley's Lover*, N. Armstrong argues, female orgasm becomes 'the boldest expression of human desire . . . because it happens within the body, but . . . eludes visibility, because what happens on the surface of the body stands in for an entirely different order of events' (*Fiction* 267). Seeing becomes a kind of guilty pleasure in Lawrence's work, North argues. This is especially clear in the poetry he wrote while travelling in South Asia. Visual depiction dominates in a poem like 'Elephant', which leads North to contend, 'What brings Lawrence halfway around the world is a search . . . for a passionate life lived in the blood

with her 'sensitive finger-tips', Ursula treats Rupert the way Rupert treats exotic goods (313). Just as his feel for things makes apparent their occluded nature, her ministrations produce a substance that can only be identified as 'the mystery that was bodily him' (314). Rupert's most authentic self is an amalgam of modern consumer and primitive symbol. He sits 'still like an Epyptian Pharaoh, driving the car. He felt as if he were seated in immemorial potency, like the great carven statues of real Egypt, as real and as fulfilled with subtle strength, as these are, with a vague inscrutable smile on the lips' (318). What Ursula and Rupert have is not ordinary sex, we may conclude, but a ritual every bit as specialized as the connoisseurial appreciation of objects whose technique it borrows.[22]

By claiming that sex is the most basic part of our humanity, that it reveals a repressed connection with antiquity, and then representing it in a syntax of notable obscurity, Lawrence may have been seeking to acquire for his fiction a version of the special authority also being sought by psychoanalysis and sexology.[23] We would do well to identify his novel as participating in what Michel Foucault calls an early twentieth-century 'shift in tactics', in which intellectuals from any number of disciplines helped define sexuality as that which 'constituted the soul's most secret and determinant part' (*History of Sexuality* 124). As much as it collaborates with other disciplines, it would not be wrong to read Lawrence's fiction as being in competition with them, a reading bolstered by the appearance of *Psychoanalysis and the Unconscious* in 1921 (the year after *Women in Love*). In his introduction to this volume, Philip Rieff observes that Lawrence's effort was treated by contemporaries as an attempt 'to supersede the then not very old testament of psychoanalysis' and to put in its place what

---

and not in the cerebral cortex or the eye, and yet when he finds it he can do nothing more than stare' at the Ceylonese subjects who cross his path (*Reading 1922* 124–5).

22 Since the publication of *Women in Love*, readers have puzzled over its sex scenes. They have attempted to understand the practice of touching the 'palpable, real otherness' contained within the human form, and offered various theories of what it means to manipulate a portion of the male anatomy described as the 'suave perfect loins and thighs of darkness' (320, 319). They have noted that it is a woman's job to put her 'arms round [her partner's] loins', to admire 'the beauty of the subjection of his loins', to acquire 'full mystic knowledge' by 'pressing mysteriously over his loins, over his flanks' (313; 181; 318, 316). Though critics have long glossed such passages as Lawrentian vernacular for titillating anal play, Bersani cautions us not to get too attached to any singular interpretation. '[I]t seems silly to argue about what's "really" going on', he concludes in a summary of critical approaches to the sex scenes, 'when in fact all that's going on is some impenetrably mystifying language' (173).

23 It is no accident that such touching takes place in a dream-like setting. Sex is as primal in Lawrence as the unconscious is in Freud. And having sex produces uncanny effects, the blurring of subject and object, sign and thing, much like those Freud discovers in dreams.

continues to strike most readers as 'a bizarre and often incomprehensible new testament in the religion of sex' (vii).

When Lawrence competed with psychoanalysis, he was not alone. Suzanne Clark describes the project of refashioning love into the product of sexual desire rather than stereotypically Victorian sympathy as a typically modernist maneuvre (1–3). In *Women in Love*, Ursula is central to this effort. She eggs Rupert on in his repudiation of couples that live 'the house-keeping way' and who express their affection in the form of 'sentimental cant' (152). She picks Rupert out of the crowd on the basis of 'physical attractiveness' and the 'hidden richness, that came through his thinness and his pallor like another voice' (44). From the very beginning, her assessment of him relies on the combination of enticing surface and primitive depth that proves so very compelling in the novel's sex scenes. 'It was in the curves of his brows and his chin, rich, fine, exquisite curves, the powerful beauty of life itself. She could not say what it was', but is ready to expend considerable energy finding out (44). Her tactics are straightforwardly erotic: in a later scene, to 'show him she was no shallow prude', Ursula held him 'tight, hard against her, and covered his face with hard, fierce kisses of passion' (187). Rather than a road to ruin, as it was in Victorian fiction, Ursula's sexual appetite leads to marriage.[24]

Sex has no more curious effect in *Women in Love* than this. Where it gives Rupert the appearance of a Pharaoh, it turns Ursula into a housewife. Erotic satisfaction helps her settle into domestic rituals she previously avoided: 'She was usually nervous and uncertain at performing these . . . duties, such as giving tea. But today she forgot, she was at her ease, entirely forgetting to have misgivings. The teapot poured beautifully from a proud slender spout. Her eyes were warm with smiles as she gave him [Rupert] his tea. She had learned at last to be still and perfect' (315). That licentious behaviour equips her to be a wife suggests the Victorians only got it half right: satisfying one's appetite does release female nature, but that nature is none other than the essence of femininity.

By refiguring the ideal man and woman, Lawrence's novel revises the sexual division of labour as well. Where Victorian novels such as *Jane Eyre* held women responsible for educating their male partners in techniques of consumption, *Women in Love* treats the man of taste as inculcator of female desire. In a model that Hollywood would eventually standardize and embody in the likes of Cary Grant and Sean Connery, Lawrence

---

24 Their nuptials occur soon after she and Rupert first go to bed.

supposed that men with an eye for exotic things might serve to generate and channel female appetite. Such men teach women that desire can be both tasteful and a little bit dirty, while showing other men that tasteful appreciation is not feminizing but rather represents a robust masculinity. In this way, Rupert and Ursula demonstrate a model in which men of the world cultivate the desires of women well practised at repressing their lusts.

Though such innovation aspires to do away with the Victorian opposition between European feminine and non-European female, it relies on a new distinction that has equally sweeping geopolitical connotations. Lawrence's world is divided between connoisseurs and people with least-common-denominator tastes. In a chapter entitled, 'A Chair', which follows closely on the heels of Ursula and Rupert's pivotal sex scene, Lawrence suggests that his reformed domestic couple might help disseminate an appreciation of the primitive to those whose consumer desires were considerably less imaginative. To Rupert, the connoisseur is as talented as any artist. 'You have to be like Rodin, Michael Angelo', he avers, to find antiquities 'amid the heaps of rubbish' on display at the Monday afternoon jumble sale he and Ursula visit (356, 354). He displays extraordinary aesthetic ability, then, in discovering the piece of furniture that prompts the following reverie:

My beloved country – it had something to express even when it made that chair . . . When I see that clear, beautiful chair, and I think of England, even Jane Austen's England – it had living thoughts to unfold even then, and pure happiness in unfolding them. And now, we can only fish among the rubbish-heaps for the remnants of their old expression. (355)

By granting the chair 'living thoughts', Rupert rewrites Georgian style in a modernist vernacular, demonstrating that the material form of any object has the uncanny ability to bring the dead to life.[25] This passage is also an instance of what Chaudhuri diagnoses as a consistent strategy in Lawrence of refusing 'to acknowledge a fundamental difference between the

---

25 For Lawrence's contemporaries, 'Jane Austen's England' stood for an authentic English style dominated by sparse, clean lines in fiction and furniture alike. Just as 'Austen's streamlined Georgian fiction . . . showed how a new English novel might recover from the Victorian age', early twentieth-century designers recycled Georgian furniture such as Rupert's chair; like him, they offered Sheridan and Chippendale as the answer to garish, cluttered Victorian décor (Lynch, 'At Home' 174). As Lynch reminds us, modernist critics such as the Leavises saw the author of *Persuasion* and *Emma* as the 'property of a minority' privileged in their understanding of the value of organic community and literary style . . . ('At Home' 183).

masterpiece . . . and the ephemeral material object . . . [which] deliberately confus[es] the line that separates tradition and culture from the tastes
and functions of . . . everyday life' (144). We might recall a similar rhetoric
behind the composition of the Barnes Foundation, which features its own
discordant arrangements of chairs and masterpieces. Though Chaudhuri
finds that such strategy brings us 'closer to the atmosphere of the Mexican
market-place than to that of the academic institution' (145), I would argue
instead that Lawrence productively conflates these two. For Rupert and
Ursula, the jumble sale is a sort of museum whose display items may be
debased but which easily satisfy the eye taught to appreciate them.

Purchasing such things is beside the point. Recognizing their value is
infinitely more important, as Rupert and Ursula show when they offer
their newly salvaged antique to a working-class couple that happens to be
frequenting the same sale. The couple recognizes the object as a strange
piece of art rather than a functional thing and, as such, they conclude that
the chair cannot possibly be right for them. 'Why don't you want it for
yourselves, if you've just bought it', they ask warily, 'Frightened it's got
something in it, eh?' (358–9). What follows is a pedagogy in taste, which
Pierre Bourdieu helpfully describes as 'what brings together things and
people that go together' (*Distinction* 241).[26] 'Don't you think it's pretty?'
Ursula asks (360). Her question is necessary because though the two
couples are shopping at the same jumble sale they are not shopping for
the same reason. Ursula and Rupert's consumption puts a premium on
style, and when they seek to pass on the chair they find themselves faced
with consumers more practised at valuing things according to their use.
Lawrence treats this difference as a reflection of qualities within the
human subject as much as simple economics. Taste can be taught because
it depends on an innate if often repressed aesthetic faculty. The capacity
to appreciate the beauty of things is as profoundly human according to
Lawrence as is the recognition of utility according to Marx. When Rupert
and Ursula succeed in persuading their interlocutors to find the chair's
strangeness attractive, they do so in spite of the fact that it is not a useful
item. 'Keep it for an ornyment', the young man says, expressing his
capacity to understand such a thing in the way Rupert and Ursula

---

26 Litvak further advances the thesis that imbuing apparently distasteful material with new appeal is
the habitual task of the sophisticate. '[T]he most advanced or refined taste', he observes, 'would
therefore be, not the "pure" taste that most fastidiously *casts out* the tastes of others, but the
omnivorous taste that most aggressively *incorporates* them, taking them in fantasmatically so as
constitute itself as their *Aufhebung*, as the simultaneous experience and transcendence of them
implied by the term consumption' (61).

understand it (360). Accepting this ornamental object brings about a change in the man's appearance, furthermore. He acquires an 'odd self-consciousness now he had the slim old arm-chair to carry' (361). This transformation reiterates the connoisseur's theme: consumption alters us. It makes even the most ordinary of men appear somewhat odd, exotic, and thus according to Lawrence more human.

There are other instances in *Women in Love* where Rupert similarly attempts to persuade his fellows to make room in their homes for uncanny furnishings, but none is quite so successful. When he tries to teach Gerald to appreciate a woodcarving – 'It is art', Rupert pronounces (78) – he fails miserably. 'You like the wrong things, Rupert . . . things against yourself', Gerald maintains (79). As much as Rupert's esteem for things distinguishes him as a connoisseur, Gerald's resistance identifies him as a man thoroughly inscribed within what Lawrence considers a competing ideology. No universal maleness, no tropical goods for him. Gerald's is a masculinity defined by its rejection of exoticism he deems 'obscene', and 'savage' life he professes to find 'duller, less exciting than the European' (74, 222). When he imports objects, he does not so much appreciate them as forcibly domesticate them. He compels his 'pure-bred' Arab mare to stand in place alongside a moving railway. Not surprisingly, the horse resists, and Gerald responds with brutality. 'He bit himself down on the mare like a keen edge biting home, and *forced* her round. She roared as she breathed . . . But he held on her unrelaxed, with an almost mechanical relentlessness' (111). This is no way to treat a mare, as even the gatekeeper who observes from the margins is able to recognize.

The descriptive language that Lawrence uses to describe Gerald's behaviour links his version of masculinity to the economics of industrialization. Gerald is disinclined toward art and exoticism, but machines fill him 'with a sort of exultation' (222). He is not at home in consumer culture but instead informs Rupert, 'I live to work, to produce something' (56). When he takes over the family coal mine, Gerald devotes all of his passion to putting 'the great industry in order' (227). Retro-fitting the family business requires '[n]ew machinery . . . brought from America' and, after the fashion of Frederick Winslow Taylor, a technique of 'accurate and delicate scientific method . . . [with] educated and expert men . . . in control everywhere . . . [and] the miners . . . reduced to mere mechanical instruments' (230; see Zapf). Both Gerald's philosophy of professional management and Rupert's connoisseurial consumption rely on expert authority and international exchange, but these similarities serve largely to identify the presence in Lawrence's novel of a bluntly schematic opposition between two antithetical economic models. American know-how and Taylorization do not so much establish a contrast between machine and nature, nor one between English and foreign, but rather single out Gerald's competing technique for administering English life in the midst of global commerce. Where Rupert seems inclined to elevate levels of consumption, a tactic that resonates with demand-centred theories of economic development, Gerald struggles to salvage heavy industry.

That these two approaches compete rather than complement one another may be deduced from a brief glance at Taylor's *Principles of Scientific Management*, which describes an administrator blessed with a sense for the inner value of objects that rivals Rupert's own. He 'can see and feel the waste of material things', writes Taylor, as well as the 'awkward, inefficient, or ill-directed movements of men . . . [which] leave nothing visible or tangible behind them. Their appreciation calls for an act of memory, an effort of the imagination' that only the best managers can muster (5–6). To many early twentieth-century British manufacturers and financiers, scientific management was an unwelcome interloper that threatened to encroach on administrative styles derived from Britain's long colonial experience (see Merkle 225). Where connoisseurship, the cultivation of markets in imported goods, and an instinct for overseas investment were bred during an imperial history with no equal, Taylorization depended on the newfound expertise of Britain's global competitors. John Lee, the director of several British telecommunications companies, led the resistance against American corporate theory by invoking a 'human nature too complex for the crude [models] of Scientific Management' (quoted in Guillén 221). Taylorization could not compete with English culture in understanding the vagaries of human subjectivity. Social critics and business executives echoed Lee's claims and appealed to their fellows to preserve 'personal ways of management' and shun the 'inhuman principle' of American organization (Chandler, *Scale* 242). Lawrence would seem to agree. Rupert alleges that Gerald's sort of industrial development makes 'life . . . a blotch of labour' and turns common Englishmen and women into 'insects scurrying in filth' (55). 'No flowers grow upon busy machinery', Ursula muses. 'And all life was a rotary motion, mechanised, cut off from reality' (193).

SEXUAL SELECTION

The context of evolutionary writing will help us to understand why this schematic account is important to Lawrence's novel. *Women in Love* invokes such writing with its description of the miners as 'powerful, underworld men' who could not help but remind readers of the Morlocks, those 'bleached' apes that populate the caves of H. G. Wells's *The Time Machine* (115, Wells 48). Such an allusion links industrial development to degeneration, which the Time Traveller describes as the inevitable result of a process he calls over-civilization, the 'work of ameliorating the conditions of life' gone horribly awry.[27] In Lawrence's version, industrial innovation ends with dehumanization, which can only lead to Britain's decline.

For the concept of degeneration, Lawrence was indebted to a model laid out not only by Wells but also by Thomas Huxley, who himself borrowed heavily from the father of evolutionary thought. In *On the Origin of Species*, Charles Darwin famously outlined two interlocking mechanisms that worked together to keep evolution on track: natural selection, or the 'survival of the fittest', and sexual selection, which 'depends not on a struggle for existence, but on a struggle between the males' for the attention of the females (168, 173). Sexual selection may be 'less rigorous' than natural selection, but remains of at least equal importance. '[I]n many cases', Darwin observes, 'victory will depend not on general vigour, but on having special weapons, confined to the male sex' (174). *On the Origin of Species* provides a host of examples of such special features, from tusks and horns to the less threatening attributes possessed by the 'rock-thrush of Guiana, Birds of Paradise, and some others [that] display their gorgeous plumage and perform strange antics before the females, which . . . choose the most attractive partner' (175).

As Gillian Beer notes, *On the Origin of Species* exudes confidence in the mechanism of sexual selection. In that volume, 'Darwin's account is always upon . . . generation, rather than on [any unpredictable aspect of] sexual desire' (Beer, *Darwin's Plots* 125). By the time he returned to the topic in *The Descent of Man*, however, Darwin appears to have become less sure. The moment when females select the most agreeable partners gives him pause to worry that in certain circumstances their choices will not be for the best. Given a population roughly divided according to sex, he fears, even 'the worst-endowed males will ultimately find females . . .

---

27 The Time Traveller expands on this process as he looks at the devastation surrounding him in the world of the distant future, 'the true civilizing process that makes life more and more secure – had gone steadily on to a climax . . . It seemed to me that I had happened upon humanity upon the wane . . . For the first time I began to realize an odd consequence of the social effort in which we are at present engaged.'

and leave as many offspring . . . as the best-endowed males' (261). Though this makes sexual selection appear a poor means of guaranteeing species health, especially under conditions of relative monogamy, there is a check built into the system. Darwin insists that the more virile mechanism of natural selection ensures that persistent violent struggle will keep the weakest of offspring from surviving long enough for females to become attached to them (278).

Huxley was not sanguine about this solution. His *Evolution and Ethics* reveals little confidence that natural selection will dominate sexual selection. Doubt leads him to jettison Darwin's self-correcting 'cosmic process' in favour of what he describes as a 'horticultural process' governed by an intrusive gardener, a eugenicist who 'restricts multiplication . . . and . . . attempts to modify the conditions, in such a manner as to bring about the survival of those forms which most nearly approach the standard of the useful, or the beautiful, which he has in mind' (14). Nothing vexes Huxley's gardener more than sex, in which the 'mighty instinct' that drives natural selection is undermined by a recognizably feminine 'sympathy' (20, 30). So long as female taste is involved in sexual selection, uneven development can be the only result, as a 'surplus population' of the 'hopelessly diseased, the infirm aged, the weak or deformed in body or in mind' gets reproduced along with the more robust members of the species (21).[28]

This same scenario explains the future depicted in *The Time Machine*. Women pick weak partners with whom they can readily sympathize rather than mate with more virile men from outside their social set. Such inbreeding causes the master–slave relationship to reverse as merely social differences between classes transform into differences between species, with robust Morlocks living below ground and fragile Eloi residing on the ruins of former civilization, consuming whatever their subterranean cousins choose to produce, and occasionally being picked off and consumed by those tunnel-dwellers in return.[29] The Time Traveller recounts,

---

28 According to Huxley, the excessive cultivation of 'sympathy' would blunt natural selection by enabling affection for the weakest souls it was so good at winnowing out (30). He asks his readers to put themselves in the place of nature, to imagine that they have been elected managers of the evolutionary process, and to recognize how the 'golden rule' of sympathy allows the survival of species detrimental to the general welfare. 'What would become of the garden if the gardener treated all the weeds and slugs and birds and trespassers as he would like to be treated, if he was in their place?' (32–3).

29 'The Eloi, like the Carlovingian kings, had decayed to a mere beautiful futility', the Time Traveller reports. 'They still possessed the earth on sufferance: since the Morlocks, subterranean for innumerable generations, had come at last to find the daylit surface intolerable. And the

not a little ironically, 'it seemed clear as daylight to me that the gradual widening of the present merely temporary and social difference between the Capitalist and the Labourer, was the key to the whole position . . . So, in the end, above ground you must have the Haves, pursuing pleasure and comfort and beauty, and below ground the Have-nots, the Workers getting continually adapted to the conditions of their labour' (49–50). In the opening decades of the twentieth century, Wells assured his readers, the 'widening gulf . . . between class and class' is still frequently breached 'by intermarriage which at present retards the splitting of our species along lines of social stratification', but he predicts that such mixing must become 'less and less frequent' (49–50). Unmanaged sexual selection, in short, threatens to turn the 'merely temporary and social difference' of owners and workers into species difference (49).

By thus problematizing reproduction, Huxley and Wells asked a question requiring an administrative answer and created an opening for any number of professional disciplines to intervene. Freudian psychoanalysis was among the most aggressive of all Europe's new specializations in turning degeneration to its advantage. Freud defined neuroses as 'individual solutions' to social problems, thereby granting psychoanalysis the authority to weigh in on matters that otherwise might have been the purview of sociology or political science.[30] When Freud suggests, 'what we call civilization is largely responsible for our misery', he stands ready with a therapeutic cure (*Civilization* 86). Nordau is similarly opportunistic. His five-hundred-plus-page chronicle of the 'disease of degeneracy' culminates in the plan for a new 'Society for Ethical Culture . . . composed of the people's leaders and instructors, professors, authors, members of Parliament, judges, high functionaries' to address the ills *Degeneration* describes (556–8). Huxley's *Evolution and Ethics* itself is a kind of manifesto calling for administrative solutions to social illness evidenced by events such as the 'Great Depression' of the 1870s and 80s, the Trafalgar Square riots of 1887, and ongoing working class demonstrations (Helfand 162).[31]

Morlocks made their garments, I inferred, and maintained them in their habitual needs, perhaps through the survival of an old habit of service' (58)

30 Freud goes so far as to claim that the 'whole history of civilization is no more than an account of the various methods adopted by mankind for "binding" their unsatisfied wishes' ('Claims of Psycho-analysis' 186). He even appropriates Huxley's degeneration thesis, but he does so in such a way to make decline seem like a boon to psychoanalysis.

31 For an overview that also provides extended readings of modernism's affinity for certain strands of eugenic thought, see Childs.

Of all the offers to manage degeneration Lawrence's had the merit of addressing what Darwin and Huxley agreed was its root cause: the disreputable feminine taste so integral to sexual selection and, not incidentally, the privileged object of domestic fiction.[32] *Women in Love* modelled examples of women's judgments both good and bad. In addition to portraying Ursula's selection of Rupert, Lawrence lavishes attention on the poor choices made by her sister. Gudrun agrees with Ursula that expertise is sexy, but the two disagree on what kind of expertise is most desirable. Their differences are as significant as the opposition between them is broadly schematic. Where Ursula is turned on by Rupert's connoisseurship, Gudrun is drawn to Gerald's industrial management. His control of the mines heightens the already considerable appeal of his rippling muscles and the 'vigorous, thrusting motion' he makes when he swims (47). Gudrun is enthralled by the 'foul beauty' of production, the industrial landscape 'silted with black dust' (115). She is captivated by the sight of colliers 'naked down to the loins' and the 'glamourous thickness of labour and maleness, [that] surcharged in the air' (115). It is no accident that when she and Gerald first kiss, they do so beneath the railway where 'the young colliers stood in the darkness with their sweethearts' (330). 'And now', Gudrun gushes, 'the master of them all pressed her to himself!' (330). She mimics those collier sweethearts who 'hang their heads back limp', knocked 'almost unconscious' by the force of their lovers' embraces (330–1).

Though Gudrun gets a certain thrill out of such rough treatment, this passage ought to remind us of that other scene of violence by the railway, in which Gerald beats his Arab mare. By linking these two passages, Lawrence hints that while Gudrun may seem the aggressor in her relationship with Gerald, she is actually its victim. Gudrun comes to this conclusion herself soon enough, when she discovers that sex with Gerald is far from the regenerative pleasure it was for Ursula and Rupert. It is, instead, 'an ecstasy of subjection' (344). One can only lie placidly as Gerald's 'terrible frictional violence' batters and wounds (344). Gerald 'pour[s] all his pent-up darkness and corrosive death' into Gudrun, leaving her to wonder why she wanted him in the first place (344). She is overwhelmed with 'nausea of him' and wishes 'his warm, expressionless

---

32 'It is not too much to say that he built his whole intellectual life on the foundation of this tradition', Williams contends in his analysis of Lawrence's debt to Victorian evolutionary thought (*Culture* 204).

beauty did not so fatally put a spell on her, compel her and subjugate her' (348).

Gudrun's desire for Gerald is not fully her own but is rather the product of some magic that leads even smart wilful women to make bad choices when it comes to men. Her appetite for the 'dangerous underworld' of production is every bit as profound, furthermore, as Rupert and Ursula's craving for the alien and the exotic (115). The barely repressed desire that burns in Ursula with the 'strange brightness of an essential flame' has its counterpart in her sister's 'subterranean desire . . . [a] strange black passion [that] surged up pure' and gave industrial labourers and industrial managers alike an undeniable voluptuousness (9, 287). If Ursula's desire testifies to the regenerative potential of England's exotic cravings, Gudrun's erotic life reveals how an appetite for industry can only damage the English self. Her habit of sexual selection is the surest indication that industrialization positions humanity on the slippery slope to degeneration.

The best evidence for such a conclusion is Gudrun's subsequent object of desire. Though Loerke and Gerald could not appear more different, they share a common fate. Loerke is a man 'further on than we are', as Rupert puts it, 'down some ghastly tunnel of darkness' (428). His tortured shape offers a glimpse of how industrial capitalism contorts the body's exterior to complement the sort of corrupt and corrosive interior Gerald possesses. Though Loerke shares certain characteristics with the Eloi, *The Time Machine*'s degenerate capitalists, he is even less appealing. He is 'an odd little boy-man' with 'small, sculptured feet', 'a wisp of elf-like, thin black hair', 'his body weak and furtive . . . eyes demonical with satire' (468, 433, 468, 471). As Christopher Craft puts it, Lawrence 'works overtime to secure the reader's revulsion' with a series of over-the-top complaints that Loerke 'lives like a rat, in the river of corruption', that he is a 'mud-child', and that he is a 'gnawing little negation' (Craft 179; *Women in Love* 428, 427, 428).

If slumming with Gerald made Gudrun's heart beat faster, Loerke's degeneracy makes her swoon. His mere presence prompts a 'certain violent sympathy' in her, and she 'quivered and flushed' at his dictum that 'Art should *interpret* industry, as art once interpreted religion' (427, 424–5). She is excited by the way he translates all humanity into a vernacular of mechanical production. The sort of 'West African wooden figures' in which Rupert discovers a 'Pure culture in sensation' exhibit for Loerke 'a curious sort of mechanical motion' (448, 79, 448). After spending time with him, even Gudrun takes on the appearance of a machine.

She appears to herself 'like a little, twelve-hour clock'. 'Didn't her face really look like a clock dial – rather roundish and pale, and impassive', she considers. Didn't her 'heart palpitate with a real approach of madness. The terrible bondage of this tick-tack of time, this twitching of the hands of the clock' (465, 464). It is as if lust has transformed her into something akin to the machine woman who stalks Fritz Lang's *Metropolis*. As with Lang's robotic 'sexual vamp,' mechanization gives Gudrun a violent edge (Huyssen, *After the Great Divide* 79–81; Elsaesser 54–6). It lends her a 'diabolic coldness' and makes her threatening to the men who lust after her (442).

Where *Metropolis* burns its cyborg at the stake, *Women in Love* exiles Gudrun to Dresden. The geographic dispersal of the novel's characters at its close helps to clarify the stakes of Lawrence's economic cum evolutionary argument. Gudrun follows Loerke to Germany, which next to the United States posed the biggest threat to British industry. Rupert and Ursula go back home to live in an old mill, the skeletal remains of an older industrial moment in the life of their rural town. And Gerald dies frozen in the Tyrolese Alps, looking over the ridge at the 'great Imperial road leading south into Italy' (478). As his characters migrate, Lawrence delineates a rough and ready international division of labour, with America and Germany defined by their status as manufacturing powerhouses, and Britain struggling to shake off a dying industry in favour of an Empire whose innumerable dangers represented new promise. This was a snapshot of the global economy to complement the equally schematic view from firms in the City of London, whose interest in domestic industry had chilled even as their craving to fund imperial adventures increased (Cain and Hopkins 1: 195).[33]

Unlike their counterparts in the United States and Germany, British bankers and manufacturers never worked well together: 'there was no welding of the joint-stock banks, money markets and Stock Exchange with provincial manufacturing industry', note Cain and Hopkins (1: 191).[34] Their goal was to advise on the industrial pursuits of others

---

33 Partisans of imperial investment in the opening decades of the twentieth century had ample evidence that Britain's manufacturing sector was no longer capable of competing. Old foes in Europe and the Americas were being joined by newly industrializing producers in Asia who moved in on historically British dominated areas like the manufacture of textiles (Kumar). Domestic production of coal was under pressure from the increasingly efficient use of foreign oil (A. J. P. Taylor 182). Because industrial losses were for the time being at least offset by gains in the financial sector, however, 'Great Britain could, as it were, afford both higher unemployment and a higher standard of living at the same time' (A. J. P. Taylor 182).

34 Cf. Anderson, 'Figures', 44; see Arrighi 234–5.

rather than to fund local factories, and to administer a 'growing pluralism of the world economy' whose 'dependence on the financial, trading and shipping services' centred in southeast England (Hobsbawm 51).[35] This dream could only become reality, however, if Britain could find a sufficient number of experts blessed with an intimate knowledge of foreign things to help distinguish between good investments and bad. A. J. P. Taylor describes the slow emergence of a such an ever 'more sophisticated' population, trained to desire products Britain's 'often antiquated' industries could not provide (182–3).

In the small way that banned, sensation-causing novels might, *Women in Love* seems designed to assist in this effort. It offered reasons to choose connoisseurs when engaging in the sexual selection so vital to the evolution of both species and societies. For those inclined to listen, it made plain the advantages of following Ursula and leaning towards an aesthete possessed of considerable experience with exotic goods. And it could not have been more strident in making the case against Gudrun and her choice of the industrial capitalist. *Women in Love* contains numerous instances of Lawrence's eligible bachelors preening before their audience – the better to compare them – but most striking is a passage that also invites readers to reiterate their appreciation for the sort of Primitive sculpture on display in every fashionable London apartment.

The scene's centerpiece is a wooden carving of a 'negro woman in labour', which Rupert describes using his habitual language of intimacy and abstraction (78). He invites us to notice the 'utterly sensual' quality of the sculpture, which reveals the West African work as an exemplar of 'centuries and hundreds of centuries of development in a straight line . . . an awful pitch of culture, of a definite sort' (79). Such treatment of Primitive art is typical. Sally Price contends that 'art in Primitive societies has generally been thought to represent communal ideas conveyed through communally developed modes of expression' (46). This stark contrast to the presumed individualism of European cultural production allowed connoisseurs to cast Primitive societies 'into the mold of an

---

35 Even as its manufacturers lost ground to foreign competition in the beginning of the twentieth century, Hobsbawm observes, 'On the international capital market, Britain remained overwhelmingly dominant. In 1914 France, Germany, the USA, Belgium, the Netherlands, Switzerland and the rest between them had 56 per cent of the world's overseas investments; Britain *alone* had 44 per cent' (51). As Lee puts it, 'The peculiar orientation of the British financial system to international trading services and overseas investments thus provided a handsome balance of payments surplus for and economy running a large and increasing deficit on commodity trade' (114).

artistic counterculture' (47). Primitive cultural deviance appears material-
ized in statuary like that described in *Women in Love*. Since such deviance
most frequently takes a sexualized form, it results in a 'tendency to see in
every breast an obsession with fertility and in every penis a fixation on
eroticism' (Price 47). The figure upon which Rupert gazes is a perfect
example of what Rita Felski dubs the 'prehistoric woman', 'an erotic-
mythic creature, an enigmatic incarnation of elemental and libidinal
forces that exceeded the bounds of reason and social order' and left
European aficionados in absolute thrall (50).

Lawrence's twist on such rhetoric is to place the connoisseur himself
on display. In the midst of his disquisition, Rupert becomes the object
of attention. He stands before us totally naked, 'white and strangely
present', and he is not alone (78). Alongside stand two other men, both
'stark naked' (78). Gerald is here too, although he remains clothed,
puzzled about 'everybody being so deliberately nude' (79). Through his
eyes, we gaze upon the bodies of the other men and, then, at the exotic
statue:

They all drew near to look. Gerald looked at the group of naked men, the
Russian golden and like a water-plant, Halliday tall and heavily, brokenly
beautiful, Birkin very white and immediate, not to be defined, as he looked
closely at the carven woman. Strangely elated, Gerald also lifted his eyes to the
face of the wooden figure. And his heart contracted. (79)[36]

Though all of the men study the carving, Gerald scrutinizes Rupert before
following his friend's eyes. Just like Ursula in the novel's climactic sex
scene, Gerald approaches Rupert the way Rupert approaches primitive
things. But where she touches, he only looks. Looking deeply at Rupert's
flesh leaves Gerald at a loss. Rupert exudes a buzz of sensual immediacy,
but Gerald can no more capture his abstract essence than he can appreciate Primitive sculpture. He never masters the technique of tapping

---

36 See Boscagli on the display of male bodies in this scene (170). As Coombes points out, colonial
sculptures like that Rupert and his cohorts cluster around had a special value for British
intellectuals. They served as three-dimensional Rorschach blots for specialists competing over the
right to interpret Great Britain's apparent decline. '[The] intersection of anthropological, medical
and aesthetic discourse around the issue of degeneration, coupled with the exigencies of the
demands for a professional status for ethnography . . . transformed [African, Oceanic, and Asiatic
artifacts into indicators of national health, symbols] of national pride within Britain' (57).
Lawrence utilizes the 'Fetish' sculpture in precisely this manner, and as much as he directs us to
'look' at the male bodies, he also asks these men to offer a variety of opinions on the object they
happen to be viewing (68).

Rupert's inner wild man as Ursula does. And, in truth, Gerald's impotent stare helps to underscore the productivity of Ursula's touch.

In a role reversal every bit as significant as Rupert's usurpation of the Victorian domestic woman's management of exotic goods, Gerald exercises what evolutionary theory had defined as the feminine duty to single out desirable men. Lawrence's version of sexual selection turns inside out the homosocial triangle famously described by Eve Kosofsky Sedgwick. Instead of calling on a woman to mediate the desire between two men, homoeroticism is a necessary preamble to straight romance. '[S]ubmerged homosexual desire', Craft explains, 'resurfaces in (sometimes extra-urgent) heterosexual guise' guided by a neat rhetoric of 'where man was, there woman shall be' (166). This substitution even appears in the novel's title, Craft observes, 'which silently ingests, all the better to occlude, the open secret of the novel's secret subject: men in love' (166).

Lawrence invokes homoeroticism in a series of chapters that roughly parallel the novel's heterosexual love story, as Rupert encourages Gerald's attention and presses him to become intimate. The integration of these two narratives of courtship further demonstrates how thoroughly Lawrence has revised the domestic romance. Just as he does with Ursula, Rupert goads Gerald to released repressed desire. Gerald resists. When Rupert talks to him of 'Blutbrüdershaft', he does not comprehend – 'We'll leave it till I understand it better', he says 'in a voice of excuse' (206–7). When Rupert says that he finds him 'beautiful', this only perplexes Gerald: 'You think I am beautiful – how do you mean, physically?' (273). Rather than threatening his affair with Ursula, Rupert's pursuit of Gerald supplements their love. At the novel's close, Rupert remains entranced by the possibility of 'eternal union with a man too' (481). What he proposes is not a choice between queer and straight but rather an eroticism in which the possibility of appreciating diverse objects energizes domestic monogamy.

Rupert's free and easy desire confirms that he is a man cut to a different measure than the habitual hero of domestic fiction who, in the culmination of novels such as *Jane Eyre*, incorporates a code of self-discipline modelled by his feminine partner. With its homoerotic subplot, *Women in Love* provides an account of discipline that has a thoroughly masculine source. No passage in the novel works harder to make this point than Lawrence's infamous nude wrestling scene. Just like the sex scene between Rupert and Ursula, this scene too begs to be interpreted in light of early twentieth-century geopolitics. As Sarah Cole argues, it is one of many passages that evoke World War I. 'The fighting in "Gladatorial" . . .

invokes war language, with Birkin repeatedly stressing the intimacy of battle, at the same time that it remains far away from war's actual horrors' (234). Cole detects a similarly loaded idiom in Rupert's mourning over Gerald's deathbed.[37] And this is not the only national allegory that the novel conjures up.

Gerald and Rupert grapple as crude caricatures of their respective modes of capitalism. Gerald stands naked 'with a proper, rich weight on the face of the earth' and moves with a 'rich, frictional kind of strength, rather mechanical' (269). Rupert, in contrast, appears so 'abstract as to be almost intangible' (269). According to the schematic logic that returns throughout this novel, Gerald's 'heavy' body connotes the solidity of industrial production, while Rupert's lithe form has benefited from the consumption of exotica (269). Rupert uses his familiarity with 'Japanese wrestling' to 'imping[e] invisibly upon the other man . . . and then suddenly pierc[e him] in a tense fine grip that seemed to penetrate into the very quick of Gerald's being' (268, 269–70). As happens when Rupert touches primitive things, physical contact demonstrates intimate knowledge. Rupert presses 'upon the other man with an uncanny force, weigh[s] him like a spell put upon him . . . [and] interfuse[s] his body through the body of the other, as if to bring it subtly into subjection, always seizing with some rapid necromantic foreknowledge every motion of the other flesh, converting and counteracting it, playing upon the limbs and trunk of Gerald like some hard wind' (270). Like the animistic priests Freud describes in *Totem and Taboo*, Rupert has the power of 'omnipotence of thought' or mind over matter. Expertise grants him the ability to manipulate Gerald through sheer force of will. In Lawrence's words, 'It was as if Birkin's whole physical intelligence interpenetrated Gerald's body, as if his fine, sublimated energy entered into the flesh of the fuller man, like some potency, casting a fine net, a prison, through the muscles into the very depths of Gerald's physical being' (270). By triumphing in this manner, Rupert demonstrates that knowledge of the exotic is what makes a man strong and, further, that homoerotic play gives him the opportunity to flex his intellectual muscles.

Such exercise is not an end in itself, however, as Lawrence indicates when at the end of the fight Rupert looks at 'the handsome figure of the other man' and finds he is only 'half thinking about the difference between it and himself . . . really it was Ursula, it was the woman who

---

37 In a related argument, Freedman contends that the 'circumstances of the war are, for Lawrence, pretext; the psychology of the war is its substance' (68).

was gaining ascendance over Rupert's being, at this moment' (273–4). The wrestling scene sets the stage for the culmination of Rupert's affair with Ursula by modelling a combination of tactile pressure and exotic knowledge their sex scene will showcase as well. The desire to penetrate and 'touch the quick of the mystery of darkness' that *Women in Love* inculcates in its heroine takes as an example the penetration of one man by another. Ursula's rhetorical question, 'Why not be bestial, and go the whole round of experience?' followed quickly by an exclamation, 'How good it was to be really shameful!' is the ultimate proof that she has learned to see the world as Rupert sees it and to appreciate the primitive sexuality Gerald calls base (413).

Instead of concluding with male desire cut to the measure of sentimentality, therefore, *Women in Love* revises the formula of *Jane Eyre* and generates female desire that is explicitly sexual. According to this revision of the domestic romance, cultural reproduction no longer depends on the civilization of men by tasteful women like Jane, but rather relies on the sexual liberation of women by lustful men. Instead of training men to be sentimental, Lawrence wishes to teach women to engage in thoroughly aestheticized expressions of primal sexuality. Relying on his pet analogy between the subject and the nation, he argues that the future of English culture depends on nothing short of this revolution, on the willingness of ordinary women to 'conquer the fear of sex, and restore the natural flow' ('State of Funk' 68).

As much as *Women in Love* reiterates tropes of degeneration and national decline – comparing the departure of exiles, for instance, to 'lice crawl[ing] off a dying body' (396) – this is a novel that encourages readers to treat such peril as an opportunity. Rupert's closing soliloquy ends on such a note: 'If humanity ran into a cul de sac, and expended itself, the timeless creative mystery would bring forth some other being, finer, more wonderful, some new, more lovely race, to carry on the embodiment of creation' (479). Lawrence explained what his effort to reimagine the love story had to do with such grandiose speculation. 'England is on the brink of great changes', he wrote in 'The State of Funk'. 'What the world of our grandchildren will be, fifty years hence, we don't know. But in its social form it will be very different from our world of to-day. We've got to change . . . make new intelligent adaptation to new conditions . . . give expression to new desires and new feelings' (63). In considering the breadth and potential reach of Lawrence's appeal, it is worth reiterating what *Women in Love* means when it uses the term 'English'. Lawrence presents English culture rightly conceived as a category formed by imperial commerce.

LOCAL PRIMITIVISM

Though it focuses on a select group of characters and is substantially situated in a single Nottinghamshire town, *Women in Love* is national if not planetary in its scope. Lawrence's version of domestic romance has as much to say about changing relations between English culture and British Empire as the Victorian plot it revises. More than the core periphery model of the nineteenth century, however, Lawrence's world vision is invested in locality. His thick description of the Midlands is as full of lived-in detail as Hardy's Wessex or Faulkner's Yoknapatawpha. Not unlike those other writers, Lawrence supplements ethnography with economy. In *Women in Love*, the 'strong intonation' and 'broad dialect' of Beldover is produced in a 'whole atmosphere' of heavy labour that is 'universal in the district, and therefore unnoticed by the inhabitants' (115). Given such attention to regional distinction, it would be incomplete to assert that Lawrence revised English culture without also noting the way his writing helps us to recognize variation within that general category. The global map of cultural essences Rupert imagines does not begin to account for such nuance. Even though *Women in Love* presents him as a model of connoisseurial skill, the novel also lays the groundwork for a far more detailed sense of *terroir* than its leading man seems capable of articulating.

Lawrence distils culture, economic history, and even philosophy from the places he portrays, but this is not the only sort of abstraction going on in his attentive descriptions. As we follow his characters from Beldover to London to the Tyrolese Alps, and as we further connect the locations of *Women in Love* to places visited in Lawrence's travel writing, we follow him in elaborating a world map of local differences. As readers, therefore, we do not confront Lawrence's locations in isolation but always in concert. From the opening of *Women in Love* to the end, we are always on the move. Gudrun's return home is the event that begins the novel; Gerald and Rupert have their first substantial discussion in the early chapter titled 'In the Train'; Rupert and Ursula have sex during a road trip through the countryside; Gerald meets his demise on vacation in the Alps. Things are in motion too: the arrival of machinery from America inaugurates a new period of industrialization in Beldover's mines; the display of statuary imported from West Africa is what lets us know we are in one of London's most au courant quarters; Hermione's desire to instal a new Persian carpet in Rupert's apartment occasions one of several tense discussions leading to that couple's ugly breakup. Such traffic is far from incidental. The global circulation of people and things fundamentally shapes the places the novel depicts.

Women in Love's sweeping assertions about sexuality, subjectivity, and humanity demand to be read in this context, against a backdrop of regions shaped by movement and exchange. Lawrence relies on the local colour of bathing colliers and imported American machinery to define sexuality he finds debased; the urban fashion of exotic décor helps designate the primitive sexuality he would celebrate. To conclude this chapter, I want to spend more time on the question of what it means for sexuality to be so localized. Instead of running over ground already covered in Lawrence, I turn to another modernist novel. Rhys's *Wide Sargasso Sea* takes both early twentieth-century writing and its Victorian precursor as explicit objects of study, and for this reason it is the perfect choice to wind up an argument that began in the middle of the nineteenth century with *Jane Eyre*.[38]

Wide Sargasso Sea recycles certain elements of domestic romance, most significantly, the genre's habit of treating female desire as narrative's driving force. The portion of the story told by the unnamed character whom readers reasonably identify as Rochester follows *Jane Eyre* in associating sexual craving with the female and the primitive, an equation that Rhys does not so much dismiss as localize.[39] Antoinette's degeneration appears congenital, an inheritance both genetic and sociohistorical.[40] Her Creole family is conspicuously excluded from the emergent Victorian landowning class. They are 'marooned', Antoinette's mother

---

38 When Parry reminds us that *Wide Sargasso Sea* focuses on a 'specific settler discourse, distinct from the texts of imperialism', her emphasis is on the 'specific': this is not any settler discourse, but a West Indian one at a pivotal moment in its history ('Problems' 37). Literary context is important too: the connection to *Jane Eyre* is obvious, but Raiskin links the novel to Rhys's earlier work, to Conrad's 'Heart of Darkness', to Michelle Cliff, Albert Camus, and Olive Shreiner. Spivak produces another equally heteroglot textual field – one in which *Frankenstein* figures prominently – and I, of course, would include *Women in Love* (*Critique*).

39 By novel's end, Antoinette appears very much as she does in *Jane Eyre*, transformed into Bertha with her 'hair [hanging] uncombed and dull into her eyes which were inflamed and staring, and her face very flushed and . . . swollen' (146). Rochester feels himself degenerating under her influence: 'the sight of a dress which she'd left lying on her bedroom floor' leaves him 'breathless and savage with desire' (93). Antoinette's efforts to spark Rochester's interest include dosing his cocktail with a drug made by Christophine, her longtime nurse and exactly the sort of native woman that Europeans would associate with primal lust and the black magic likely to induce it. The 'imaginative inheritances' that license Rhys's account of *Obeah* exude what the novelist Wilson Harris calls a 'Caribbean catholicity that includes Haitian *vodun* . . . and many versions or energetic translations of Christianity' (52).

40 Her mother is sent to the 'country' early in the novel, convalescence made necessary by the shock of seeing her dreams of domestic bliss dashed when her estate is burned to the ground and her infant son killed in an uprising among recently freed slaves (46).

laments (26).[41] Alienation leads to insanity, according to Judith Raiskin, who reasons that 'Antoinette's madness can be read as the psychological conflict between . . . desire to belong to opposing communities and . . . recognition that [she] belongs to neither' (111).

It can also be read as evocative of the uncanny, although this too gets localized in the novel's frequent references to zombis.[42] Like so many primitive ideas, the notion of zombification owes at least as much to European conviction about what natives think as to indigenous culture.[43] Raiskin reminds us of the association in West Indian literature between zombification and slavery. 'Metaphorically', she argues, 'the zombi can be seen to represent the condition of both the slave and the colony itself; like the colony, the zombi is a functioning economic body serving the demands of the master while its soul . . . has been forcibly put to sleep' (132). If Freud's story about the crocodile table that comes to life in a London apartment is the perfect uncanny tale for the metropole – where the emphasis is on consumption – stories of zombified labour are exactly appropriate for the colonies – with their equally pronounced emphasis on agricultural production. Even as the novel may be said to invoke such a stark economic geography, however, it also demands that we grapple with the interconnections between these separate spheres.

It does so by way of the tropical figure that perhaps best captures Antoinette's plight: a parrot named Coco whose fiery plunge from the family estate's roof foreshadows Bertha's demise in *Jane Eyre*. In addition

---

41 Burrows writes, 'The earliest definition of the word *maroon*, in use by the early seventeenth century, refers to fugitive or runaway slaves and their descendants in the West Indies, and all other islands of the New World in which slavery was practised. A hundred years later, the term had come to refer to the act of putting a person ashore, leaving him or her on an island or coast as punishment for an infraction on a voyage, abandoned without resources or hope to almost certain death. It is this second usage that Rhys employs as a metaphor for the white creole historical trauma of post-Emancipation' (32). 'From the start, Antoinette and her family exceed mythological racial categories of colonialism', Raiskin argues. 'They spill beyond the confines of white society and are certainly not part of the black society they so recently believed they "owned"' (109). See Wickramagamage for a careful reading of Rhys's racial terminology.

42 Rochester provides us with a definition from a book he is reading entitled *The Glittering Coronet of Isles*: '*A zombi is a dead person who seems to be alive or a living person who is dead*' (107). Although his source attributes the notion to local belief, it notes tellingly that '*negroes as a rule refuse to discuss the black magic in which so many believe*' (107). According to Freud, 'an uncanny experience occurs either when infantile complexes which have been repressed are once more revived by some impression, or when primitive beliefs which have been surmounted seem once more to be confirmed' ('Uncanny' 249). Rhys's novel offers examples of both varieties of uncanny experience. When she was 'still babyish', Antoinette remembers, she was 'sure everything was alive, not only the river or the rain, but chairs, looking-glasses, cups, saucers, everything' (37).

43 Evidence of such unstable provenance appears in the ubiquity of the zombi figure as exhaustively traced by critics such as Burrows, Choudhury, Raiskin, and Wickramagamage.

to his spectacular appearance early in the novel, Coco also pops up in Antoinette's dream towards the end. She hears 'the parrot call as he did when he saw a stranger, *Qui est là? Qui est là?*' (189). As if inspired by the parrot's mimicry, Antoinette begins to transform: 'The wind caught my hair and it streamed out like wings', she dreams. 'It might bear me up, I thought, if I jumped to those hard stones' (189–90). Her avian appearance suggests to Graham Huggan that we might wish to question the critical consensus about what is happening here at the end of Rhys's novel. 'Should we take Rhys's Antoinette for Brontë's Bertha', he asks, 'and interpret the ending of *Wide Sargasso Sea* accordingly as the prelude to an inevitable act of self-sacrifice? Or should we listen to the resurrected Creole parrot? "Che Coco, Che Coco". Answering back, cheekily, to Her Mistress's Voice' (657).[44]

If we interpret Antoinette as mimicking rather than prefiguring Bertha's actions in *Jane Eyre*, we must revise our understanding of what it means to read *Wide Sargasso Sea* as the back story to Brontë's canonical plot. We must reconsider the notion that the Caribbean produces raw material for *Jane Eyre* to work over, in other words, and conclude instead that it represents one of many locations where Brontë's novel itself gets consumed. To make such an argument is to employ a notion of consumption like that I have identified in other fictions, wherein consuming involves appropriation, display, and ultimately transformation. If this reasoning seems persuasive, we may see how *Wide Sargasso Sea* does not reinforce the imperial division of labour between European consumers and colonial producers, but invites reconsideration of that relationship by drawing attention to colonial consumption as well.

Although Huggan singles out Gayatri Spivak as one of the best-known critics too quick to presume that Antoinette must commit suicide, her argument about the setting for *Wide Sargasso Sea*'s final act helps make Huggan's point about Rhys's mimicry. Spivak treats Antoinette's description of Thornfield as a house 'made of cardboard' as an invocation of the actual book that Rhys sets out to rewrite. We can interpret Antoinette as 'having been brought into the England of Brontë's novel', Spivak theorizes, and thus into a 'cardboard house' – 'a book between cardboard covers' – that Antoinette is right to call 'not England' (Spivak, *Critique* 127; Rhys 181).

---

44 Choudhury argues that Bertha's torching of Thornfield Hall appears an exercise in keeping touch with tropical roots, an example of 'how the suicidal burning down of an English manor house should signify West Indianness' (319).

Recognizing the fictive quality of Brontë's England does more than put Rhys's West Indies on a par with that other location. It distinguishes her tactic of describing desire as part of local colour from the standardizing technique of *Jane Eyre* and its Victorian brethren. Because *Wide Sargasso Sea* leaves Thornfield so under-detailed, it signals the importance of fleshing out localities within England to match the texture Rhys's novel gives the Caribbean. There were in fact plenty of writers in the early twentieth century engaged in such an effort to thicken and pluralize English culture. Lawrence was one of these. In my final chapter I treat others who refused to consider English culture the standard by which all civilization should be measured and instead described it as startlingly strange and various.

CHAPTER 5

Local authority after Empire

The writer's only service to the disintegrated society of today is to create little independent systems of order of his own.

Evelyn Waugh

Though major studies of literary modernism offer varying responses to the question 'When was modernism?' they answer in one voice to the sequitur 'Where was modernism?' Raymond Williams's 1989 *The Politics of Modernism* confirmed the critical standard set by such landmarks as Marshall Berman's 1982 *All that is Solid Melts into Air* by treating location as a settled issue. Though the title of Williams's chapter 'Metropolitan Perceptions and the Emergence of Modernism' does not rule out the possibility that modernism might have emerged from other positions, the opening sentence certifies that debate on the issue is closed. Williams writes, 'It is now clear that there are decisive links between the practices and ideas of the avant-garde movements of the twentieth century and the specific conditions and relationships of the twentieth-century metropolis' (*Politics* 37).

One might have expected such prominent fictions as *Sons and Lovers* and *Brideshead Revisited* to check the critical propagation of the 'metropolitan modernism' thesis. That they have not, I hypothesize, can be traced to our sense that country writing is modernism in a minor key, a body of work that pales in comparison to the urban literature at the canon's core. That we persist in thus dividing the field signals an assumption that a stark opposition between rural and urban remains an organizing principle in the twentieth century. It does, but I argue that this geopolitical distinction derives its importance from another opposition, to which it is secondary: a division of labour between native inhabitants and travelling experts.

As Williams explains in *The Country and the City*, in previous centuries representations of a bucolic and unchanging rural milieu served as an antithesis to developments taking place in urban centres and imperial ports. For a growing middle class, the Victorian countryside offered not only a retreat from the worlds of manufacturing and colonial endeavour but also a resource for securing the nation's conceptual foundation. It is tempting to think that this notion of the country persisted, since this would allow us neatly to distinguish a modernism in tune with global commerce from an apparently anachronistic preference for the pastoral.

Indeed, recent scholarship often succumbs to this temptation when it interprets interwar interest in the countryside. A proliferation of guide-books, mysteries set in county seats, and even such elite investigations as Virginia Woolf's *Orlando* – with its imaginative reconstruction of Vita Sackville-West's house, Knole – prop up a literary genealogy in which rural writing represents a conservative reaction to the urbanism of the 1910s and 20s.[1]

But two factors belie this thesis: first, although there was considerable publication about rural locales after World War I, the audience for such work did not appear overnight. Preservationists such as G. Baldwin Brown, political thinkers like C. F. G. Masterman, and novelists such as Mary Webb began to cultivate an audience around the turn of the century.[2] Second, and more importantly, this body of prose did not in the main conceive of Britain's provincial regions as occupying a separate sphere. Rather, writers often depicted a countryside inflected by the same technological, commercial, and geopolitical forces that were reshaping the metropolis.

---

1 Williams describes modernist regionalism as a 'defensive reflex', a knee-jerk response to the 'loss of a credible common world' (*Country and the City* 253). The rural milieux of modernist fiction are '"unspoiled" places' generated by and for urban readers 'under [the] spell of pastures' (253). These are readers who fear the sort of working-class communities that have sprung up in the cities and towns, and whose nostalgia goes hand in hand with 'hatred of the mob, of the unions, of the subverters of "Old England"' (254). Later critics have amplified this association of regionalism with conservatism by describing a modernist rural nostalgia that makes sense only as a retreat in the face of imperial decline. Baucom focuses on nervous and often outright jingoistic fetishizing of places that appear to demonstrate 'the nation's essential continuity over time' (4). Light describes an interest in the local and the domestic that reacts 'against loss and . . . ideological rupture which is marked by the Great War', while Esty identifies a 1930s 'transition in English literature from metropolitan modernism to minor culture' precipitated by a crisis of British imperialism in the interwar era (Light 211; Esty, 'Amnesia' 269). He argues, further, that post World War I England's provincialism in the world economy made it 'newly possible for intellectuals of all kinds to conceive of England as possessing the kind of cultural boundedness, unity, and knowability previously restricted to peripheral regions like Hardy's Wessex or to subject nations like Yeats's Ireland' (*Shrinking Island* 46).

2 I concentrate my attention in this chapter on Webb's popular late novel *Precious Bane*, which was published in 1924. Her earlier writing, such as her collection of essays *The Spring of Joy* and her 1917 novel *Gone to Earth*, reveals a continuing thematic concern and an ongoing commitment to rural setting. On preservation prose, see Matless and Mandler.

Although he is in the critical minority, Robert Crawford rightly contends that modernism's famed metropolitanism and its equally insistent if less heralded attention to the periphery were not opposite but rather complementary tendencies. 'Modernism's cosmopolitanism can be seen as partly the result of "provincial" concerns', Crawford argues. '[A]iming to outflank the Anglocentricity of established Englishness through a combination of the demotic and the multicultural, Modernism was an essentially provincial phenomenon' (270). Modernism brought provincialism to the metropole – in the form of dialect and regional idiom punctuating modernist prose and poetry – and reciprocated by bringing the city to the country – via the cosmopolitanism that frames modernist literature as a whole and shapes the outlook of so many of its characters, no matter where they find themselves.

The social landscape itself revealed a marked reciprocity between rural and urban. Highway projects and electrification forged new ties among parts of the British Isles that had long relied on slower and less reliable commercial and communication networks. Those networks extended far beyond the shores of Britain, moreover, and linked towns small and large into a grid that seemed to stretch around the world. Williams explains that earlier rural idealism tended to occlude such assemblage, and to paper over the 'increasing penetration by capitalist social relations' (*Country and the City* 98). In contrast, writers in the opening decades of the twentieth century focused on development in an effort to take charge of it.

In a 1930 volume entitled *The Face of the Land*, the Council for the Preservation of Rural England and the Design and Industries Association relied on an aesthetic vernacular to document similar troubles of 'ugliness' and 'vulgarity' in spots from Sheffield to Stonehenge to Leicester (Design 9). Whether confronting the 'vexed questions of electric pylons' in the South Downs, the 'evolution of the Underground station' in St James's Park, or the layout of the Imperial Chemical Industries 'factory village' at Billingham, these commentators sought an administrative approach capable of securing distinctions among rural and urban places that were increasingly interconnected (Designs 36, 131, 139).[3] If we are to reconsider the location of modernism, it will be essential to understand the implications of such integration.

---

3 These aims lead Matless to contend that early twentieth-century preservation efforts constituted not 'a conservative protection of the old against the new but an attempt to plan a landscape simultaneously modern and traditional' (25).

This chapter studies how modernist commentators and their contemporaries understood early twentieth-century changes in the nature of locality. I show that novelists, historians, and suburban planners juggled what seemed twin imperatives to demonstrate, first, that global forces were altering the fabric of life within the British Isles and, second, that local culture could accommodate such influence. If these writers agreed that imperial commerce and capitalist expansion had profoundly affected places large and small, they also concurred that rural and urban localities could no longer simply be opposed to one another. Commentators posed the problem of figuring out how local places were related at the same time as they considered how locality could be preserved.

In noting that novels contributed to this effort, we must not overlook their disciplinary distinction. This is no doubt most apparent in the urban fictions *Ulysses* and *Mrs Dalloway*, which challenge readers with literary references and a density of language as different from the scholasticism of social science as the narrative accessibility of travel writing. To help make this comparison, I contrast literary accounts of the city with that appearing in Georg Simmel's sociology. I concentrate on the 'Wandering Rocks' chapter of James Joyce's novel and Clarissa's famed walk through the streets of Westminster in the opening pages of Woolf's narrative. These metropoles serve to highlight the difference between modernism's notion of place and the earlier conception described in *The Country and the City*. Williams observes a rural standard against which the city was defined. Modernism tended to work the other way around, relying on the urban to designate the shape of change in rural regions.

In addition to this reversal, I highlight another. Williams concluded his argument with a description of how the city/country opposition was exported to the colonies. 'Familiar problems of the chaotically expanding city recur, across the world, in many of the poorest countries', he observed.[4] What Williams does not discuss is the reciprocal import of imperial material from those poorest countries to the metropolis. I have highlighted various aspects of that trade in the previous chapters of this

---

4 This was his response to a critical approach that read colonial and postcolonial literature 'through the alienating screens of foreignness and race [and] all too often . . . [took] the particularity of these stories as merely exotic' (288). Though surely an important corrective, Williams reproduces an equally chronic tendency to turn overseas writing into a reiteration of Europe's past. 'We can remember our own early literature of mobility and of the corrupting process of cities', he writes, 'and see many of its themes reappearing in African, Asian and West Indian literature, itself written, characteristically, in the metropolitan languages which are themselves among the consequences of mobility' (288).

book, and now attend to another example of imperial influence by beginning with Dublin, that 'lapsed European capital' as Crawford calls it (252).

There is little doubt that Woolf thought she and Joyce were mining a similar vein. In a diary entry composed soon after she received a copy of his manuscript, Woolf 'reflected how what I'm doing is probably being better done by Mr Joyce. Then I began to wonder what it is that I am doing: to suspect, as is usual in such cases, that I have not thought my plan out plainly enough' (*Diary* 2: 69). Whatever doubts Woolf might have had, it seems clear that she and Joyce offer a common approach to the question of what makes a city feel distinct. Both *Ulysses* and *Mrs Dalloway* treat cosmopolitanism as a boon to local culture and each novel describes a native population that is not less particular for being multifarious.

Such a gesture is also apparent in the rural materials I turn to in the second section of this chapter. Prose about the country portrayed natives whose commerce with the larger world left them no more capable of representing themselves than the colonial subjects who appear in anthropology. Most everyone agreed that sympathetic and observant outsiders could best appreciate the particularity of England's provincial regions, and I treat Rose Macaulay's *Pleasure of Ruins* and Waugh's *Brideshead Revisited* as exemplars of that consensus. Travel writing unites with fiction in attending to the traffic between urban and rural that promises to revamp both. Unlike the conventions of travel writing, however, Waugh's novelistic prose allows him to develop a meta-commentary on the expert observation necessary to track such change. *Brideshead Revisited* reckons that an outsider might well end up going native, as its protagonist does in one of England's more curious county seats.

Throughout this book, I have remarked on the kinship between modernist fiction and anthropology. Each discipline in its own way transmuted the Victorian chiasmus of centre and periphery into an infinitely more complex set of transactions, always in need of management, among diverse localities. By the late 1930s, anthropology had begun to rethink the distribution of this expertise through the project of auto-ethnography. Mary Louise Pratt is perhaps most responsible for reviving interest in this term in recent decades, while James Buzard traces its use to 1938, to debate surrounding the publication of Jomo Kenyatta's *Facing Mount Kenya: The Traditional Life of the Gikuyu* and to 'Mass-Observation, a social research movement devoted to the anthropological study of British culture by ordinary Britons' ('On Auto-Ethnographic Authority' 66).[5] Buzard notes, 'Rather amazingly, this amateurish populist enterprise gained the qualified imprimatur of Malinowski himself, who declared the "Home-Coming of Anthropology" to be the "inevitable [and intended] consequence" of his own path-breaking researches among tribal peoples half a world away' (66). At base, for Buzard, auto-ethnography names the modern movement 'by which Western societies seek to know themselves as "cultures"' (450). Such knowledge cannot help but trouble the status of the knower.

Buzard and other scholars reveal a connection between the narrative work of fiction and that of ethnography. I demonstrate why this must have been a two-way street. Modernist fiction does not simply 'borrow' from auto-ethnography or vice versa; one sort of writing transforms the material of the other when the two collabourate across their differences. In this chapter's final section, I call upon Mary Webb's *Precious Bane* and George Orwell's *Coming Up for Air* to explain that when these novels turn figures we have learned to recognize as social scientific stereotypes – the native informant and the participant observer – into novelistic characters, they refigure the kind of knowledge one might expect to derive from the local as well as implicitly defend the need for a specifically literary expertise to know it. They confirm fiction's aptitude for delineating local particularity in the city, the country, and even in the suburb. Like *Brideshead Revisited*, these novels treat locality as an administrative problem and ask, furthermore, what qualifies someone to represent it. Where travel writing and the Mass-Observation movement sought to disseminate auto-ethnographic authority, in novels the task of fully representing a locality remains an author's function. I will elaborate on this contention, but to take the first step in explaining how fiction distinguished its effort to define local culture, I begin with Joyce's Dublin.

THE CITY AS NEIGHBOURHOOD

The tales told by modernist novelists, critics, and commentators about the status of local culture confirmed that centuries of colonial traffic had introduced new and strange material to Europe's cities and towns and that such commerce had made it difficult to declare the composition of any

---

5 The 'anthropological turn', as Esty calls it, brought a consistency to the terminology employed when describing social life in places that from all outward appearances remained absolutely alien (*Shrinking Island* 2). Anthropology did not discount the stark differences between colonial and metropolitan life, but did offer to articulate them with a related critical vocabulary.

locality autochthonous. But these same writings also suggested that the obliteration of autochthony could engender a new vocabulary of regional distinction. We may see this reasoning at work in representations of the urban locations imperialism was said to have modified most of all. There are no better examples than Joyce's Dublin and Woolf's London. As much as these two places testify to imperialism's influence, it is impossible to overlook what differentiates them within the Empire. But they also show that much links metropolitan life on either side of the Irish Sea. Rereading *Ulysses* and *Mrs Dalloway* together allows us to compare them without assuming that London can be conceived only as the centre to Dublin's periphery.

'Wandering Rocks' has much to teach us about managing metropolitan locales. Enda Duffy notes that two sorts of surveillance frame Joyce's chapter (73). Father Conmee's perambulation starts us off, while the Viceregal cavalcade brings the chapter to a close. As these two authorities move through the streets, Joyce describes denizens who react in far from compliant ways. The cavalcade provides a special impetus to public display – from Tom Kernan's vain greeting, to Simon Dedalus's discreet effort to cover his open fly, to John Wyse Nolan's 'unseen coldness' (10: 1176–282). By emphasizing the idiosyncrasy of local response to such unmistakably British authority, *Ulysses* notes that Dublin is part of a colony while simultaneously revealing variety within the categories 'Irish' or 'colonial'. By demonstrating that the cavalcade's passage has nothing like a singular effect on the natives, *Ulysses* questions what British authority means in this setting and whether the procession gives the impression of a Viceroy in charge of his surroundings.

The Earl of Dudley is not the only one whose authority appears in question. Our mastery as readers is similarly under pressure. In her trenchant review of scholarly attempts to grasp everything that goes on in 'Wandering Rocks', Bonnie Kime Scott observes that part of the challenge lies in the high profile the chapter grants to the most insignificant of players: 'Despite its (almost) central placement, "Wandering Rocks" contains numerous moments of being that enact the marginal experiences of minor characters' (136). This paradox implies a larger truth. 'Wandering Rocks' reminds us that *Ulysses* is composed almost exclusively of marginal characters, famously ordinary figures whose insignificance on the world stage is precisely the point.[6] What counts as the Dublin average, however, is not uniform but rather a mish-mash produced by commerce

6 Manganaro argues that the novel's emphasis on 'average' Dublin life is what keys us into its status as auto-ethnography (106).

with Scotland, England, Europe, and the larger world.[7] Characters walk Dublin's streets fresh from Italy, back from soldiering in India, and on the verge of emigrating to the United States – 'America . . . What is it? The sweepings of every country including our own' (10: 734–5). The languages invoked within the chapter's pages include French, Latin, Gaelic, and Italian, not to mention Joyce's idiosyncratic English (10: 182, 197, 1006, 344). Wildly various commerce takes place in the lapidary shop with its 'lozenges of cinnabar . . . rubies, leprous and winedark stones', at the Empire Theatre where the English comedienne and singer Marie Kendall is scheduled to perform, and in the bookstall where Bloom peruses *Aristotle's Masterpiece* and von Sacher Masoch, not to mention the volume he selects, *Sweets of Sin* (10: 800, 495, 585).

The social fabric that Joyce deduces from this material is, as Michael Tratner puts it, 'radically pluralistic, formed of myriad blocks that are bound together by myriad conflicting "laws" that are constantly shifting' (*Modernism* 184).[8] Because the situation is so fluid, we need to tread carefully when ascribing geopolitical importance to what we read in *Ulysses*. 'Wandering Rocks' in particular refuses to authorize one vantage point, preferring instead to proliferate perspectives capable of shedding light on Dublin ritual and habit.[9] Everybody looks at everybody else.

---

7 This mongrelized populace was a longstanding interest of Joyce's, Manganaro shows. He refers readers to Joyce's 1907 lecture 'Ireland, Island of Saints and Sages', which describes the mingling of 'old Celtic stock' with Scandinavian, Anglo-Saxon, and Norman influences (119).

8 There is, of course, no avoiding nationalism either British or Irish in *Ulysses*: the myriad monuments to Irish nationalism noted through the chapter are hard to miss: they include sites associated with Wolfe Tone, Silken Thomas, and Robert Emmet (10: 378, 409, 765). The 'Returned Indian officer [who b]ravely . . . bore his stumpy body' while begging from Molly reminds us that Ireland demands to be situated in the midst of a broader Empire (10: 756). Klein makes this point with his gloss of the dancing algebraic symbols that move 'in grave morrice' across a student copybook in *Ulysses*'s second chapter (2: 155). As the numbers and letters 'give hands' and 'bow to partner', they create 'a metaphorical community' (2: 156–57; Klein 83). Lest we be tempted to conclude this community is Irish, Klein unpacks the reference: 'The "grave morrice" is not merely Moorish, but the "mummery" of the Morris-dance, a ritual performed in villages in the English Midlands . . . [part of] a tradition that had largely lapsed' (83). By recalling it, Joyce 'implies the possibility of cultural rebirth – here ironically under a British imprimatur' (Klein 83).

9 Instead of discouraging a comprehensive reading, *Ulysses*'s intricacies have long enticed scholars of a mind for totalization. The most thorough-going attempts to master 'Wandering Rocks' date from the 1970s. These include the fold-out chart of times and places compiled by Hart and the maps that accompany Gifford and Seidman's annotations. In the decades since, the masterly aspiration of such projects has been treated with scepticism. Mahaffey's 1988 *Reauthorizing Joyce* describes *Ulysses* as tending towards stylistic and linguistic diffusion that 'has rendered criticism most helpless' (136). Our desire to master *Ulysses* and our urge to note how it exceeds critical containment are two sides of the same tendency. Hart's charts encompass from outside the complexity in which Mahaffey contends we are ourselves encompassed. Either way, we consider every shrug or flourish that appears over the course of 'Wandering Rocks' as part of a cultural

Buck Mulligan spots the city marshal at the Bakery Company, Dilly and Stephen examine one another with glances simultaneously wary and sentimental, Lenehan and Mc'Coy snicker at Bloom behind his back as he shops at the bookstall (10: 497–8). No one is simply an observer, nor is anyone simply observed. Instead, Father Conmee provides the first link in a chain to which each character contributes: he spies the 'gentleman with glasses' on the tram, and speculates on what exactly he might have been telling the woman next to him, as he is simultaneously subjected to a grimace from Mr Eugene Stratton (10: 120–41).[10]

By evoking this dense network of social observation, Joyce depicts his Dubliners organizing their town largely without outside supervision. Whatever else they may be, Father Conmee and Bloom are both amateur city planners. They mull over innovations to Dublin's infrastructure that include Conmee's tramline for 'such an important thoroughfare' as the Circular road, Bloom's hydroelectric plant to catch the tide, 'petropropelled riverboats' for tourists, and bovine trolley for the Cattle Market (10: 73; 17: 1710–43).

Though the novel generously distributes the capacity to observe and to organize, it is equally liberal in disseminating incompetence. Much of the urban development proposed in its pages seems ill-conceived, while potentates and ordinary denizens alike have gaps in their local knowledge. Sometimes Joyce's city dwellers know those they encounter – Father Conmee renews his acquaintance with 'three little schoolboys at the corner of Mountjoy square' (10: 40) – and sometimes they don't – Conmee does not recognize the 'flushed young man' who emerges from a hedge along with a 'young woman with wild nodding daisies in her hand' (10: 199–200).[11] Dublin may have been a smallish colonial town in the early years of the twentieth century, and *Ulysses* may have made it feel smaller still by presenting us with so many interconnected characters, but no one in the place has a complete grasp of everything going on.[12] By

whole – which we describe variously as one of life's 'comically unstable webs' or as a 'spatio-temporal pattern' rendered in the form of a spreadsheet (Mahaffey 191, Hart 215).

10 Some of this does have the feel of surveillance, Duffy is surely right, especially when the observing gaze is that of Conmee or the Viceroy – Ireland's 'two masters' as Stephen calls them (1: 638) – and when the object of their stare is Bloom, whose flânerie we might well recognize as 'evasive action' (Duffy 73).

11 On such limitation, Mahaffey notes 'Joyce's relentless exposure of the easefully oblivious Conmee showcases a double irony: the irony of acting according to one's own lights, a euphemism for acting ignorantly, and of using the unfocused notion of individual lights as a vague defense for one's own ignorance' (119).

12 Lehan points out that in 1904 Dublin had a population barely a fraction of the size of London's. 'Dublin, in fact, was closer to a peasant than an industrial world – a fact Joyce caught nicely in

noting their failure, we also note the emergence of a division of labour. The characters' limited purview serves as an invitation for someone else to put their observations to good use.

Readers have laboured to do so, arguably at Joyce's urging.[13] Buzard argues that readers analyze Joyce's novels the way anthropologists analyze culture, adopting a 'vantage point that we might call an *outsider's inside-ness*' ('"Culture" and the Critics' 52). There is no denying the similarity between the anthropologist's relationship to the native informant and our relationship to the characters whose observations we supplement. Unlike the anthropologist's 'culture' in its observed state, however, *Ulysses* offers a more authoritative description. Unlike the anthropologist's published texts, furthermore, Joyce's description itself demands interpretive activity on the part of its readers. Joyce provides less an explanation of Dublin than the opportunity to reflect on the process of apprehending it. And the seemingly inexhaustible interpretability of *Ulysses* leaves little chance of mistaking this with a more narrowly polemical anthropological approach to the process of cultural apprehension. As Derek Attridge comments, the novel routinely draws attention to its status as a specifically literary document. Joyce habitually foregrounds the aesthetic means through which he generates a persuasive representation of Dublin, emphasizing the 'linguistic and literary processes through which this effect is achieved' (81). Precisely because we understand what has gone into achieving it, we readers know far too well that we cannot reproduce Joyce's labour.

What we can do is to sort through sublime and ridiculous symbols, metaphors, and widely ranging references to literature – English and other-wise. Oblique and overt nods to Odysseus' voyage butt up against puns about passing wind. The gritty realism of colonial life confronts anecdotes caged from bodice-rippers. The symbolic famously intermingles with the

---

Ulysses with the old milkwoman at the beginning of the novel, with Mr. Deasy on foot-and-mouth disease, and with the cattle crossing the street that stop the funeral procession on its way to Glasnevin cemetery' (107). For a model dynamic between the notion of competence and that of expertise, see de Certeau 7.

13 Helped along by the plurality of guides published since Stuart Gilbert's first offering, readers have done such a thorough job of fleshing out Joyce's Dublin that his novelistic version threatens to usurp the actual town. Evidence that modernist copies have gone a long way to authorizing versions of the cities they represent can be found in the social sciences, where Donald asserts the city has taken on a distinctly literary form. 'There is a free migration of images and narratives between archive and library', he attests (187). The urban sociologist Cohen, meanwhile, asserts that a growing attention to what he calls the 'prosaics and poetics' of city analysis has challenged geographers to concentrate their attention on 'lived cultures and narratives through which the daily business of living, loving, working travelling and playing around in the city are conducted' (74–5).

material. The water flowing through a pipe from 'Roundwood reservoir in County Wicklow of a cubic capacity of 2400 million gallons, percolating through a subterranean aqueduct of filter mains' is every bit as important – or trivial – as the various conclusions one might deduce from having Bloom described as 'waterlover, drawer of water, water-carrier' and knowing that he draws this water on returning home at the end of his long day's journey (17: 164–83).

To respond to such juxtaposition we want a provisional means of discrimination, one capable of on-the-fly adjustments. Jennifer Wicke shows how Joyce has provided a model in the form of the 'bookstall placed within its chapters, so that as readers hold the book in their hands they are inevitably repeating the distracted colportage encountered in the text, sometimes literalized as Stephen and Dilly and Bloom's bookstall moments' ('Appreciation' 399). As these characters root through books jumbled together for display on the city street, so we sift through descriptions of people and things.[14] Though we learn from Joyce's characters, these moments are precisely the sort that remind us of what it is to be a reader, flipping more or less attentively through a novel. They are also moments that Franco Moretti argues 'show the . . . absence of order and hierarchies', transforming Dublin into the equivalent of a 'second-hand bookstore' (203). There may be little innate value to much of what Joyce puts before his readers, but there is a good deal that encourages an analytic process capable of ascribing verifiable worth. As any used-book shopper knows, the whole point of trolling through second-hand merchandise is that one person's cast-off is another's rare find. The same can be said of the disorder that one encounters in *Ulysses*.

This labour is eminently reproducible, as we may see by turning to *Mrs Dalloway*. To describe *Ulysses* and *Mrs Dalloway* as collabourators flies in the face of Woolf's antagonism toward Joyce's novel. She famously peppered her diary, letters, and essays with dismissive jabs at the 'poverty of the writer's mind' and characterizations of *Ulysses* as 'terrific in disaster', when not 'pretentious . . . underbred', and the product of 'Genius . . . but of the inferior water' ('Modern Novels' 34, 'How it Strikes a Contemporary' 356, *Diary* 2: 199). Like some contemporary critics, Woolf professed to find the novel 'diffuse'; unlike more recent scholars she found little to like about *Ulysses*'s 'brackish' resistance to systematicity (*Diary* 2: 199). Perhaps most notoriously, she railed against Joyce's 'dull indecency', a

14 See Wirth-Nesher on the way Woolf also puts us in a comparable position to her characters.

complaint that does as much to reinforce an image of Woolf as staid elitist as it does to confirm the stereotype of Joyce as window-breaking provocateur ('Character in Fiction' 434).

Notably, however, the same essays and diary entries also provide good reason to think of *Mrs Dalloway* as being in dialogue with *Ulysses*. These occasional writings show Woolf working on a problem she associated with Joyce and that Ann Banfield describes as the 'multiplication and assemblage of perspectives' (343). Woolf worries about the 'danger [of] the damned egotistical self; which ruins Joyce & [Dorothy] Richardson['s]' attempts to solve the same problem (*Diary* 2: 14). In addition to recognizing a shared endeavour, Woolf discovered in Joyce a common interest in the everyday. 'Let us not take for granted that life exists more in what is commonly thought big than in what is commonly thought small', she wrote in her essay 'Modern Novels'. 'Any one who has read . . . *Ulysses* . . . will have hazarded some theory of this nature as to Mr Joyce's intention' (34).

In *Mrs Dalloway*, readers find a corner of London thoroughly exoticized and populated exclusively with eccentric characters: Peter Walsh just 'back from India', Doris Kilman the German sympathizer, Septimus Smith the shell-shocked soldier with the Italian wife Rezia, the anonymous 'Colonial' who insults the House of Windsor, even Richard Dalloway the 'pillar of the metropolitan establishment' who craves nothing but escape (5, 21). Every intersection throbs with exchange, a good portion of which parallels that observed in the lapidary's shop and the bookstall of *Ulysses*: diamonds 'tempt Americans'; bookstore windows display *Soapy Sponge* cheek by jowl with *Big Game Shooting in Nigeria*; luminous arrangements of exotic blooms flaunt themselves for Clarissa's benefit (7, 12, 15–16). Woolf populates the minds of her characters with thoughts ranging from bitchy complaints about those 'nincompoop' Anglo-Indian women, to memories 'of the dead; of the flag; of Empire,' to longings to reside in 'foreign parts' (10, 21, 32). Such is the local culture of Westminster.

Though Woolf portrays a place that is surely metropolitan, neither she nor Joyce dwell on the unsettling affect that critics have come to associate with life in the city. When Clarissa 'plunges' into the streets she does not perceive their blur and buzz as 'threatening currents and discrepancies of [her] external environment', unlike Georg Simmel who describes urban 'intensification of nervous stimulation' in his classic 1903 essay, 'The Metropolis and Mental Life' (*Simmel on Culture* 175). She takes extraordinary delight in London's 'beating . . . stirring . . . tapping' (7). For her,

Westminster is 'absolutely absorbing', and in a good way, 'loving it as she did with an absurd and faithful passion, being part of it' (ii, 7). Clarissa does not become 'blasé', as Simmel suspects the city dweller must become, in order to protect herself from such stimulation, nor does she throw in her lot with 'the asocial' in a bid to mimic the flâneur described by that other great theorist of modern city life, Walter Benjamin. Rather, like Joyce's Leopold Bloom, Woolf's Mrs Dalloway engages in ad hoc urban planning.[15] Just as in *Ulysses*, characters in *Mrs Dalloway* help give discordant raw material a local feeling and turn a collection of blocks into a distinguishable place. Woolf follows Joyce in taking conditions that commentators had come to associate with urban chaos and converting them into something equally familiar, the city neighbourhood.[16]

The apparent contradiction between the founding theories of the modernist city and its definitive novels is yet another sign of productive collabouration. Taken together, fiction and theory solidified a new way of speaking of the city as, first, what finally does away with the older form of locality the Victorians associated with village life and, second, what paradoxically preserves in its heterogeneity the conditions we associate with the local, namely, irrefutable distinction, knowability, and above all a full-body sensation one can only describe as the 'feel' of a place.

At the risk of collapsing very different intellectual projects, allow me to observe that fiction and theory shared a conviction that the significance of metropolitan life resided in what Benjamin calls 'the new experiences of the city' (*Arcades* 447). Simmel privileges experience as well, crafting what he dubs a 'sociology of the senses': of the eye and its attraction to 'branches swaying in the wind', of the ear 'condemned to take in everything that comes into its vicinity', of the nose and the intimacy of smells (*Simmel on Culture* iii, 114). It is not difficult to see *Mrs Dalloway* as a literary companion to such a critical model, so full is it with the booming

---

15 In a manner indicative of Woolf's approach, even landmarks like Big Ben that might be habitually thought of as representing the nation seem more importantly thought of as part and parcel of a neighbourhood.
16 Woolf plays upon what Buell describes as the 'myth of urban experience' that imagines the twentieth-century city as a substantial degree 'more unstable, challenging, and problematic' than anything humans had experienced before (112). Buell points the finger at Simmel and Benjamin, among others, as the parties responsible for generating this account, but observes that it lives on in literary and cultural criticism to this day. 'Whatever one says about the obsolescence of [these] early treatments of the psychology of urban alienation, disorientation, loss of mastery', he comments, 'clearly they remain precursive of loss-of-mastery discourse in contemporary urban thinking' (112–13). Appadurai makes a similar observation: 'It is one of the grand clichés of social theory (going back to Toennies, Weber, and Durkheim) that locality as a property or diacritic of social life comes under siege in modern societies' (*Modernity* 179).

of Big Ben, the 'strange high singing' of aeroplanes, odiferous tar, 'earthy-garden sweet' flower shops, and throbbing 'motor engines like a pulse irregularly drumming through an entire body' (6, 15, 17). Recent scholarship like that of Banfield and Jesse Matz has done much to solidify our philosophical and aesthetic grasp on the sensory data of modernist fiction, while Sara Danius's technologically inflected reading allows us to understand *Mrs Dalloway,* like *Ulysses,* as a 'modernist monument to the eye and the ear' (149). We can equally confirm Woolf's intervention in sociology by contrasting Clarissa, an active participant in the 'touch-and-go' life of the metropolis, with Benjamin's urban types the 'badaud' and the gawker, an 'impersonal creature . . . no longer a human being [but] part of the public, of the crowd', and Simmel's men and women nervously shielding themselves against outside influence with a 'reserve' so complete they 'do not even know by sight those who have been [their] neighbors for years' ('Paris' 69; *Simmel on Culture* 179).

The act of noticing those neighbours – no matter how ignorantly – remains productive according to Simmel. 'Among the individual sensory organs', he tells us, 'the eye is destined for a completely unique sociological achievement: the connection and interaction . . . that lies in the act of individuals looking at one another' (*Simmel on Culture* 111). Furtive glances and blank stares, inquisitive regards and open-mouthed ogling all contribute to the establishment of a complex structure. As Siegfried Krakauer explains, in Simmel's sociology no instance of sensory perception 'can be extricated from [a] web of social relations, since each is enmeshed in the web with all other such expressions' (232). Simmel writes, 'Every gain in dynamic extension becomes a step . . . for a new and larger extension. From every thread spinning out of the city, ever new threads grow as if by themselves' (*Simmel on Culture* 182).

As Jessica Burstein points out, *Mrs Dalloway* employs a strikingly similar metaphor. Lady Bruton imagines that her luncheon guests remain tied to her by 'thin thread[s] which would stretch and stretch', while somewhat later on in the novel Clarissa extemporizes on the 'odd affinities she had with people she had never spoken to, some woman in the street, some man behind a counter – even trees, or barns' (Burstein 242; *Mrs Dalloway* 124, 169). Though she does not know them – and laments this lack – Clarissa acquires something else through these 'odd' connections, a certain familiarity. On hearing of Septimus's death, for instance, she displays an ability to enter the minds of characters, to reflect on that practice, and to derive a thrill from the identification that results. As she moves through the city and fixes her attention here and there she demonstrates what Wicke calls a way of 'seeing that literally makes and remakes life moment by moment' ('Mrs Dalloway' 13). She is not the only character to thus interpret and order her surroundings, moreover.

As Clarissa walks through Westminster forging links to whatever the day has to offer, her fellow pedestrians join in this habit. They all observe, to take an example reminiscent of the Viceregal Cavalcade from 'Wandering Rocks', an automobile that carries a presumably royal personage from Bond Street towards Buckingham. Sarah Bletchley, 'with her baby in her arms', thinks of the Prince's fealty to his mother (*Mrs Dalloway* 23). 'Tall men' who 'seemed ready to attend their Sovereign, if need be, to the cannon's mouth' stand awkwardly 'in the bow window of White's with their hands behind the tails of their coats' (21). 'Shawled Moll Pratt', meanwhile, 'would have tossed . . . a bunch of roses . . . out of sheer light-heartedness and contempt of poverty had she not seen the constable's eye upon her, discouraging an old Irishwoman's loyalty' (22). Septimus, finally, sees in the stares of his fellow pedestrians a horrifying vision 'about to burst into flames' (18). These idiosyncratic responses indicate the heterogeneity of the local population, but they also represent a collective interpretive activity.

What makes a place, Michel de Certeau reasons, is an 'inward-looking' attitude (108). Though a set of city blocks may be full of alien stuff, recycled matter, the 'world's debris', it is the way such leftovers get localized that engenders a neighbourhood (107). Whatever else the denizens of *Mrs Dalloway* may think of royalty, like the natives of *Ulysses* they all possess a practical knowledge of how queens and princes fit into their daily lives. Just as the Viceregal Cavalcade indicated the colonial status of Joyce's burg, moreover, habitual royal sightings are part of what makes Westminster distinct. Here, one expects to labour, shop, and loiter in the presence of the crown. What the Queen means in Westminster, thus, is not the same as what she means in the world at large.

Signs of the local abound in this novel, although critics have disagreed over how to describe the Westminster populace they encompass. A sky-writing plane creates 'smoke words' that draw everyone's attention (25). Michael North reads them as 'but one of a number of devices . . . [that] knit together subjectivities', and adds that '[t]hese symbols of the public seem only accidentally to contain the very different subjectivities of Mrs Dalloway and Septimus Smith, [since] it is the purpose of the novel to show that these are not distinct' (*Reading 1922* 84). Emily Dalgarno disagrees, contending that the aeroplane 'reveals the heuristic gap between Septimus and other readers of signs' (75). Where their observations pull the plane into the neighbourhood, 'Septimus seems unable to create the position of viewer . . . Rather he hovers on the boundary between subject and object, his body "rooted to the pavement", becoming the object of the gaze' (75). Though she may well be correct, Dalgarno's reading also reinforces North's point that the aeroplane like the automobile defines a population. Through these vehicles Woolf links perspectives, discriminates among them, and establishes a hierarchy of viewers.

While Clarissa at times seems to share the authority of narration, at others her behaviour becomes a text for us to read and interpret. We can return to Big Ben for an example. The clock sounds with a tone that 'wafted over the northern part of London; blent with that of the other clocks, mixed in a thin ethereal way with the clouds and wisps of smoke . . . twelve o'clock struck as Clarissa Dalloway laid her green dress on the bed, and the Warren Smiths walked down Harley Street . . . The leaden circles dissolved in the air' (104). At first blush Big Ben's ringing seems to signal Westminster's integration with the city or nation beyond. Clarissa's familiarity with the bell interrupts this reading. She knows Big Ben so well she can intuit its ring the moment before it sounds. She understands it as her neighbourhood bell. As much as its 'leaden circles' serve to locate her, furthermore, she uses them as a guide. They spark reflection about her capacity to organize the city. 'For heaven knows why one loves it so', she muses, 'how one sees it so, making it up, building it round one, tumbling it, creating it every moment afresh' (6).[17] If the bell places her, Clarissa simultaneously uses it to chart her progress managing a small a corner of the world in her own inimitable way.

There are limits to what Clarissa can do. Though she has the gift of 'knowing people almost by instinct', Septimus is among those who pose a distinct interpretive challenge (11). To look at him is to see a man who 'might have been a clerk', who is clearly 'a border case, neither one thing nor the other' (93). He is nearly impossible to place in a city that 'has swallowed up many millions of young men called Smith; thought nothing of fantastic Christian names with which their parents have thought to distinguish them' (94). All one can say in the end is that 'something was up' with him (95).

While Septimus makes apparent the limits of Clarissa's understanding, Peter Walsh feels even more forcefully constrained. For him, walking the streets of the city involves encountering an ordering presence beyond the

---

17 Though it may represent national discipline, Big Ben also seems to indicate something like a panopticon in reverse. On this sort of reversal, see de Certeau 108.

ken of any single pedestrian. 'It struck him coming back from the East –
the efficiency . . . of London', he thinks. 'Every cart or carriage of its own
accord drew aside to let the ambulance past' (167). In contrast to the
metaphor of an ever extending web of interpersonal relations, passages
like this figure social organization on a larger scale as a substantially
impersonal affair. 'Swiftly, cleanly the ambulance sped to the hospital',
as Peter watches, 'having picked up instantly, humanely, some poor devil;
some one hit on the head, struck down by disease, knocked over perhaps a
minute or so ago at one of these crossings, as might happen to oneself'
(167). Peter senses an administrative force behind this sequence of events, a
force that intervenes in the neighbourhood but is conspicuously not of it.

'Insofar as neighborhoods are imagined, produced, and maintained
against some sort of ground', Arjun Appadurai argues, they require
'contexts against which their own intelligibility takes shape' (*Modernity*
184). Social science describes such contexts as 'social, material, environ-
mental', and surely these terms are relevant for fiction too, but literature
also brings with it a terminology of its own (Appadurai, *Modernity* 184).
Woolf's characters rub up against their own limitations in a manner that
recalls the constraints placed on Joyce's characters and, furthermore, what
Michael Levenson calls a distinctively modernist 'division of narrative
labour' (*Genealogy* 8). This is a division between the richly textured
'consciousness' of first-person narration 'enshrine[ed] . . . as the repository
of meaning and value' and a 'plane of incident' transmitted in some
novels via third-person narrator and implied in those without consistent
third-person narration by scenes like the one involving Peter Walsh and
the ambulance (*Genealogy* 22).[18]

In this hierarchy, characters may 'assume the traditional functions of
the omniscient narrator . . . to direct attention, to interpret incidents, to
evaluate behavior', but they invariably do so 'on a more modest scale'
(*Genealogy* 9). Their authority is always tempered by the idiosyncrasy of
individual perception and predilection, limitations that Woolf and Joyce
are at pains to demonstrate even as they collate and contrast multiple
characters' perspectives. This limit is a strength, since the partiality of each
perspective makes it clearer that we as readers confront what Levenson –
reading 'The Waste Land' – calls a 'system of points of view' (*Genealogy*
185). Faced with such a system, 'We find ourselves in a position to

---

18 It is worth noting that this argument leads Levenson to an investigation of what he calls a
'"psychologistic" theory of literary meaning' rather different from the ethnographic emphasis I
find in the same narrative innovation (21).

confront . . . the problem of . . . unity' without losing 'the plurality of voices that sound in no easy harmony' (*Genealogy* 191). This is a familiar problem for readers of modernist fiction as well as poetry. As much as it is the author's function to put a variety of character perspectives in play, we are used to being called upon to describe the relationship between those perspectives and in so doing to characterize the system in which they are embedded. *Ulysses* and *Mrs Dalloway* supplement this habitual project by localizing it in the neighbourhoods of Dublin and London. Because the characters they assemble are so firmly rooted in place, it only follows that by characterizing the systems of points of view that we find in these novels we characterize the localities in which they are set as well.

Describing in literary terms what otherwise might seem a social scientific hierarchy – between the subjectivity of native viewpoints and the editorial position that assembles such perspectives – helps reveal the distinctive fashion of fiction's engagement in early twentieth-century revision of local culture. Modernism treated what Levenson calls its division of narrative labour as generally applicable and relied on it to represent the particularity of all sorts of settings, not only the urban milieux on which I have concentrated thus far. Levenson discovers its origin, in fact, in Conrad's imperial tales. And we may see its importance to the country estate novel *Brideshead Revisited*, which I treat at the end of the next section. Before approaching that modernist novel, however, I will look at how early twentieth-century writing in general portrayed the country.

MAKING RURAL LOCALITIES

The most efficient way to demonstrate the difference between twentieth-century accounts of rural locations and previous versions of the country will be to take a cursory glimpse at their portrayal of England's ruins. Early nineteenth-century romantic and picturesque writing helped to establish the meaning of decrepit abbeys and cottages as what Anne Janowitz calls 'the ground of nationhood' (119). Wordsworth's 'The Ruined Cottage' and 'Tintern Abbey', among other poems, treat scenes of material decay as imaginative resources that poetry makes available to readers who have 'forfeited their ancient English dower / Of inward happiness' ('London, 1802' 579). The thirteenth book of 'The Prelude' contains Wordsworth's influential formula of a poet standing 'By Nature's side among the Men of old', calling forth 'Objects unseen' from moss and ivy-covered structures (lines 297–304). In romantic poetry,

Janowitz explains, ruins 'subsume cultural and class difference into a conflated representation of Britain as nature's inevitable product' and thus provide 'an historical provenance for the conception of the British nation as immemorially ancient' (Janowitz 4).[19] The thirteenth book of 'The Prelude' demonstrates just this rhetoric as the poet imagines a 'single Briton clothed in Wolf-skin vest', striding 'across the wold' towards Stonehenge (lines 322–3).

For many twentieth-century writers, the alternately sublime and picturesque quality of ruin suggested a contrastingly local past. This era's treatment differed from the romantic one, but it shared an important feature. Like Wordsworth, many rural writers a century later also privileged the viewpoint of the visitor. Commentators thought of themselves as part of a mobile population whose experience comparing places allowed them to appreciate rural variety. Unlike Wordsworth's evocation of a primal Briton, the ruin offered twentieth-century visitors the opportunity to see modern natives: villagers who still inhabited the hinterlands. These residents added a thrilling possibility on loan from more tropical prose: the possibility of going native among the locals.

Rose Macaulay's 1953 *Pleasure of Ruins* offers a perfect example of the era's treatment of ancient piles. She consolidates an account of the 'peculiarly emotion-stirring' sight of 'graceful elegance . . . fallen on barbarous days' (334).[20] Like Wordsworth, Macaulay favours an idiom of haunting, but the ghostly figures she describes evince something both more and less than British spirit. 'In the dull modernity of the biscuit town', she writes, 'in the most banal of public gardens, these massive towering vestiges of greatness strike an alien note of fear and gloom' (354). Though 'demeaned into the pleasure park of a hideous Leeds suburb', the abbey of Kirkstall enshrines an 'ordered beauty' that gives this mundane setting a sense of historical distinction and depth (345). Nationalism, according to Macaulay, has little to do with the world contained in such peculiar spots. Nations, she avers, tend to spend their 'all on weapons, so brutal and barbarous, of war', rather than allocating funds for the 'exquisite expenditure' of satisfying 'our appetite for ruinous beauty' (346). From Macaulay's perspective, the nation enables one to see the globe as territory to be conquered, but it might be better understood as

19 Material on such use of ruins in early nineteenth-century poetry, fiction, and art is extensive. See, for instance, the relevant contributions to Mitchell's *Landscape and Power*.
20 Simmel's 1911 essay 'The Ruin' is an early continental model of this rhetoric; it describes the 'immediately perceived presence' brought on by the sight of decayed buildings (265).

composed of myriad regions filled with curious ruins worthy of detailed observation.

To fully appreciate such geographical heterogeneity requires a focus on historical distinction as well. Every dilapidated church dotting the countryside shelters an eccentric heritage. The ancient chapel at Knowlton Circles, for instance, is heir to an 'age-old sequence of religious buildings standing on the same sites, in the same sacred thickets, through who knows how many wild centuries of strange cults' (336). Instead of bolstering the nation, Macaulay's ruins take their place in a field of regionalized antiquity: 'all over the country manor houses, farms and cottages are haunted with strange intimations from shadowy vanished worlds; long refectories are piled with hay and strewn with agricultural tools; and in cow-house walls are niches where once saints stood' (335). Macaulay links place and past in the town as well as the country. 'In the slums about Oxford railway station', she notes, 'lies the site of the magnificent Osney, beloved of the sixteenth- and seventeenth-century antiquarians' (359). *Pleasures of Ruins* culls together myriad districts of all sizes, but this variance belies a common condition. Every spot on Macaulay's world map marks the presence of a discrete history.

That map stretches far beyond the borders of Great Britain, it is important to note. To fully grasp the 'excessively English' flavour of ruins in Oxford and Leeds, she argues, one must understand what they lack (359). 'What we miss in British church ruins are the fragments of Rome', she contends, which means consulting Italian structures will give us a better grasp of what lies at home (367). A capable observer of the British homeland needs to travel outside it. Macaulay is no slouch, moving as she does from Cartujas to Cochin, and from Syria to Ceylon, balancing a drive to compare with an insistence that every quarter be valued for its own sake. She embeds ruins in elabourate temporal and geographic contexts, 'a romanesque barn amidst . . . orchards, woods and villages', a Cambodian tomb along with the 'golden city of lotus-crowned towers' sprung up around it (368, 377). The result is a differential system whose depth equals its breadth.[21]

---

21 This system itself has a history. As *Pleasure of Ruins* takes us from Tintern Abbey to San Antonio at Tivoli, Macaulay hints that she is not the first globetrotter to bring such varied places together. The well-trodden nature of the routes that she traces implies a longstanding traffic between rural English plots and foreign rustic sites. 'English landscape gardens', she notes, are 'so strangely and so often [decorated with the] elegant and exotic charms' of Chinese antiquities (393).

A wealth of more or less popular writing dating from the earliest years of the twentieth century reiterated a comparable account of rural locality. Preservationist literature, travel writing, and auto-ethnographic speculation elabourated a network of places featuring both deeply rooted history and heterogeneity engendered by centuries of commercial contact with neighbouring villages and faraway realms. Like Macaulay's tome, many earlier volumes modelled techniques for observing such places. Taken as a whole, this body of work may be understood as disseminating the authority to observe local culture. It was joined in this endeavour by Mass-Observation, the interwar boom in hiking and rambling clubs, and the Youth Hostel Association, which encouraged visitors to appreciate the diverse 'countryside under definite rules of conduct' (Matless 94–7).

The preservationist G. Baldwin Brown's 1905 *The Care of Ancient Monuments* is one early entry to urge popular appreciation of England's reconceived countryside. It maintains that the 'worth of a monument . . . does not always reside in its importance for the art or the history of the whole land, but not seldom in its value for a much smaller area, or for the actual place where it stands' (17). At the same time, however, Brown imagines that such discrete localities could have wide appeal. He imagined 'an ever-increasing stream of visitors to this country . . . [eager to] seek out in quiet nooks our ancient monuments' (31). Travel writers avidly rehearsed this line. Volumes such as H. V. Morton's 1927 bestseller *In Search of England* – a compilation of his *Daily Express* columns – drummed up support for travel around a nation composed of infinitely various locales. 'England', Morton informs, 'has the knack of changing her expression in a mile' (196). The BBC broadcaster S. P. B. Mais strikes a similar note in *The Unknown Island*, which relays the impression of 'a country quite startling in its diversities and quick changes' (xiv).[22] Picture volumes like 1945's *How to See the Country* by Harry Batsford further

---

22 Reminding ordinary Britons that they could now reach all corners of the islands was part of Mais's propaganda effort. He primed his audience to take advantage of regions formerly 'remote and inaccessible' that had been made available by the 'remarkable system of motor-coach services which now penetrate every part of the country' (Mais ix). Mais and Morton did not address a solely domestic audience, moreover, for their books appeared in American and colonial editions as well. To a transnational readership, they displayed a nation whose fascination lay in its disintegration. 'It is my very strong belief', Mais confessed, 'that almost every corner of this island is full of interest and beauty, and that it is proximity and accident that bring one area into prominence and leave another unvisited' (viii). The BTA's propaganda sounded a similar note by gathering together seemingly unremarkable if picturesque images in its brochures and thus hinting, as Buzard remarks, that 'substitutes or counterparts might be found "wherever [the tourist] may go" in that country' ('Culture for Export' 123).

educated tourists, while the entrepreneur Harry Peach published 1930's *Let Us Tidy Up* to help them maintain what they saw.

Magazines and guidebooks, clubs and associations all repeated the idea that England's regions were as exotic as any place abroad. 'Those who assert that they prefer continental travel on the ground that they require . . . a complete change, strangeness, and a "foreign" atmosphere', Mais lectures, 'cannot surely ever have explored this island, for the atmosphere of Cornwall is as strange and foreign as that of Hamburg' (xiv). Mais and Morton offer ample evidence that English villages had benefited from longstanding and intimate connection to the larger world. Mais prefers to dwell on traces of European influence. To him Norwich appears 'exactly like Rouen, a higgledy-piggledy medley of very old and very new' (113). Morton, on the other hand, craves traces of Norman invasion. He finds a tower in Ludlow where Marion de la Bruyère may have prayed (197). Both guides remind readers that England was colonized by Rome. Morton, for instance, asks us to observe the 'right-angled streets' of Gloucester as engineering feats of 'the Second Legion of the Roman Expeditionary Force' (188).[23]

Architectural surveys confirmed England's mongrel past. Ralph Dutton notes that over the course of English history most influential designers imported their techniques. '[T]he Duke of Northumberland sent John Shute to study in Italy in 1550 to the great advantage of English taste', he reports, 'Lord Pembroke sent Inigo Jones on the same mission half a century later' (6). A similarly foreign flavour may be detected in gardens. Vita Sackville-West's *Country Notes* depicts grounds blooming with 'new introductions from . . . China, Japan, Tibet . . . South America and Africa' (108). Tropical flowers blossom in pastures where flocks graze 'whose origin has been variously attributed to Syria, Portugal, North Africa, Zululand, Persia, Egypt, and Barbary' (26). Given the prevalence of such mongrel flora and fauna, not to mention the continental styling

---

23 A sense of innate mongrelism was also the point of departure for one of the more influential histories to appear in the early twentieth century. George Macauley Trevelyan's 1926 *History of England* begins with a section titled 'The mingling of the races' and proceeds from the 'commonplace . . . that the British are a people of mixed blood' (1). The model for the *Outline of History* that Mrs Swithin reads in *Between the Acts* was none other than Trevelyan's. It is thus not surprising to discover traces of a colonial past on the landscape around the house where Miss La Trobe's pageant is performed: 'From an aeroplane . . . you could still see, plainly marked, the scars made by the Britons; by the Romans; by the Elizabethan manor house; and by the plough, when they ploughed the hill to grow wheat in the Napoleonic wars' (4). Brenda Silver charts the influence of Trevelyan's volume on this novel and Woolf's unpublished short history, 'Anon'. (Woolf, 'Anon.' 401n1).

of country homes, it may seem unclear what was particularly English about the English regions all of these writers were encouraging tourists to visit.

Auto-ethnographic inquirers took up this question. One of the most notable to do so was Ford Madox Ford, whose 1907 *England and the English* amplifies the argument for English cosmopolitanism by briefly reviewing its history:

England, almost more than any other, is the land that has been ruled by foreigners . . . Almost every continental race – and at least one Asiatic one – can take a kindly interest in English territory, because almost every continental race of importance can say: 'At one time we conquered England.' French, Latin, German, Dutch, Scot, Welshman – all can say it. Even the Spaniards can say, 'Once a King of Spain was King of England.' (254)

From perpetual colonization comes triumph and a decided comfort with the idea of an English society that is not fully English, not completely foreign:

But if you put these facts to an Englishman, he may confess to their truth . . . Nevertheless . . . he will say, 'All these fellows *are* "ourselves". We, being English, have swallowed them up. We have digested them.' (254)

Ford demonstrates the efficacy of English digestion with a series of anecdotes in which a 'touch of the English soil' turns William the Conqueror English; attending 'our school' Anglicizes a Dahomeyan migrant; and a fondness for the imbroglios of district politics makes Joan of Arc 'in spirit, an Englishwoman' (256, 261). In these stories, 'English' appears less the name for a singular population than for a philosophy that embraces the inevitability of heterogeneous mixture. It is thus most appropriate for the English to have, 'shown the nations how mankind, composed as it is of differing individualities, might, with a sort of rule-of-thumb agreeableness, live together in great congeries' (274). In this way, Ford defines English culture not as a primitive essence excreted from the soil of southeast Britain but as a medium that encourages mongrelization. It makes little sense, therefore, to describe English places as either pure or polluted. Ford invites us to contemplate how local distinction is engendered rather than endangered by cosmopolitan exchange. Whether they had fully assimilated this theoretical principle or not, commentators of all stripes extolled the pleasures of a multifarious England.

In treating every ordinary tourist as a potential ethnographer on safari amidst England's mongrel populations, writers revealed they were not afraid to characterize the locals in a manner reminiscent of ethnography's colonial origin. 'We are gradually learning', the political commentator C. F. G. Masterman explains in his 1909 *The Condition of England*, 'that "the people of England" are as different from, and as unknown to, the classes that investigate, observe, and record, as the people of China and Peru' (89). Native Englishmen and women live 'amongst us and around us', he argues, 'never becoming articulate, finding even in their directly elected representatives types remote from their own' (89). As a result, the attentive rural tourist may easily discover in these indigenes the 'most remarkable differences in habits, customs, productivity, and statistics of birth and death' (81).

Having populated the land with English primitives and launched tourists on their way to being amateur ethnographers, it was perhaps inevitable that early twentieth-century commentary would begin to extol the pleasure of going native in the rural regions. The Liberal crusader turned farming columnist H. J. Massingham, for instance, tells a story of developing intimacy in the western hills:

When you first travel Cotswold, its wolds and vales and streams and villages bring the impact of first love, a lyrical delight. Then follows the middle period, when you begin to understand the lay and structure of the land, to find things where you expect, the period of recognition and more familiarity: and perhaps then you become a little used to what you see. But after that comes the last phase and the last love of all, when intimacy reveals a newness unexpected, freshness unexplored, graces undivulged; and this is the love that is both last and lasts, for its fountains are inexhaustible. (quoted in Grace 79)

For Massingham, the observer's attention to geographic details helps him to anchor social habits. In an appropriation of the tried and true literary technique of making setting reveal character, Massingham's method allows him to imagine that however heterogeneous its derivation, English culture still finds perfect complement in bucolic environs. As important as such confirmation may be, it must be said that this passage emphasizes the observer who describes the Cotswold as much as it sheds light on the locality itself. Massingham's tale of going native reminds us that every account of local culture contends at least implicitly with the question of who has the authority to write such a description.

Modernist fiction tended to make that question of authority explicit. Though Massingham champions rural residence, Evelyn Waugh treats it as a sticky business. *Brideshead Revisited* considers what happens to one rural observer who goes native. In this novel, any profit to be gained in settling down is offset by a loss of critical distance. This lesson emerges as Waugh details the changing relationship between Charles Ryder and the estate that he grows to think of almost as his own. In contrast to the nationalist uniformity of type Wordsworth finds in the history of British structures, Waugh gives Brideshead a history as eclectic as Macaulay's ruins. Owned by a wealthy Catholic family, with a 'Painted Parlour', Egyptian obelisk in the garden, and fountain from 'a piazza in Southern Italy', Brideshead is a mongrelized and super-sized version of museum-houses like *Jane Eyre*'s Thornfield (77, 81). Though Ryder could not be more different from the Flyte family in financial situation and religious inclination, he is enthusiastic about their multifarious house: 'It was an aesthetic education to live within those walls, to wander from . . . the Soanesque library to the Chinese drawing-room, adazzle with gilt pagodas' (80).

Ryder makes the leap from observation to participation by decorating one of the house's rooms with a small 'romantic landscape' (82). Then, when the Flytes' second home Marchmain is torn down to 'put up a block of flats', he preserves it in watercolour, which launches an artistic career (217). A string of 'splendid folios' follows, demonstrating his mastery of a plurality of settings, from *Ryder's Country Seats* to *Ryder's Village and Provincial Architecture* (227). Waugh identifies his hero as an active participant in the process of dismantling England into so many distinct pieces, and reassembling it into a virtual composition of expertly depicted localities. Though his books present Ryder as an authority securely among the class of travelling observers, the possessive in their titles suggests something more complicated is happening to him. His relationship to the Flyte estate shows that for Ryder expertise and intimacy are aligned. He is so familiar with the details of their home and their lives, in fact, that he comes to think of himself as more like them than we might have ever thought imaginable. By the end of the novel, he seems as much rightful heir to their estate as he does a specialized observer of regional habit and local style. In the novel's final scene, Waugh presents Ryder's acclimation as a form of conversion. In those final pages, he returns to Brideshead after it has been outfitted as a military base. He walks around the house, considering anew how the Flytes 'enriched and extended' the 'stones of the old castle' that formed the building's foundation. In the midst of his tour Ryder visits Brideshead's chapel, and there says what to him is an unfamiliar 'prayer, an ancient, newly learned form of words' (350). In his mind, he as much as the Flytes belongs on this plot of land.

Though Waugh may have shared his leading man's nostalgia, his novel cultivates detachment from Ryder's situation. Ryder inherits none of the Flytes' former wealth when he appropriates their rituals, repeats their prayers, and extols their questionable taste. By making this clear, *Brideshead Revisited* lends the distinction between expert and native a solidity not apparent in travel writing such as Massingham's Cotswold reverie. Going native is not the same as becoming a native. It implies a change of position, a loss of critical distance, and a decreased capacity to make the value and interest in a place intelligible to others. Ryder ends the novel with a quickened step and a look that causes his second-in-command to observe, 'You're looking unusually cheerful to-day' (351). Though Ryder's subordinate may be in the dark, readers of *Brideshead Revisited* learn that Ryder's intimate relationship to the house is a secret. In a stroke, Waugh demotes his protagonist from the position of authority indicated by his published books of drawings and paintings. Ryder shifts from observer to observed. As the novel wraps up, we find ourselves scrutinizing his behaviour the way we also examined that of Clarissa Dalloway and Leopold Bloom. Whereas guidebooks and treatises on ruins *enact* the stance of the authoritative travelling observer, modernist fiction *depicts* observers of various sorts. Both turn England into a plurality of local cultures in need of descriptive preservation by outsiders, but they reflect differently on what one knows when one describes them.

LOCAL AUTHORITY AND POPULAR CULTURE

Though novelists portrayed figures reminiscent of anthropological stereotypes such as the participant observer and the native informant, they treated every one of them in the manner Levenson describes as typical of modernist character. Capable of performing some of the functions associated with the omniscient narrators of Victorian fiction, these figures 'direct attention . . . interpret incidents . . . [and] evaluate behavior', but their labour also serves to excite the interest of readers ready to interpret what modernist characters put before them (Levenson, *Genealogy* 9). In this last section, I offer two final examples of this relation: Orwell's *Coming Up for Air*, which extends my survey of early twentieth-century localities to the suburbs, and Webb's under-read bildungsroman *Precious Bane*. Where anthropology's author function made local cultures available by yoking together the personae of the fieldworker and the writer for a reader who could appreciate the labour of each, these last literary examples help to clarify literature's different approach. Modernism's portrayal of locality hinged on an author's capacity to represent a variety of local perspectives and to mobilize a reader to recognize regional distinction in such fictional points of view. Both in our era and in the age of modernism proper, there were plenty of readers willing to play their part in this division of labour.

The audience that treated fiction as such a resource included the Tory Prime Minister Stanley Baldwin, who in the late 1920s went out of his way to associate his administration with Webb's novels. Baldwin turned to Webb as he was trying to contain the fallout from one of the most significant development schemes England had ever witnessed. As the historian Peter Mandler observes, 'Baldwin presided over a massive road-building and electrification programme that shredded the countryside' (241). In what demands to be read as an attempt to diffuse opposition to such infrastructure construction, Baldwin took every available opportunity to demonstrate his abiding support for regionalism. At a speech to the Royal Society of St George in 1924, he proclaimed, 'if our differences are smoothed out and we lose that great gift, we shall lose at the same time our power. Uniformity of type is a bad thing' (*On England* 5). Baldwin's critics saw right through his rhetoric. They mocked his 'yards and yards of sob-stuff about the beauties of the countryside' and went even further, Mandler reports, 'denouncing his "hypocrisy" and "stupidity"' (241). What Baldwin clearly wanted was someone capable of helping him to persuade voters that the goals of developing England and preserving regional variation were not incommensurate.

He found such a resource in Webb, whose novel *Precious Bane* Baldwin helped make a bestseller when he penned its introduction in 1928.[24] He praised the book for depicting provincial existence as a 'mingling of peoples and traditions and turns of speech and proverbial wisdom' ('Introduction' 11–12). Reiterating an argument that modernist fiction and travel guides were making familiar, he focused on the ways *Precious Bane* historicized the heterogeneous by unveiling 'earthly beauty in one bit of the England of Waterloo' ('Introduction' 12). As Webb gave Shropshire a very particular past, she perhaps less intentionally offered Baldwin evidence that rural customs were sufficiently well established and durable that electricity and new roadways could never wipe them out. Webb's novel did not depict a pastoral utopia, however. She was unafraid to reveal the seamier side of county culture. Violence and abuse are

---

24 Not that Webb herself profited from this additional exposure; she died the year before. See S. Miller on Baldwin's appropriation of Webb.

commonplace in *Precious Bane*. For this reason, the novel must also be seen as providing ammunition for a contention that England's natives were incapable of taking care of themselves. One suspects that such sentiment was exactly what Baldwin wanted to hear. It implied that the country could only benefit from a little development and that development could find a willing ally in a well-versed native informant.

Precious Bane narrates the adolescence of Prue Sarn, a young woman whose passion for chronicling goings-on in her village ultimately forces her to leave it. The novel defines what anthropology would call the position of the native informant as an awkward one. Prue is poised between her immediate surroundings and a larger context of literate Englishmen and women. The great difficulty in her life is that facility with language does not grant her authority among the people of Shropshire but rather leads to ostracization. She is no latter-day Pamela or Jane Eyre. Instead, her attempts to improve and instruct those around her earn only disapproval. When she points out the cruelty involved in a 'bull-baiting', for example, Prue is attacked for her trouble. Because *Precious Bane* persuades us of its protagonist's correctness in such matters, it also convinces us that rural habits will need to be reformed. The novel's depiction of resistance to Prue's activities, furthermore, helps us to see that the village cannot be reformed from within.

Prue is the perfect guide for experts who would wish to administer her corner of England. She indigenizes a metaphor borrowed from Emerson and Olive Shreiner when she presents the land 'like a great open book with fair pages . . . written in a secret script' and promises to translate it for her readers (156).[25] If the city was a text for Joyce and Woolf, Webb confirms that the country can be thoroughly textualized too. Prue composes in the attic, surrounded by crops waiting for market. In the fall she writes between crates of apples – 'codlins and golden pippins, brown russets and scarlet crabs' – and pears – 'Worcester pears and butter pears, jargonelle, bergamot and Good Christian' (73). Amidst a glow 'bright as a church window, all reds and golds', she translates her surroundings into 'tall and short script' (294). Organic though they may be, Prue's letters make her neighbours nervous. Combined with a growing reputation as a rabble-rouser and an unfortunately distinguishing facial mark – she has a

---

25 For her part, Webb blurs the distinction between innate and book knowledge of a place by using her introduction to the novel to thank the authors of Shropshire Folk Lore for the 'verification of various customs' and William Sharpe for the 'consummate art' of his description of sin-eating (15).

harelip – Prue appears strange enough to be branded a witch. She has little choice in the end but to elope to London with an itinerant weaver. Such is life in the country.

Though she may manifest some of the skills of authorship, Prue is sure that she does not have an expert's authority. She marvels at the 'mystery about an educated man' and observes that she is 'not anything of a scholar' (276, 294). From the novel's first page, moreover, where she self-consciously addresses a reader who will not know what a 'love-spinning' is and has never 'slept in a cot of rushes', Prue relies on provincial vernacular (17). She translates local practice, but only from one dialect to another. She invites us to compare the game of 'conkers', for instance, to one 'you play with chestnut cobs' (26). Bound as she is by idioms belonging to the backwards lot who tried to burn her at the stake, Prue finds her capacity to write herself out of her situation and into the stance of the auto-ethnographer profoundly limited. With Prue's story, *Precious Bane* promulgates doubt about the extent to which the authority to observe can be extended to a general population. Though she surely provides a service to some reader eager to understand how the natives think, Prue experiences the position of the native informant as a desperate one indeed.[26]

Modernism dwelled on the fate of such local observers in suburban settings as well. Nowhere was the management of local culture more of a pressing matter than in the burgeoning suburbs. During the interwar period, executives like William and George Cadbury collaborated with

---

26 Where Webb may not have intended her novel as an invitation for expert intervention, other modernists were deliberate in their appeals. In his 1934 travelogue *English Journey*, the novelist and dramatist J. B. Priestley plays the part of matchmaker between professionals and regions with very specific needs. Two early chapters focus on signature provincial 'tricks': in the Cotswolds villages are composed of buildings that seem to keep 'the lost sunlight of centuries glimmering'; in the Black Country the natives show a remarkable knack of 'keeping up with the times' (38; 55). The Cotswolds looks 'as if it had decided to detach itself from the rest of England about the time of the Civil War' (46). Its houses 'huddle' together in valleys that appear designed precisely to hold them (46, 43). Coventry's history in contrast is 'stated emphatically' by steeples and smokestacks that set off 'the green hollow and the silken sky' and provide the perfect habitat for men who build without 'any obvious supervision . . . motor cars [that] seemed to flower out of cast iron, steel, aluminum, as naturally as dandelions flower in a field' (53, 57). What a borough like Coventry requires is an administrator able to coordinate human capital and industrial technology. Changes in manufacturing have led to a situation in which schools churn out 'boys . . . turned into square pegs, when unfortunately industry itself is arranging that there shall be only more and more round holes' (58). A consultant could help smooth communication between education and the assembly line. Such a specialist would have little work in the Cotswolds, in contrast. That quarter wants a district officer like 'F. L. Griggs, the artist, who has spent time, energy and money for the last twenty-five years, keeping the place beautiful' (41). For more on Priestley's travelogue, see J. Taylor 133–4.

architects and self-appointed visionaries such as 'the Garden City geyser' Ebenezer Howard to design tracts that would exude a sense of place comparable to that of the city neighbourhood and the village. Previous development failed in this regard, these planners contended, because the elected officials behind it were 'out of touch with the views of citizens' and because the citizens themselves were guilty of incredibly bad taste (Beaufoy 146). The result was haphazard construction, which generally took the form of 'pink asbestos bungalows' strung along the trunk roads in and out of England's cities (Williams-Ellis 16).

To rectify matters, developers sought to establish 'some sense of community [that] might be achieved by means of aesthetic control' (Meacham 29). The historian Standish Meacham describes a campaign to awaken 'in the consciousness of housedwellers a best self derived from their everyday surroundings' (72). The architect Raymond Unwin sought to advance this aim by organizing residential plots around picturesque high streets, small parks, and squares he called 'places' (Meacham 105). He contended that these could generate an inward-looking community worthy of the name. His efforts were influential in the Garden City movement, which favoured suburbs of considerable internal complexity – winding residential streets, varied housing, interesting choices of flora – organized adjacent to or surrounding a shared 'place'. The result of such planning was a combination of inviting public display and 'dense suburban jungle' that might comfort locals while leaving strangers feeling like the outsiders they were, lost in a suburban maze (J. M. Richards 32).[27]

In what is easily the most biting novelistic critique of Garden City planning, George Orwell's *Coming Up for Air* dissects the application of Howard and Unwin's ideals while appropriating their inspiration. His novel takes up the challenge to treat the suburb as if it might be a place along the lines of the urban neighbourhood and the rural village. This novel's suburban informant is a salesman who resides just outside London and spends most of his time on 'cross-country journeys [to] suburbs of midland towns that you'd never heard of in a hundred normal lifetimes' (149). George Bowling is the perfect vehicle for a plot that locates the suburb in a comparative field. By following George around the midlands, *Coming Up for Air* finds that to compare suburbia to the likes of Woolf's Westminster or Webb's Shropshire is to find it lacking. Such

---

27 Winding lanes should break up lines of sight, says the suburban enthusiast J. M. Richards, substantial hedges and tight fences should combine to create a 'romantic technique of concealment and surprise, of charms enhanced because they are grudgingly revealed' (32).

developments as West Bletchley, where George lives, evince neither the haunted feeling nor the vibrant cosmopolitanism that modernism treated as essential to local culture. Instead, West Bletchley offers a regularized and blandly contemporary feel, with its grid of semi-detached houses each with the 'stucco front, the creosoted gate, the privet hedge, the green front door' (11). This is the suburban norm, George complains, and it is taking over not only the city fringe but also the provinces.[28]

According to Orwell, instead of distinction suburbia brings standardization. Even commercial exchange, that vehicle for cosmopolitanism, has been homogenized. Gone is the remarkable variety of penny sweets, the Penny Monsters and Caraway Comfits that made George's childhood consumption an adventure. Gone too are the curiosities of local produce, those sundry berries and nuts that 'you used to find in the hedges' (41–4). What remains is mass-produced, nationally distributed, 'streamlined', and – this is the final straw – 'American' (26). The United States stands for the very opposite of the multifarious market George remembers nostalgically. It produces and distributes 'phantom stuff that you can't taste and can hardly believe in its existence of' (26). What is wrong with the suburban community, Orwell's novel hints, may not lie in the idea but in its execution. Howard and Unwin may have been on the right track when they developed the notion of the Garden City, but the unchecked dissemination and unmanaged implementation of their idea distorted it. Though George does not reach this conclusion himself, the novel as a whole may lead us to deduce that what the suburbs demand is not a new theory but better regulation. The rural ideal of small-scale heterogeneity and multifarious local commerce for which George is nostalgic is itself the model Howard and Unwin sought to bring to the suburbs. What we make of this resemblance may remain open to interpretation, which could be precisely the point. As much as *Coming Up for Air* is a critique of the actually existing suburb, the novel is also an invitation to debate its future.

Interpretability is perhaps the most significant difference between literature and the social scientific writing that also participated in rezoning local culture during the early twentieth century. We are not wrong to treat literary and anthropological approaches together, but doing so risks losing what is specific to literature in this enterprise. Worse, it can

---

28 The homogeneity of suburban life has crept into rural enclaves like George Bowling's hometown in Oxfordshire. There a 'forest city' of uniform bungalows has sprung up around a small patch of trees that used to be dense woodland; the Big House has been turned into a sanatorium; and the downtown has been re-zoned with new 'rather mean, shabby kind[s] of street[s]' (214).

commit us to the errant presupposition that focusing on local ritual and habit, whether symbolic or material, is a properly anthropological enterprise even when it appears in fiction. We ought to remember that when anthropology sought to become more self-reflexive about the notion of culture, it often turned to literature. In his influential essays on ethnographic authority, James Clifford relies on the 'notoriously interpretable' quality of Conrad's 'Heart of Darkness' to introduce a new sense of flexibility to critical understanding of Malinowski's foundational work (*Predicament* 99). Though this gesture may appear to treat anthropology as literature, the opposite is in fact the case. Having turned to Conrad to help launch his project, Clifford retroactively transforms 'Heart of Darkness' into ethnography, the representative instance even of 'the ethnographic standpoint, a subjective position and a historical site of narrative authority' without which modern anthropology could not tell its stories about local culture (*Predicament* 99).

More recently, Clifford has seemed wary about blurring the boundary between these disciplines, as demonstrated in the question and answer session appended to his essay 'Traveling Cultures' and particularly in his response to Homi Bhabha's query about the role of exile in his analysis. 'I suppose I've steered away from a focus on "exile" because of the privilege it enjoys in a certain modernist culture', Clifford comments (*Routes* 43). He clearly means to give space to literature here, to the 'special uprootedness, pain, authority' of 'Joyce, Beckett, Pound, Conrad' and to the notion of the modernist author as exile (*Routes* 43). Though he promises to leave modernist authority to one side, he cannot help but further conflate it with that of his discipline. He observes that 'Conrad's extraordinary experience of travel, of cosmopolitanness, finds expression only when it is limited, tied down to a language, a place, an audience' and notes that movement allows Conrad – like Clifford the anthropologist – to recognize how the notion of place 'needs to be reconceived' (*Routes* 43–4).

Modernist elaboration of Dublin, London, and Shropshire natives in their element endowed localities with textual richness and the sort of interpretative challenges properly termed literary. It was not simply Conrad's exile that led him to rethink the idea of place, moreover, but also the economic and geopolitical changes contemporary with his efforts. Modernism was neither simply the cause nor the effect of these changes, but its fiction accommodated, investigated, and extended them. Without them, there would have been neither possibility nor need for Conrad to imagine a transnational and elite readership for his novels, for Lawrence to figure the primitivism of English domesticity, or for Woolf to render the cosmopolitanism of *Mrs Dalloway*'s urban neighbourhood. Changes in transportation and communication, politics and marketing made it possible and, perhaps, necessary for modernist fiction to enjoin readers worldwide to feel just as strongly about the need to preserve a vanishing urban way of life, like the Dublin of *Ulysses*, as the village rituals Webb finds in Shropshire.

As my comparison of *Ulysses* and *Mrs Dalloway* is meant to suggest, such an emphasis on the importance of local culture did in fact extend across the greater divide between places conventionally distinguished as home and colony. That we still recognize the difference between these types of local culture clarifies – if there was any doubt – that electrification programmes and network connectivity did not do away entirely with the country/city distinction or that between colonizer and colonized. But that we consider regional particularity on either side of these oppositions worthy of preservation shows how thoroughly such older geopolitical distinctions have become mediated by the division of labour so habitually figured in modernist fiction between mobile observers and local subjects whose lot it was to have their way of life observed. Such mediation was vital to the modernist dream that I invoked at the beginning of this book. In that dream, Great Britain's decline provided the pretext for the birth of a decentred network of places and peoples described, analyzed, and managed by a cosmopolitan cast of English-speaking experts.

A great many people shared in this vision. Inclusiveness was perhaps the most critical distinction between the professional ideal that Harold Perkin describes as triumphing in the early decades of the twentieth century and previous social ideals associated with the aristocrat and entrepreneur. 'Whereas their ideal citizen had been a limited concept', Perkin contends, 'the professional ideal could in principle be extended to everyone. Every landlord and industrialist could be transformed into a professional manager, every worker into a salaried employee' (*Rise* 8). That ideal was altered in its realization, however. Professionalism did not, in the end, create an egalitarian society. 'To paraphrase George Orwell', Perkin writes, 'all professionals are equal but some are more equal than others' (*Rise* 9). Modernism's version of this contradiction entailed so-liciting readers from all walks of life and from every region of the planet but arranging that audience hierarchically. Further distinguishing be-tween qualified readers and writers capable of fulfilling the discrete functions of a modernist author confirmed a commitment to expertise and hierarchy both. Modernism was not alone in this commitment, of course. Anthropology, economics, and a host of other disciplines shared it as well, which is why it makes sense to understand them as collabourating, however inadvertently, in the dissemination of professionalism. Indeed, modernism did not simply reflect the triumph of professional society but helped to spread it to every spot inhabited by readers capable of being persuaded to analyze and appreciate works of difficult fiction written in English.

Bibliography

Achebe, Chinua. 'The Novelist as Teacher.' 1965. *Hopes and Impediments*. New York: Doubleday, 1988. 40–6.

Adams, James Eli. *Dandies and Desert Saints: Styles of Victorian Manhood*. Ithaca: Cornell University Press, 1995.

Adu Boahen, A., ed. *Africa Under Colonial Domination. Unesco General History of Africa*. Vol. VII. Berkeley: University of California Press, 1990.

Afigbo, A. E. *The Warrant Chiefs: Indirect Rule in Southeastern Nigeria 1891–1929*. New York: Humanities, 1972.

Aguirre, Mark. 'Cold Print: Professing Authorship in Anthony Trollope's *An Autobiography*.' *Biography* 25.4 (2002): 569–92.

Ahuma, Attoh. *Gold Coast Nation and National Consciousness*. 1911. London: Cass, 1971.

Anderson, Amanda. *The Powers of Distance*. Princeton: Princeton University Press, 2001.

Anderson, Benedict. *Imagined Communities*. Rev. Ed. New York: Verso, 1991.

Anderson, Perry. 'Figures of Descent.' *New Left Review* 161 (1987): 20–77.

Appadurai, Arjun. *Modernity at Large: Cultural Dimensions of Globalization*. Minneapolis: University of Minnesota Press, 1996.

Appadurai, Arjun, ed. *The Social Life of Things: Commodities in Cultural Perspective*. Cambridge: Cambridge University Press, 1986.

Arata, Stephen. *Fictions of Loss in the Victorian Fin De Siècle*. New York: Cambridge University Press, 1996.

Archer, Mildred and Ronald Lightbowm. *India Observed: India as Viewed by British Artists, 1760–1860*. London: Victoria and Albert, 1982.

Ardis, Ann L. *New Women, New Novels: Feminism and Early Modernism*. New Brunswick: Rutgers University Press, 1990.

Armstrong, Nancy. *Desire and Domestic Fiction: A Political History of the Novel*. New York: Oxford University Press, 1987.

Fiction in the Age of Photography. Cambridge: Harvard University Press, 1999.

Armstrong, Tim. *Modernism, Technology, and the Body*. Cambridge: Cambridge University Press, 1998.

Arrighi, Giovanni. *The Long Twentieth Century*. New York: Verso, 1994.

Arrighi, Giovanni, Beverly J. Silver, et al. *Chaos and Governance in the Modern World System.* Minneapolis: University of Minnesota Press, 1999.

Attridge, Derek. *Joyce Effects: On Language, Theory, and History.* Cambridge: Cambridge University Press, 2000.

Auerbach, Erich. *Mimesis: The Representation of Reality in Western Literature.* Trans. Willard R. Trask. Princeton: Princeton University Press, 1953.

Austen, Jane. *Pride and Prejudice.* 1813. New York: Penguin, 1972.

Baldwin, Stanley. Introduction. 1928. *Precious Bane.* Mary Webb. Notre Dame: University of Notre Dame Press, 1980. 10–12.

On England. London: Allan, 1926.

Banfield, Ann. *The Phantom Table: Woolf, Fry, Russell and the Epistemology of Modernism.* Cambridge: Cambridge University Press, 2000.

Barthes, Roland. *Writing Degree Zero and Elements of Semiology.* Trans. Annette Lavers and Colin Smith. Boston: Beacon, 1968.

Batchelor, John. *The Life of Joseph Conrad.* Cambridge: Blackwell, 1994.

Baucom, Ian. *Out of Place: Englishness, Empire, and the Locations of Identity.* Princeton: Princeton University Press, 1999.

Bayly, C. A. *Indian Society and the Making of the British Empire.* New York: Cambridge University Press, 1988.

Beaufoy, Helena. '"Order out of chaos": the London Society and the planning of London, 1912–1920.' *Planning Perspectives.* 12 (1997): 135–64.

Beard, Charles A. and Mary R. Beard. *The Rise of American Civilization.* New York: Macmillan, 1930.

Beer, Gillian. *Darwin's Plots: Evolutionary Narrative in Darwin, George Eliot, and Nineteenth-Century Fiction.* London: Ark, 1983.

Bell, Quentin. *Virginia Woolf: A Biography.* 2 vols. New York: Harcourt, 1972.

Benjamin, Walter. *The Arcades Project.* Trans. Howard Eiland and Kevin McLaughlin; from German volume, ed. Rolf Tiedemann. Cambridge: Harvard University Press, 1999.

'Paris, Capital of the Nineteenth Century.' *Reflections.* New York: Harcourt, 1978.

Berman, Marshall. *All that is Solid Melts into Air: The Experience of Modernity.* 1982. Rev. edn. New York: Penguin, 1988.

Bermingham, Ann. *Landscape and Ideology: The English Rustic Tradition, 1740–1860.* Berkeley: University of California Press, 1986.

Bernal, Martin. *Black Athena.* Vol. I. New Brunswick: Rutgers University Press, 1987.

Berry, Sara. 'Hegemony on a Shoestring: Indirect Rule and Access to Agricultural Land.' *Africa* 62.3 (1992): 327–55.

Bersani, Leo. *A Future for Astyanax.* New York: Columbia University Press, 1994.

Bhabha, Homi K. *The Location of Culture.* New York: Routledge, 1984.

Bhagwati, Jagdish. 'The Diminished Giant Syndrome: How Declinism Drives Trade Policy.' *A Stream of Windows: Unsettling Reflections on Trade, Immigration, and Democracy.* Cambridge: MIT University Press, 1998. 95–104.

A Stream of Windows: Unsettling Reflections on Trade, Immigration, and Democracy. Cambridge: MIT University Press, 1998.

Wealth and Poverty. Ed. Gene Grossman. Cambridge: MIT University Press, 1985.

Birken, Lawrence. *Consuming Desire: Sexual Science and the Emergence of a Culture of Abundance, 1871–1914*. Ithaca: Cornell University Press.

Birkett, Dea. *Spinsters Abroad: Victorian Lady Explorers*. New York: Blackwell, 1989.

Bivona, Daniel. *British Imperial Literature, 1870–1940*. Cambridge: Cambridge University Press, 1998.

Black, Charles E. D. *A Memoir of the Indian Surveys, 1875–1890*. London, 1891.

Boone, Joseph Allen. *Libidinal Currents: Sexuality and the Shaping of Modernism*. Chicago: University of Chicago Press, 1998.

Bongie, Chris. *Exotic Memories: Literature, Colonialism, and the Fin de Siècle*. Stanford: Stanford University Press, 1991.

Boscagli, Maurizia. *Eye on the Flesh: Fashions of Masculinity in the Early Twentieth Century*. Boulder: Westview, 1996.

Bossche, Chris R. Vanden. 'The Value of Literature: Representations of Print Culture in the Copyright Debate of 1837–1842.' *Victorian Studies* 38.1 (1994): 41–68.

Bourdieu, Pierre. *Distinction: A Social Critique of the Judgement of Taste*. Trans. Richard Nice. Cambridge: Harvard University Press, 1984.

The Field of Cultural Production: Essays on Art and Literature. Ed. Randal Johnson. New York: Columbia University Press, 1993.

The Logic of Practice. 1980. Trans. Richard Nice. Stanford: Stanford University Press, 1990.

Rules of Art. Trans. Susan Emanuel. Stanford: Stanford University Press, 1992.

'The Uses of the "People."' *In Other Words*. Trans. Matthew Adamson. Stanford: Stanford University Press, 1990. 150–5.

Brantlinger, Patrick. *Rule of Darkness: British Literature and Imperialism, 1830–1914*. Ithaca: Cornell University Press, 1988.

Bristow, Joseph. *Effeminate England: Homoerotic Writing after 1885*. New York: Columbia University Press, 1995.

Brittain, Vera. *Testament of Youth*. 1933. London: Virago, 1978.

Brontë, Charlotte. *Jane Eyre*. 1847. New York: Oxford University Press, 1998.

Brown, Bill. 'The Secret Life of Things: Virginia Woolf and the Matter of Modernism.' *Modernism/Modernity* 6.2 (1999): 1–28.

'The Tyranny of Things (Trivia in Karl Marx and Mark Twain).' *Critical Inquiry* 28.2 (2002): 442–69.

Brown, G. Baldwin. *The Care of Ancient Monuments*. Cambridge: Cambridge University Press, 1905.

Buell, Lawrence. 'Crosscurrents of Urban Theory.' *Configurations* 7.1 (1999): 109–18.

Burrows, Victoria. *Whiteness and Trauma: The Mother–Daughter Knot in the Fiction of Jean Rhys, Jamaica Kincaid and Toni Morrison*. London: Palgrave, 2004.

Burstein, Jessica. 'A Few Words About Dubuque: Modernism, Sentimentalism, and the Blasé.' *American Literary History* 14.2 (2002): 227–54.

Buzard, James. *The Beaten Track: European Tourism, Literature, and the Ways to Culture, 1800–1918*. Oxford: Clarendon, 1993.

'"Culture" and the Critics of *Dubliners*.' *James Joyce Quarterly* 37.1–2 (2000): 43–62.

'Culture for Export: Tourism and Autoethnography in Postwar Britain.' *Studies in Travel Writing* 2 (1998): 106–27.

'Ethnography as Interruption: *News from Nowhere*, Narrative, and the Modern Romance of Authority.' *Victorian Studies* 40.3 (1997): 445–74.

'Mass-Observation, Modernism, and Auto-ethnography.' *Modernism/Modernity* 4.3 (1997): 93–122.

'On Auto-Ethnographic Authority.' *Yale Journal of Criticism* 16.1 (2003): 61–91.

Cain, P. J. and A. G. Hopkins. *British Imperialism*. 2 vols. New York: Longman, 1993.

Callaway, Helen. 'Purity and Exotica in Legitimating the Empire.' *Legitimacy and the State in Twentieth-Century Africa*. Ed. Terence Ranger and Olufemi Vaughan. London: Macmillan, 1993. 31–61.

Chandavarkar, Anand. 'Money and Credit, 1858–1947.' Kumar 762–804.

Keynes and India: A Study in Economics and Biography. London: Macmillan, 1989.

Chandler, Alfred D. *Scale and Scope: The Dynamics of Industrial Capitalism*. Cambridge: Harvard University Press, 1990.

Chatterji, Basudev. *Trade, Tariffs, and Empire*. Delhi: Oxford University Press, 1992.

Chaudhuri, Amit. *D. H. Lawrence and 'Difference'*. New York: Oxford University Press, 2003.

Childs, Donald J. *Modernism and Eugenics: Woolf, Eliot, Yeats, and the Culture of Degeneration*. Cambridge: Cambridge University Press, 2001.

Ching, Leo. 'Globalizing the Regional, Regionalizing the Global: Mass Culture and Asianism in the Age of Late Capital.' *Public Culture* 12.1 (2000): 233–58.

Choudhury, Romita. '"Is there a Ghost, a Zombie There?": Postcolonial Intertextuality and Jean Rhys's *Wide Sargasso Sea*.' *Textual Practice* 10.2 (1996): 315–27.

Clark, Suzanne. *Sentimental Modernism: Women Writers and the Revolution of the Word*. Bloomington: Indiana University Press, 1991.

Clifford, Hugh. 'The Clifford Minute.' 1922. *The Principles of Native Administration in Nigeria: Selected Documents 1900–47*. Ed. A. H. M. Kirk-Greene. London: Oxford University Press, 1965. 174–86.

Clifford, James. *The Predicament of Culture: Twentieth-Century Ethnography, Literature, and Art*. Cambridge: Harvard University Press, 1988.

Routes: Travel and Translation in the Late Twentieth Century. Cambridge: Harvard University Press, 1997.

Cohen, Phil. 'Out of the Melting Pot into the Fire Next Time.' *Imagining Cities*. Ed. Sallie Westwood and John Williams. London: Routledge, 1997. 73–85.

Cole, Sarah. *Modernism, Male Friendship, and the First World War.* Cambridge: Cambridge University Press, 2003.

Colley, Linda. *Britons: Forging the Nation, 1707–1837.* New Haven: Yale University Press, 1992.

Comaroff, John and Jean. *Ethnography and the Historical Imagination.* Boulder: Westview, 1992.

Conrad, Joseph. *The Collected Letters of Joseph Conrad.* Vols. I–VI. Ed. Frederick R. Karl and Laurence Davies. New York: Cambridge University Press, 1983–2002.

'Heart of Darkness.' 1899. *Youth.* 1902. New York: Doubleday, 1928. 45–162.

'Karain: A Memory.' *Tales of Unrest.* 1898. New York: Scribner's, 1906. 1–90.

Letters to William Blackwood and David S. Meldrum. Ed. William Blackburn. Durham: Duke University Press, 1958.

Lord Jim. 1899. New York: Doubleday, 1963.

The Nigger of the 'Narcissus.' 1897. Ed. Cedric Watts. New York: Penguin, 1989.

Nostromo. 1904. New York: Penguin, 1963.

Notes on Life and Letters. Garden City: Doubleday, 1923.

A Personal Record. Garden City: Doubleday, 1934.

'Preface.' 1897. *The Nigger of the 'Narcissus.'* Ed. Cedric Watts. New York: Penguin, 1989. xlvii–li.

Coombes, Annie E. *Reinventing Africa: Museums, Material Culture, and Popular Imagination.* New Haven, Yale University Press, 1994.

Cottom, Daniel. *Abyss of Reason: Cultural Movements, Revelations, and Betrayals.* New York: Oxford University Press, 1991.

Craft, Christopher. *Another Kind of Love: Male Homosexual Desire in English Discourse, 1850–1920.* Berkeley: University of California Press, 1994.

Crawford, Robert. *Devolving English Literature.* Oxford: Clarendon, 1992.

Crowder, Michael. *The Story of Nigeria.* London: Faber, 1962.

Crowder, Michael, and Obaro Ikime. 'West African Chiefs.' *Colonial West Africa: Collected Essays.* Michael Crowder. London: Cass, 1978.

Crystal, David. *English as a Global Language.* New York: Cambridge University Press, 1997.

Cucullu, Lois. 'Shepherds in the Parlor: Forster's Apostles, Pagans, and Native Sons.' *Novel* 32.1 (1998): 19–50.

Curl, James Stevens. *The Egyptian Revival.* London: Allen, 1982.

Dalgarno, Emily. *Virginia Woolf and the Visible World.* Cambridge: Cambridge University Press, 2001.

Dalsimer, Katherine. *Virginia Woolf: Becoming a Writer.* New Haven, Yale University Press, 2001.

Daly, Nicholas. 'That Obscure Object of Desire: Victorian Commodity Culture and Fictions of the Mummy.' *Novel* 28.1 (1994): 24–51.

Danius, Sara. *The Senses of Modernism: Technology, Perception, and Aesthetics.* Ithaca: Cornell University Press, 2002.

Darwin, Charles. *The Descent of Man and Selection in Relation to Sex.* New York: Appleton, 1879.

On the Origin of the Species. 1859. Cambridge: Harvard University Press, 1964.

Das, G. K. *E. M. Forster's India.* Totowa, NJ: Rowman, 1977.

David, Deidre. *Rule Britannia: Women, Empire, and Victorian Writing.* Ithaca: Cornell University Press, 1995.

Davidson, Basil. *The Black Man's Burden.* New York: Times, 1992.

Let Freedom Come. Boston: Little, 1978.

Davis, Lance E., and Robert A. Huttenback. *Mammon and the Pursuit of Empire: The Political Economy of British Imperialism, 1860–1912.* Cambridge University Press, 1987.

Dean Carolyn J. 'The Great War, Pornography, and the Transformation of Modern Male Subjectivity.' *Modernism/Modernity* 3.2 (1996): 59–72.

de Certeau, Michel. *The Practice of Everyday Life.* Trans. Steven Rendall. Berkeley: University of California Press, 1984.

DeKoven, Marianne. *Rich and Strange: Gender, History, Modernism.* Princeton: Princeton University Press, 1991.

Dellamora, Richard. 'E. M. Forster at the End.' *Fictions of Masculinity: Crossing Cultures, Crossing Sexualities.* Ed. Peter Murphy. New York: New York University Press, 1994.

Desai, Gaurav. *Subject to Colonialism.* Durham: Duke University Press, 2001.

Design and Industries Association. *The Face of the Land.* London: Allen, 1930.

Dewey, Clive. 'The End of the Imperialism of Free Trade.' *The Imperial Impact.* Ed. Dewey and A. G. Hopkins. London: Athlone, 1978.

Diawara, Manthia. 'Toward a Regional Imaginary in Africa.' Jameson and Miyoshi 103–24.

Diepeveen, Leonard. *The Difficulties of Modernism.* New York: Routledge, 2003.

Dollimore, Jonathan. *Sexual Dissidence: Augustine to Wilde, Freud to Foucault.* Oxford: Clarendon, 1991.

Donald, James. 'This, Here, Now: Imagining the Modern City.' *Imagining Cities.* Ed. Sallie Westwood and John Williams. London: Routledge, 1997. 181–201.

Dore, Ronald. 'Will Global Capitalism Be Anglo-Saxon Capitalism?' *New Left Review* 6 (2000): 101–19.

Doyle, Laura. *Bordering on the Body.* New York: Oxford University Press, 1994.

Duffy, Enda. *Subaltern Ulysses.* Minneapolis: University of Minnesota Press, 1994.

Dutton, Ralph. *The English Country House.* London: Batsford, 1936.

Eagleton, Terry. *Exiles and Emigrés.* New York: Schocken, 1970.

Edney, Matthew H. *Mapping an Empire: The Geographical Construction of British India, 1765–1843.* Chicago: University of Chicago Press, 1997.

Edwards, Amelia. *A Thousand Miles Up the Nile.* London: Longmans, 1877.

Egerton, George. *Keynotes.* New York: Garland, 1977.

Ekechi, F. K. *Tradition and Transformation in Eastern Nigeria.* Kent: Kent St. University Press, 1989.

Eliot. T. S. 'The Metaphysical Poets.' 1921. *Selected Prose* 59–68.

'On the Place and Function of the Clerisy.' Appendix. *T. S. Eliot's Social Criticism.* By Roger Kojecky. New York: Farrar, 1971 240–9.

Selected Prose. Ed. Frank Kermode. New York: Harcourt, 1975.

'Tradition and the Individual Talent.' 1919. *Selected Prose* 37–44.

'Ulysses, Order, and Myth.' 1923. *Selected Prose* 175–8.

Ellison, Julie. *Cato's Tears and the Making of Anglo-American Emotion.* Chicago: University of Chicago Press, 1999.

Elsaesser, Thomas. *Metropolis.* London: BFI, 2000.

Errington, Shelly. *The Death of Authentic Primitive Art and Other Tales of Progress.* Berkeley: University of California Press, 1998.

Esty, Joshua. 'Amnesia in the Fields: Late Modernism, Late Imperialism, and the English Pageant Play.' ELH 69 (2002): 245–76.

'National Objects: Keynesian Economics and Modernist Culture in England.' *Modernism/Modernity* 7.1 (2000): 1–24.

A Shrinking Island. Princeton: Princeton University Press, 2004.

Fabian, Johannes. *Out of Our Minds: Reason and Madness in the Exploration of Central Africa.* Berkeley: University of California Press, 2000.

Time and the Other: How Anthropology Makes its Object. New York: Columbia University Press, 1983.

Fagan, Brian. *The Rape of the Nile.* New York: Scribner's, 1975.

Felski, Rita. *The Gender of Modernity.* Cambridge: Harvard University Press, 1995.

Feltes, N. N. *Literary Capital and the Late Victorian Novel.* Madison: University of Wisconsin Press, 1993.

Ferguson, Niall. *Empire.* London: Lane, 2002.

Fishman, Joshua A., Andrew W. Conrad, and Alma Rubal-Lopez, eds. *Post-imperial English: Status Change in Former British and American Colonies, 1940–1990.* New York: Mouton de Gruyter, 1996.

Fletcher, John. 'Forster's Self-Erasure: *Maurice* and the Scene of Masculine Love.' *Sexual Sameness: Textual Difference in Lesbian and Gay Writing.* Ed. Joseph Bristow. New York: Routledge, 1992.

Flint, John E. 'Frederick Lugard: The Making of an Autocrat (1858–1943).' Gann, L. H., et al. eds. *African Procounsels: European Governors in Africa.* New York: Free, 1978. 290–312.

Ford, Ford Madox. *England and the English.* New York: McClure, 1907.

Forster, E. M. *Commonplace Book.* Ed. Philip Gardner. Stanford: Stanford University Press, 1985.

A Passage to India. 1924. New York: Harcourt, 1952.

Foucault, Michel. 'The Discourse on Language.' *The Archaeology of Knowledge and the Discourse on Language.* Trans. A. M. Sheridan Smith. New York: Pantheon, 1972. 215–37.

The History of Sexuality: An Introduction. Vol. 1. Trans. Robert Hurley. New York: Vintage, 1990.

'What is an Author?' *Language, Counter-Memory, Practice.* Ithaca: Cornell University Press, 1977. 113–38.

'What is Enlightenment?' *The Foucault Reader*. Ed. Paul Rabinow. New York: Pantheon, 1984. 32–50.

France, Peter. *The Rape of Egypt*. London: Barrie, 1991.

Franey, Laura. 'Ethnographic Collecting and Travel: Blurring Boundaries, Forming a Discipline.' *Victorian Literature and Culture* (2001): 219–39.

Freedgood, Elaine. 'E. M. Forster's Queer Nation: Taking the Closet to the Colony in *A Passage to India*.' *Genders* 23 (1996): 123–44.

Freedman, Ariela. *Death, Men, and Modernism: Trauma and Narrative in British Fiction from Hardy to Woolf*. New York: Routledge, 2003.

Fried, Michael. 'Almayer's Face: On "Impressionism" in Conrad, Crane, and Norris.' *Critical Inquiry* 17 (1990): 193–236.

'Painting Memories: On the Containment of the Past in Baudelaire and Manet.' *Critical Inquiry* 10.3 (1984): 510–33.

Freidson, Eliot. 'The Futures of Professionalisation.' *Health and the Division of Labour*. Ed. Margaret Stacey, et al. London: Croom Helm, 1977. 14–40.

Freud, Sigmund. *Civilization and its Discontents*. 1930. *The Standard Edition of the Complete Psychological Works of Sigmund Freud*. Trans. James Strachey. Vol. XXI. London: Hogarth, 1953. 59–145.

'The Claims of Psycho-analysis to Scientific Interest.' 1913. *The Standard Edition of the Complete Psychological Works of Sigmund Freud*. Trans. James Strachey. Vol. XIII. London: Hogarth, 1953. 165–90.

'Fragment of an Analysis of a Case of Hysteria.' 1905. *The Standard Edition of the Complete Psychological Works of Sigmund Freud*. Trans. James Strachey. Vol. III. London: Hogarth, 1953.

The Interpretation of Dreams. 1900. *The Standard Edition of the Complete Psychological Works of Sigmund Freud*. Trans. James Strachey. Vols. IV–V. London, Hogarth, 1953.

Totem and Taboo. 1913. *The Standard Edition of the Complete Psychological Works of Sigmund Freud*. Trans. James Strachey. Vol. 13. London, Hogarth, 1953. ix–162.

'The Uncanny.' 1919. *The Standard Edition of the Complete Psychological Works of Sigmund Freud*. Trans. James Strachey. Vol. 17. London: Hogarth, 1955. 217–56.

Fryer, Peter. *Staying Power: The History of Black People in Britain*. London: Pluto, 1992.

Gagnier, Regenia. *The Insatiability of Human Wants: Economics and Aesthetics in Market Activity*. Chicago: University of Chicago Press, 2000.

Gallagher, Catherine. *The Industrial Reformation of English Fiction: Social Discourse and Narrative Form, 1832–1867*. Chicago: University of Chicago Press, 1985.

Nobody's Story: The Vanishing Acts of Women Writers in the Marketplace 1670–1820. Berkeley: California University Press, 1994.

Galton, Francis. 'Opening Remarks by the President.' *Journal of the Anthropological Institute of Great Britain and Ireland* 15 (1886): 336–8.

George, Rosemary Marangoly. *The Politics of Home: Postcolonial Relocations and Twentieth-Century Fiction*. New York: Cambridge University Press, 1996.

Giddens, Anthony. *The Consequences of Modernity*. Stanford: Stanford University Press, 1990.

Gifford, Don, with Robert J. Seidman. *Ulysses Annotated*. Berkeley: University of California Press, 1988.

Gikandi, Simon. *Maps of Englishness: Writing Identity in the Culture of Colonialism*. New York: Columbia University Press, 1996.

Gilbert, Sandra, and Susan Gubar. *No Man's Land*. Vol. I. *The War of the Words*. New Haven: Yale University Press, 1988.

Gilman, Sander L. 'Black Bodies, White Bodies: Toward an Iconography of Female Sexuality in Late Nineteenth-Century Art, Medicine, and Literature.' *'Race', Writing, and Difference*. Ed. Henry Louis Gates, Jr. Chicago: University of Chicago Press, 1985. 163–84.

No Man's Land. Vol. II. *Sexchanges*. New Haven: Yale University Press, 1989.

Gilpin, William. *Three Essays: On Picturesque Beauty; on Picturesque Travel; and on Sketching Landscape. With a Poem on Landscape Painting*. 3rd ed. London: Cadell and Davies, 1808.

Gissing, George. *The Private Papers of Henry Ryecroft*. Ed. Mark Storey. Oxford: Oxford University Press, 1987.

Glover, David. *Vampires, Mummies, and Liberals*. Durham: Duke University Press, 1996.

GoGwilt, Christopher. *The Invention of the West: Joseph Conrad and the Double-Mapping of Europe and Empire*. Stanford: Stanford University Press, 1995.

Goschen, George. *Essays and Addresses*. London, 1905.

Grace, Catherine. 'A Pleasure Ground for the Noisy Herds? Incompatible Encounters with the Cotswolds and England, 1900–1950.' *Rural History* 11.1 (2000): 75–94.

Grand, Sarah. *The Heavenly Twins*. 1893. Ann Arbor: University of Michigan Press, 1992.

Guérard, Albert. *Conrad the Novelist*. Cambridge: Harvard University Press, 1958.

Guha, Ranajit. *Dominance without Hegemony: History and Power in Colonial India*. Cambridge: Harvard University Press, 1997.

Guillén, Mauro F. *Models of Management: Work, Authority, and Organization in a Comparative Perspective*. Chicago: University of Chicago Press, 1994.

Haggard, H. Rider. *Allan Quatermain*. 1887. New York: Penguin, 1990.

King Solomon's Mines. 1885. New York: Oxford University Press, 1989.

Halberstam, Judith. *Female Masculinity*. Durham: Duke University Press, 1998.

Hall, Radclyffe. *The Well of Loneliness*. 1928. New York: Anchor, 1990.

Hall, Stuart. 'The Local and the Global.' *Dangerous Liasons*. Ed. Anne McClintock, et al. Minneapolis: University of Minnesota Press, 1997. 173–87.

Harpham, Geoffrey Galt. 'Conrad's Global Homeland.' *Raritan* 21.1 (2001): 20–33.

One of Us: The Mastery of Joseph Conrad. Chicago: University of Chicago Press, 1996.

Harris, Wilson. *The Womb of Space: The Cross-Cultural Imagination.* London: Greenwood, 1983.

Harrison, Simon. 'From Prestige Goods to Legacies: Property and the Objectification of Culture in Melanesia.' *Comparative Studies in Society and History.* 42.3 (2000): 662–79.

Hart, Clive. 'Wandering Rocks.' *James Joyce's Ulysses: Critical Essays.* Ed. Clive Hart and David Hayman. Berkeley: University of California Press, 1974.

Harvey, David. *Condition of Postmodernity.* Oxford: Blackwell, 1989.

Hay, Colin. 'Contemporary Capitalism, Globalization, Regionalization, and the Persistence of National Variation.' *Review of International Studies* 26 (2000): 509–31.

Helfand, Michael S. 'T. H. Huxley's "Evolution and Ethics": The Politics of Evolution and the Evolution of Politics.' *Victorian Studies* 20.2 (1977): 159–77.

Helsinger, Elizabeth. 'Turner and the Representation of England.' *Landscape and Power.* Ed. W. J. T. Mitchell. Chicago: University of Chicago Press, 1994. 103–26.

Herbert, Christopher. *Culture and Anomie: Ethnographic Imagination in the Nineteenth Century.* Chicago: University of Chicago Press, 1991.

Herzinger, Kim. *D. H. Lawrence in His Time: 1908–1915.* Lewisburg: Bucknell University Press, 1982.

Hilferding, Rudolf. *Finance Capital: A Study of the Latest Phase of Capitalist Development.* London: Routledge, 1981.

Hobsbawm, Eric. *The Age of Empire: 1875–1914.* New York: Vintage, 1989.

Hobsbawm, Eric, and Terence Ranger. *The Invention of Tradition.* Cambridge: Cambridge University Press, 1983.

Hobson, John A. *The Evolution of Modern Capitalism: A Study of Machine Production.* London: Scott, 1895.

Horne, Philip. *Henry James and Revision.* Oxford: Clarendon, 1990.

Huggan, Graham. 'A Tale of Two Parrots: Walcott, Rhys, and the Uses of Colonial Mimicry.' *Contemporary Literature* 35.4 (1994): 643–61.

Hume, David. *A Treatise of Human Nature.* 1739–40. Ed. David Fate Norton and Mary J. Norton. Oxford: Oxford University Press, 2000.

Huxley, Thomas H. *Evolution and Ethics.* 1894. Ed. James Paradis and George C. Williams. Princeton: Princeton University Press, 1989.

Huyssen, Andreas. *After the Great Divide: Modernism, Mass Culture, Postmodernism.* Bloomington: Indiana University Press, 1986.

Hyam, Ronald. 'Concubinage and the Colonial Service: The Crewe Circular.' *The Journal of Imperial and Commonwealth History.* 14 (1986): 170–86.

Ingham, Geoffrey. 'Commercial Capital and British Development.' *New Left Review* 172 (1988): 45–72.

Isichei, Elizabeth. *A History of the Igbo People*. New York: St Martin's, 1976.

Jacobson, Dan. 'Going Native.' *London Review of Books* 21.23 (1999): 29–30.

Jaffe, Audrey. *Scenes of Sympathy: Identity and Representation in Victorian Fiction*. Ithaca: Cornell University Press, 2000.

James, Henry. Preface. *The Golden Bowl*. New York: Penguin, 1981.

Jameson, Fredric. 'Culture and Finance Capital.' *Critical Inquiry* 24.1 (1997): 246–65.

'Modernism and Imperialism.' *Nationalism, Colonialism, and Literature*. Intro. Seamus Deane. Minneapolis: University of Minnesota Press, 1990. 43–68.

The Political Unconscious: Narrative as a Socially Symbolic Act. Ithaca: Cornell University Press, 1981.

Postmodernism or, The Cultural Logic of Late Capitalism. Durham: Duke University Press, 1991.

Sartre: The Origins of a Style. New York: Columbia University Press, 1984.

A Singular Modernity. London: Verso, 2002.

'*Ulysses* in History.' *James Joyce and Modern Literature*. Ed. W. J. McCormack and Alistair Stead. London: Routledge & Kegan Paul, 1982. 126–41.

Jameson, Fredric, and Masao Miyoshi, eds. *The Cultures of Globalization*. Durham: Duke University Press, 1998.

Janowitz, Anne. *England's Ruins: Poetic Purpose and the National Landscape*. London: Blackwell, 1990.

Jay, Gregory. *T. S. Eliot and the Poetics of Literary History*. Baton Rouge: Louisiana State University Press, 1983.

Jean-Aubrey, G. *Joseph Conrad: Life and Letters*. 2 vols. Garden City: Doubleday, 1927.

Johnson-Odim, Cheryl and Nina Emma Mba. *For Women and the Nation*. Urbana: University of Illinois Press, 1997.

Joyce, James. *A Portrait of the Artist as a Young Man*. New York: Penguin, 1976.

Selected Letters. Ed. Richard Ellman. London: Faber, 1975.

Ulysses. New York: Vintage, 1986.

Kaplan, Amy, and Donald Pease. *Cultures of United States Imperialism*. Durham: Duke University Press, 1993.

Kapur, Geeta. 'Globalization and Culture: Navigating the Void.' Jameson and Masao Miyoshi 191–217.

Karl, Frederick. *Joseph Conrad: The Three Lives*. New York: Farrar, 1979.

Kaufman, Robert. 'Red Kant, or The Persistence of the Third *Critique* in Adorno and Jameson.' *Critical Inquiry* 26 (2000): 682–724.

Keating, Peter. *The Haunted Study: A Social History of the English Novel 1875–1914*. London: Secker, 1989.

Keep, Christopher, and Don Randall. 'Addiction, Empire, and Narrative in Arthur Conan Doyle's *The Sign of Four*.' *Novel* 32.2 (1999): 207–21.

Kenner, Hugh. *A Sinking Island*. New York: Knopf, 1988.

Kermode, Frank. *Romantic Image*. New York: Macmillan, 1957.

Kern, Stephen. *The Culture of Time and Space: 1880–1918*. Cambridge: Harvard University Press, 1983.

Keynes, John Maynard. *Collected Writings of John Maynard Keynes*. 30 vols. Managing Ed. Austin Robinson. London: Macmillan, 1973–80.

Essays in Persuasion. New York: Harcourt, 1932.

Kipling, Rudyard. *Kim*. 1901. New York: Penguin, 1987.

Kittler, Friedrich. *Discourse Networks: 1800 / 1900*. Stanford: Stanford University Press, 1990.

Gramophone, Film, Typewriter. Stanford: Stanford University Press, 1999.

Klein, Scott. *The Fictions of James Joyce and Wyndham Lewis: Monsters of Nature and Design*. Cambridge: Cambridge University Press, 1994.

Kracauer, Siegfried. 'Georg Simmel.' *The Mass Ornament*. Trans. Thomas Y. Levin. Cambridge: Harvard University Press, 1995.

Krauss, Rosalind E. *The Picasso Papers*. Cambridge: MIT Press, 1999.

Krishnamurty, J. 'The Occupational Structure.' Kumar 533–52.

Kuklick, Henrika. *The Imperial Bureaucrat: The Colonial Administrative Service in the Gold Coast, 1920–1939*. Stanford: Hoover Institution Press, 1979.

The Savage Within: The Social History of British Anthropology, 1885–1945. New York: Cambridge University Press, 1991.

Kumar, Dharma, ed. *Cambridge Economic History of India*. New York: Cambridge, 1983.

Kyrk, Hazel. *A Theory of Consumption*. Boston: Houghton, 1923.

Lackner, Helen. 'Colonial Administration and Social Anthropology: Eastern Nigeria 1920–40.' *Anthropology and the Colonial Encounter*. Ed. Talal Asad. New York: Humanities, 1973. 123–52.

Lamos, Colleen. *Deviant Modernism: Sexual and Textual Errancy in T. S. Eliot, James Joyce, and Marcel Proust*. Cambridge: Cambridge University Press, 1998.

Lane, Christopher. *The Ruling Passion: British Colonial Allegory and the Paradox of Homosexual Desire*. Durham: Duke University Press, 1995.

Larson, Magali Sarfatti. *The Rise of Professionalism: A Sociological Analysis*. Berkeley: University of California Press, 1977.

Latham, Sean. *'Am I a Snob?' Modernism and the Novel*. Ithaca: Cornell University Press, 2003.

Lawrence, Christopher, and Anna-K. Mayer, eds. *Regenerating England: Science, Medicine, and Culture in Inter-War Britain*. Amsterdam: Rodopi, 2000.

Lawrence, D. H. 'A Propos of *Lady Chatterley's Lover*.' *Sex* 82–111.

'Fantasia of the Unconscious.' *Psychoanalysis and the Unconscious, Fantasia of the Unconscious*. 1921, 1922. Intro. Philip Rieff. New York: Viking, 1960.

Letters of D. H. Lawrence. Ed. George J. Zytaruk and James T. Boulton. 8 vols. Cambridge: Cambridge University Press, 1981.

Mornings in Mexico, Etruscan Places. 1927, 1932. New York: Penguin, 1981.

'Pornography and Obscenity.' *Sex* 64–81.

Sex, Literature, and Censorship. Ed. Harry T. Moore. New York: Viking, 1953.

'The State of Funk.' *Sex* 58–63.

Women in Love. 1920. Ed. David Farmer, Lindeth Vasey, and John Worthen. Cambridge: Cambridge University Press, 1987.

Lazarus, Neil. *Nationalism and Cultural Practice in the Postcolonial World.* New York: Cambridge University Press, 1999.

Leavis, F. R. *The Critic as Anti-Philosopher.* Athens: University of Georgia Press, 1983.

The Great Tradition. 1948. New York: Penguin, 1993.

Lee, C. H. *The British Economy Since 1700: A Macroeconomic Perspective.* New York: Cambridge University Press, 1986.

Lehan, Richard. *The City in Literature.* Berkeley: University of California Press, 1998.

Lesjak, Carolyn. 'A Modern Odyssey: Realism, the Masses, and Nationalism in George Eliot's *Felix Holt.*' *Novel* 30.1 (1996): 78–97.

Levenson, Michael. *A Genealogy of Modernism: A Study of Literary Doctrine 1908–1922.* New York: Cambridge University Press, 1984.

Modernism and the Fate of Individuality, Character, and Novelistic Form From Conrad to Woolf. Cambridge: Cambridge University Press, 1991.

'The Value of Facts in *Heart of Darkness.*' *Heart of Darkness.* By Joseph Conrad. Ed. Robert Kimbrough. 3rd ed. New York: Norton, 1988. 391–405.

Levine, Philippa. Introduction. *Untrodden Peaks and Unfrequented Valleys: A Midsummer Ramble in the Dolomites.* Amelia Edwards. Boston: Beacon, 1986. xv–xxviii.

Levy, Anita. 'Gendered Labor, the Woman Writer and Dorothy Richardson.' *Novel* 25.1 (1991): 50–70.

Lewis, David Levering. *The Race to Fashoda: European Colonialism and African Resistance in the Scramble for Africa.* New York: Weidenfeld, 1987.

Lewis, Pericles. *Modernism, Nationalism, and the Novel.* Cambridge: Cambridge University Press, 2000.

Lewis, Wyndham. *Enemy Salvos: Selected Literary Criticism.* Ed. C. J. Fox. New York: Harper, 1976.

Light, Alison. *Forever England: Femininity, Literature, and Conservatism Between the Wars.* New York: Routledge, 1991.

Lin, Nan. *Social Capital: A Theory of Social Structure and Action.* Cambridge: Cambridge University Press, 2001.

Litvak, Joseph. *Strange Gourmets: Sophistication, Theory, and the Novel.* Durham: Duke University Press, 1997.

London, Bette. 'Guerrilla in Petticoats or Sans-Culotte? Virginia Woolf and the Future of Feminist Criticism.' *Diacritics* 21.2–3 (1991): 11–29.

Luftig, Victor. *Seeing Together: Friendship Between the Sexes in English Writing, from Mill to Woolf.* Stanford: Stanford University Press, 1993.

Lugard, Sir F. D. *The Dual Mandate in British Tropical Africa.* Edinburgh: Blackwood, 1922.

Luhmann, Niklas. *Social Systems.* Trans. John Bednarz, Jr. Stanford: Stanford University Press, 1995.

Lukács, Georg. *The Historical Novel.* Trans. Hannah and Stanley Mitchell. Lincoln: University of Nebraska Press, 1983.

Realism in Our Time. New York: Harper, 1962.

Lynch, Deidre. 'At Home with Jane Austen.' Lynch and Warner 159–92.

    The Economy of Character: Novels, Market Culture, and the Business of Inner Meaning. Chicago: University of Chicago Press, 1998.

Lynch, Deidre, and William B. Warner, ed. *Cultural Institutions of the Novel.* Durham: Duke University Press, 1996.

Lyon, Janet. *Manifestoes: Provocations of the Modern.* Ithaca, Cornell University Press, 1999.

Macauley, Rose. *Pleasure of Ruins.* 1953. New York: Thames, 1984.

Maddox, Brenda. *D. H. Lawrence: The Story of a Marriage.* New York: Simon, 1994.

Mahaffey, Vicki. *Reauthorizing Joyce.* Cambridge: Cambridge University Press, 1988.

Mais, S. P. B. *The Unknown Island.* New York: Loring, 1933.

Malik, Charu. 'To Express the Subject of Friendship: Masculine Desire and Colonialism in *A Passage to India.*' *Queer Forster.* Ed. Robert K. Martin and George Piggford. Chicago: University of Chicago Press, 1997. 221–36.

Malinowski, Bronislaw. *Argonauts of the Western Pacific.* 1922. Prospect Heights, Illinois: Waveland, 1984.

    A Diary in the Strict Sense of the Term. Stanford: Stanford University Press, 1989.

    Freedom and Civilization. New York: Roy, 1944.

    'Native Education and Culture Context.' *International Review of Missions.* 25 (1936): 480–515.

    'The Rationalization of Anthropology and Administration.' *Africa* 3.4 (1930): 405–29.

    The Sexual Life of Savages in North-Western Melanesia. New York: Halcyon, 1929.

Mandami, Mahmood. *Citizen and Subject: Contemporary Africa and the Legacy of Late Colonialism.* Princeton: Princeton University Press, 1996.

Mandler, Peter. *The Fall and Rise of the Stately Home.* New Haven: Yale University Press, 1997.

Manganaro, Marc. *Culture, 1922: The Emergence of a Concept.* Princeton: Princeton University Press, 2002.

Mann, Kristin. *Marrying Well: Marriage, Status, and Social Change among the Educated Elite in Colonial Lagos.* Cambridge: Cambridge University Press, 1985.

Mao, Douglas. *Solid Objects: Modernism and the Test of Production.* Princeton: Princeton University Press, 1998.

Marcus, Jane. *Virginia Woolf and the Languages of Patriarchy.* Bloomington: Indiana University Press, 1987.

Marcus, Phillip. '"A Whole Healed Man": Frazer, Lawrence, and Blood-Consciousness.' *Sir James Frazer and the Literary Imagination: Essays in Affinity and Influence.* Ed. Robert Fraser. New York: St. Martin's, 1990. 232–52.

Marcus, Sharon. 'The Profession of the Author: Abstraction, Advertising, and Jane Eyre.' PMLA 110.2 (1995): 206–20.

Markham, Clements R. *A Memoir of the Indian Surveys.* 2nd ed. London, 1878.

Marx, Karl. *Capital.* Vol. I. Trans. Ben Fowkes. New York: Vintage, 1977.

Grundrisse: Foundations of the Critique of Political Economy. Trans. Martin Nicolaus. New York: Vintage, 1973.

Masterman, C. F. G. *The Condition of England.* 1909. London: Methuen, 1960.

Matless, David. *Landscape and Englishness.* London: Reaktion, 1998.

Matz, Jesse. *Literary Impressionism and Modernist Aesthetics.* Cambridge: Cambridge University Press, 2001.

McLaughlin, Joseph. *Writing the Urban Jungle.* Charlottesville: University of Virginia Press, 2000.

'Measuring Globalization.' *Foreign Policy* 122 (2001): 56–65.

Meacham, Standish. *Regaining Paradise: Englishness and the Early Garden City Movement.* New Haven: Yale University Press, 1999.

Meisel, Perry. *The Myth of the Modern: A Study in British Literature and Criticism after 1850.* New Haven: Yale University Press, 1987.

Menand, Louis. *Discovering Modernism.* New York: Oxford University Press, 1987.

Merkle, Judith. *Management and Ideology: The Legacy of the International Scientific Management Movement.* Berkeley: University of California Press, 1980.

Mignolo, Walter D. 'Globalization, Civilization Processes, and the Relocation of Languages and Cultures.' Jameson and Miyoshi 32–53.

Miller, Andrew. *Novels Behind Glass: Commodity Culture and Victorian Narrative.* New York: Cambridge University Press, 1995.

Miller, Simon. 'Urban Dreams and Rural Reality: Land and Landscape in English Culture, 1920–45.' *Rural History* 6.1 (1995): 89–102.

Mitchell, Timothy. *Colonising Egypt.* New York: Cambridge University Press, 1988.

Rule of Experts. Berkeley: University of California Press, 2002.

Mitchell, W. J. T., ed. *Landscape and Power.* Chicago: University of Chicago Press, 1994.

Moody, A. D. 'Eliot's Formal Invention.' *T. S. Eliot: Man and Poet.* Vol. I. Ed. Laura Cowan. 1990. 21–34.

Moretti, Franco. *Signs Taken for Wonders.* New York: Verso, 1983.

Morgan, Susan. *Place Matters: Gendered Geography in Victorian Women's Travel Books about Southeast Asia.* New Brunswick: Rutgers University Press, 1996.

Morrell, Lady Ottoline. *Memoirs: A Study in Friendship, 1873–1915.* Ed. R. Gathorne-Hardy. New York: Knopf, 1964.

Morrison, Mark. 'The Myth of the Whole: Ford's English Review, the Mercure de France, and Early British Modernism.' *ELH* 63.2 (1996): 513–33.

Morton, H. V. *In Search of England.* 1927. New York: Dodd, 1935.

Moser, Thomas. *Joseph Conrad: Achievement and Decline.* Cambridge: Harvard University Press, 1957.

Moses, Michael Valdez. *The Novel and the Globalization of Culture*. New York: Oxford University Press, 1995.

Mudimbe, V. Y. *The Idea of Africa*. Bloomington: Indiana University Press, 1994.

The Invention of Africa: Gnosis, Philosophy, and the Order of Knowledge. Bloomington: Indiana University Press, 1988.

Mufwene, Salikoko. *The Ecology of Language Evolution*. New York: Cambridge University Press, 2001.

Mulhern, Francis. 'English Reading.' *Nation and Narration*. New York: Routledge, 1990. 250–64.

The Moment of Scrutiny. London: NLB, 1979.

Munich, Adrienne. *Andromeda's Chains: Gender and Interpretation in Victorian Literature and Art*. New York: Columbia University Press, 1989.

Mydans, Seth. 'Nations in Asia Give English Their Own Flavorful Quirks.' *The New York Times* 1 July 2001: 1, 12.

Najder, Zdzislaw. *Joseph Conrad: A Chronicle*. Trans. Halina Carroll-Najder. New Brunswick: Rutgers University Press, 1984.

Nandy, Ashis. *The Intimate Enemy: Loss and Recovery of Self Under Colonialism*. Delhi: Oxford University Press, 1983.

Newell, Stephanie. 'Paracolonial Networks: Some Speculations on Local Readerships in Colonial West Africa.' *Interventions* 3.3 (2001): 336–54.

Nordau, Max. *Degeneration*. 1892. Lincoln: University of Nebraska Press, 1993.

Norris, Margot. *Joyce's Web: The Social Unraveling of Modernism*. Austin: University of Texas Press, 1992.

North, Michael. *The Dialect of Modernism: Race, Language, and Twentieth Century Literature*. New York: Oxford University Press, 1994.

Reading 1922: A Return to the Scene of the Modern. Oxford: Oxford University Press, 1999.

Nunokawa, Jeff. *Tame Passions of Wilde*. Princeton: Princeton University Press, 2003.

O'Hara, Daniel. 'Dancer and Dance: Romantic Modernism and Critical Theory.' *Soundings* 85.3–4 (2002): 361–80.

Ohadike, Don C. *The Ekumeku Movement: Western Igbo Resistance to the British Conquest of Nigeria, 1883–1914*. Athens: Ohio University Press, 1991.

Ong, Aihwa. *Flexible Citizenship: The Cultural Logics of Transnationality*. Durham: Duke University Press, 1999.

Orwell, George. *Coming Up for Air*. 1939. New York: Harcourt, 1950.

Pakir, Anne, ed. *English Language in Singapore: Standards and Norms*. Singapore: Unipress, 1993.

Pal, Pratapaditya, and Vidya Dehejia. *From Merchants to Emperors, British Artists and India, 1757–1930*. Ithaca: Cornell University Press, 1986.

Parry, Benita. 'Materiality and Mystification in E. M. Forster's *A Passage to India*.' *Novel* 31.2 (1998): 174–94.

'Problems in Current Theories of Colonial Discourse.' *Oxford Literary Review* 9 (1987): 27–58.

Pecora, Vincent. *Households of the Soul.* Baltimore: Johns Hopkins University Press, 1997.

Pennycook, Alastair. *English and the Discourses of Colonialism.* London: Routledge, 1998.

Perera, Suvendrini. *Reaches of Empire: The English Novel from Edgeworth to Dickens.* New York: Columbia University Press, 1991.

Perkin, Harold. *The Rise of Professional Society: England Since 1880.* New York: Routledge, 1989.

  Third Revolution: Professional Elites in the Modern World. New York: Routledge, 1996.

Phillimore, R. H., ed. *Historical Records of the Survey of India.* Volume IV, 1830–1843, George Everest. Dehra Dun: Government of India, 1958.

Pinch, Adela. *Strange Fits of Passion: Epistemologies of Emotion, Hume to Austen.* Stanford: Stanford University Press, 1996.

Pollack, Sheldon. 'Cosmopolitan and Vernacular in History.' *Public Culture* 12.3 (2000): 591–625.

Poovey, Mary. *Uneven Developments: The Ideological Work of Gender in Mid-Victorian England.* Chicago: University of Chicago Press, 1988.

Porter, Bernard. *Critics of Empire: British Radical Attitudes to Colonialism in Africa 1895–1914.* New York: St. Martin's, 1968.

Pratt, Mary Louise. *Imperial Eyes: Travel Writing and Transculturation.* New York: Routledge, 1992.

Price, Sally. *Primitive Art in Civilized Places.* Cambridge: Harvard University Press, 1992.

Priestley, J. B. *English Journey.* London: Harper, 1934.

Rainey, Lawrence. *Institutions of Modernism: Literary Elites and Public Culture.* New Haven: Yale University Press, 1998.

Raiskin, Judith L. *Snow on the Cane Fields: Women's Writing and Creole Subjectivity.* Minneapolis: University of Minnesota Press, 1996.

Rappaport, Erika. '"A Husband and His Wife's Dresses": Consumer Credit and the Debtor Family in England, 1864–1914.' *The Sex of Things: Gender and Consumption in Historical Perspective.* Ed. Victoria de Grazia with Ellen Furlough. Berkeley: University of California Press, 1986. 163–87.

Rees, Joan. *Writings on the Nile.* London: Rubicon, 1995.

Rhys, Jean. *Wide Sargasso Sea.* 1966. New York: Norton, 1982.

Richards, J. M. *The Castles on the Ground: The Anatomy of Suburbia.* 1946. London: Murray, 1973.

Richards, Thomas. *The Commodity Culture of Victorian England: Advertising and Spectacle, 1851–1914.* Stanford: Stanford University Press, 1990.

  The Imperial Archive. New York: Verso, 1993.

Richardson, Dorothy. *Pilgrimage.* Vol. I. Urbana: University of Illinois Press, 1989.

Riley, Denise. *'Am I That Name?' Feminism and the Category of Women in History.* Minneapolis: Minnesota University Press, 1988.

Robbins, Bruce. *Secular Vocations: Intellectuals, Professionalism, Culture.* New York: Verso, 1993.

Robinson, Ronald, and John Gallagher, with Alice Denny. *Africa and the Victorians: The Climax of Imperialism in the Dark Continent.* New York: St Martins, 1961.

Rosaldo, Renato. *Culture and Truth: The Remaking of Social Analysis.* Boston: Beacon, 1989.

Ilongot Headhunting, 1883–1974: A Study in History and Society. Stanford: Stanford University Press, 1990.

Rose, Mark. *Authors and Owners: The Invention of Copyright.* Cambridge: Harvard University Press, 1993.

Rubenstein, Michael. '"The Waters of Civic Finance": Moneyed States in Joyce's *Ulysses.' Novel* 36.3 (2003): 289–306.

Rubenstein, W. D. *Capitalism Culture and Decline in Britain. 1750–1990.* New York: Routledge, 1993.

Rubin, William. *'Primitivism' in 20th-Century Art.* New York: MOMA, 1984.

Rushdie, Salman. *Imaginary Homelands.* London: Granta, 1990.

Ruthven, K. K. *Faking Literature.* Cambridge: Cambridge University Press, 2001.

Sackville-West, Vita. *Country Notes.* London: Harper, 1940.

Sagar, Keith. *D. H. Lawrence: Life into Art.* Athens: University of Georgia Press, 1985.

Said, Edward. *Culture and Imperialism.* New York: Knopf, 1993.

The World, the Text, and the Critic. Cambridge: Harvard University Press, 1983.

Samarin, William J. *The Black Man's Burden: African Colonial Labor on the Congo and Ubangi Rivers, 1880–1900.* Boulder: Westview, 1989.

Sánchez-Eppler, Karen. 'Raising Empires like Children: Race, Nation, and Religious Education.' *American Literary History* 8.3 (1996): 399–425.

Sarkar, Sumit. *Modern India.* New York: St Martin's, 1989.

Writing Social History. New Delhi: Oxford University Press, 1997.

Schjeldahl, Peter. 'Untouchable: The Barnes Foundation and its Fate.' *The New Yorker.* 16 Feb 2004: 202–3.

Schor, Naomi. *Bad Objects: Essays Popular and Unpopular.* Durham: Duke University Press, 1995.

Reading in Detail: Aesthetics and the Feminine. New York: Methuen, 1987.

Scott, Bonnie Kime. 'Diversions from Mastery in "Wandering Rocks."' *Ulysses: En-Gendered Perspectives.* Ed. Kimberly J. Devlin and Marilyn Reizbaum. Columbia: University of South Carolina Press, 1999.

Sedgwick, Eve Kosofsky. *Between Men: English Literature and Male Homosocial Desire.* New York: Columbia University Press, 1985.

Epistemology of the Closet. Berkeley: University of California Press, 1990.

Shaffer, Brian. *The Blinding Torch: Modern British Fiction and the Discourse of Civilization.* Amherst: University of Massachusetts Press, 1993.

Sharpe, Jenny. *Allegories of Empire: The Figure of Woman in the Colonial Text.* Minneapolis: University of Minnesota Press, 1993.

Showalter, Elaine. *The Female Malady.* New York: Pantheon, 1985.

Simmel, Georg. 'The Ruin.' *Georg Simmel, 1858–1918.* Columbus: Ohio State University Press, 1959. 259–66.

Simmel on Culture. Ed. David Frisby and Mike Featherstone. London: Sage, 1997.

Simpson, David. *Fetishism and Imagination.* Baltimore: Johns Hopkins University Press, 1982.

Skidelsky, Robert. *John Maynard Keynes.* Vol. II, *The Economist as Savior.* New York: Penguin, 1994.

John Maynard Keynes. Vol. III, *Fighting for Britain.* London: Macmillan, 2000.

Smith, Paul. *Millennial Dreams: Contemporary Culture and Capital in the North.* London: Verso, 1997.

Spacks, Patricia. *Boredom: The Literary History of a State of Mind.* Chicago: University of Chicago Press, 1995.

Spivak, Gayatri Chakravorty. *A Critique of Postcolonial Reason.* Cambridge: Harvard University Press, 1999.

Outside in the Teaching Machine. New York: Routledge, 1993.

'Three Women's Texts and a Critique of Imperialism.' *'Race', Writing, and Difference.* Ed. Henry Louis Gates, Jr. Chicago: University of Chicago Press, 1986. 262–80.

Stafford, Barbara Maria. 'Toward Romantic Landscape Perception: Illustrated Travels and the Rise of 'Singularity' as an Aesthetic Category.' *Studies in Eighteenth-Century Culture* 10 (1981): 17–76.

Stape, J. H., and Owen Knowles, eds. *A Portrait in Letters: Correspondence to and about Joseph Conrad.* Amsterdam: Rodopi, 1996.

Stein, Gertrude. 'Composition as Explanation.' 1926. *Selected Writings.* Ed. Carl Van Vechten. New York: Vintage, 1990. 511–23.

Stewart, Susan. *On Longing: Narratives of the Miniature, the Gigantic, the Souvenir, the Collection.* Durham: Duke University Press, 1993.

Stocking, George W. *After Tylor: British Social Anthropology 1881–1951.* Madison: University of Wisconsin Press, 1995.

'The Ethnographer's Magic: Fieldwork in British Anthropology From Tylor to Malinowski.' *Observers Observed: Essays on Ethnographic Fieldwork.* Ed. George W. Stocking. Madison: University of Wisconsin Press, 1983. 70–120.

Strychacz, Thomas. *Modernism, Mass Culture, and Professionalism.* Cambridge: Cambridge University Press, 1993.

Subramani. 'The End of Free States: On Transnationalization of Culture.' Jameson and Miyoshi 146–63.

Suleri, Sara. *The Rhetoric of English India.* Chicago: University of Chicago Press, 1992.

Sunder Rajan, Rajeswari. 'The Third World Academic in Other Places; or, the Postcolonial Intellectual Revisited.' *Critical Inquiry* 23 (1997): 596–616.

Taylor, A. J. P. *English History, 1914–45.* New York: Oxford University Press, 1965.

Taylor, Frederick Winslow. *The Principles of Scientific Management*. New York: Harper, 1911.

Taylor, John. *A Dream of England: Landscape, Photography, and the Tourist's Imagination*. Manchester: Manchester University Press, 1994.

Tennenhouse, Leonard. 'The Americanization of Clarissa.' *Yale Journal of Criticism*. 11.1 (1998): (177–96).

Thomas, Ronald. *Dreams of Authority: Freud and Fictions of the Unconscious*. Ithaca: Cornell University Press, 1990.

Tidrick, Kathryn. *Empire and the English Character*. London: Tauris, 1990.

Tomlinson, B. R. *The Economy of Modern India*. New York: Cambridge University Press, 1993.

Torgovnick, Marianna. *Gone Primitive: Savage Intellects, Modern Lives*. Chicago: University of Chicago Press, 1990.

Primitive Passions: Men, Women, and the Quest for Ecstasy. New York: Knopf, 1997.

Touval, Yonatan. 'Colonial Queer Something.' *Queer Forster*. Ed. Robert K. Martin and George Piggford. Chicago: University of Chicago Press, 1997. 237–54.

Tratner, Michael. 'Cultural Studies: Virginia Woolf and Consumerism.' *Virginia Woolf and the Arts*. Ed. Dianne Gillespie and Leslie Hankins. New York: Pace University Press, 1997. 302–9.

Modernism and Mass Politics. Stanford: Stanford University Press, 1995.

Trevelyan, George Macauley. *History of England*. London: Longmans, 1926.

Trotter, David. *The English Novel in History: 1895–1920*. New York: Routledge, 1993.

Valente, Joseph, ed. *Quare Joyce*. Ann Arbor: University of Michigan Press, 1998.

Vendler, Helen. *Coming of Age as a Poet*. Cambridge: Harvard University Press, 2003.

Viswanathan, Gauri. *Masks of Conquest: Literary Study and British Rule in India*. New York: Columbia University Press, 1989.

Ward, David. *T. S. Eliot Between Two Worlds*. London: Routledge, 1973.

Watt, Ian. *Conrad in the Nineteenth Century*. Berkeley: University of California Press, 1979.

Waugh, Evelyn. *Brideshead Revisited*. Boston: Little, 1945.

Webb, Mary. *Precious Bane*. 1924. Notre Dame: Notre Dame University Press, 1980.

Webb, Sidney, and Beatrice Webb. *Problems of Modern Industry*. London: Longmans, 1898.

Wells, H. G. *The Time Machine*. 1895. *The Time Machine and The Island of Doctor Moreau*. New York: Oxford University Press, 1996 1–91.

West, Rebecca. *The Judge*. New York: Doran, 1922.

White, Allon. *The Uses of Obscurity: The Fiction of Early Modernism*. Boston: Routledge, 1981.

Wicke, Jennifer. *Advertising Fictions: Literature, Advertisement, and Social Reading*. New York: Columbia University Press, 1988.

'Appreciation, Depreciation: Modernism's Speculative Bubble.' *Modernism/ Modernity* 8.3 (2001): 389–402.

'Enchantment, Disenchantment, Re-enchantment: Joyce and the Cult of the Absolutely Fabulous.' *Novel* 29.1 (1995): 128–37.

'Mrs. Dalloway Goes to Market: Woolf, Keynes, and Modern Markets.' *Novel* 28.1 (1994): 5–24.

Wickramagamage, Carmen. 'An/Other Side to Antoinette/Bertha: Reading 'Race' into *Wide Sargasso Sea*.' *Journal of Commonwealth Literature* 35.1 (2000): 27–42.

Williams, Linda Ruth. *Sex in the Head: Visions of Femininity and Film in D. H. Lawrence*. Detroit: Wayne State University Press, 1993.

Williams, Raymond. 'The Bloomsbury Fraction.' *Problems in Materialism and Culture*. 1980. New York: Verso, 1989. 148–69.

The Country and the City. New York: Oxford University Press, 1973.

The Politics of Modernism. New York: Verso, 1989.

Williams, Rosalind. *Dreams Worlds: Mass Consumption in Late Nineteenth-Century France*. Berkeley: University of California Press, 1982.

Williams, William Appleman. *Roots of Modern American Empire*. New York: Random, 1969.

Williams-Ellis, Clough. *England and the Octopus*. 1928. Glasgow: MacLehose, 1975.

Willinsky, John. *Learning to Divide the World: Education at Empire's End*. Minneapolis: University of Minnesota Press, 1999.

Wirth-Nesher, Hana. *City Codes: Reading the Modern Urban Novel*. Cambridge: Cambridge University Press, 1996.

Woolf, Virginia. 'Anon.' Ed. Brenda Silver. *Twentieth Century Literature*. 25.3–4 (1979): 380–424.

Between the Acts. 1941. New York: Harcourt, 1970.

'Character in Fiction.' *Essays*. Vol 3. 420–38.

The Diary of Virginia Woolf. 5 vols. Ed. Anne Olivier Bell. New York: Harcourt, 1977–84.

The Essays of Virginia Woolf. 4 vols. Ed. MacNeillie, Andrew. London: Hogarth, 1986–94.

'How it Strikes a Contemporary.' *Essays*. Vol. III. 353–60.

Jacob's Room. 1922. London: Grafton, 1976.

Letters of Virginia Woolf. 6 vols. Ed. Nigel Nicolson. London: Hogarth, 1975–80.

Mrs Dalloway. New York: Harcourt, 1925.

'Modern Novels.' *Essays*. Vol. III. 30–7.

Orlando. New York: Harcourt, 1986.

To the Lighthouse. New York: Harcourt, 1989.

The Voyage Out. 1915. New York: Penguin, 1992.

Wordsworth, William. 'London, 1802.' *William Wordsworth: The Poems*. Vol. I. Ed. John O. Hayden. New Haven: Yale University Press, 1977.

Preface. 1800. *Lyrical Ballads.* Ed. Michael Mason. London: Longman, 1992. 55–86.

The Prelude. Ed. J. C. Maxwell. New York: Penguin, 1971.

Yusuf, Shahid, Weiping Wu, and Simon Everett. *Local Dynamics in an Era of Globalization.* New York: Oxford University Press, 2000.

Zachernuk, Philip S. *Colonial Subjects: An African Intelligentsia and Atlantic Ideas.* Charlottesville: University Press of Virginia, 2000.

Zapf, Herbert. 'Taylorism in D. H. Lawrence's *Women in Love.*' *The D. H. Lawrence Review* 15 (1982): 129–39.

Zeleza, Tiyambe. *A Modern Economic History of Africa.* Volume I, *The Nineteenth Century.* Dakar: Codesria, 1993.

Index